POETIC CREATION

POETIC CREATION

Language and the Unsayable in the
Late Poetry of Robert Penn Warren

John C. Van Dyke

THE UNIVERSITY OF TENNESSEE PRESS | KNOXVILLE

Selections from *The Collected Poems of Robert Penn Warren* © 1997
and *New and Selected Essays* © 1989 by the Estate of Robert Penn Warren.
Reprinted by permission of WME, Inc., on behalf of the author.

Library of Congress Cataloging-in-Publication Data
Names: Van Dyke, John C., author.
Title: Poetic creation : language and the unsayable in the late poetry of
    Robert Penn Warren / John C. Van Dyke.
Description: First edition. | Knoxville : The University of Tennessee
    Press, [2021] | Includes bibliographical references and index. |
Summary: "In *Poetic Creation*, John Van Dyke explores the turn in
    Robert Penn Warren's poetry toward the problematic nature of
    language and argues that such an attention to language discloses
    a shift away from a modernist critical paradigm (that conceives of
    language as a tool) and toward a postmodern conception of language
    as an endless play of difference. Such difference is found in Warren
    in the unresolvable tension between the 'sayable' and the 'unsayable.'
    Warren's struggle within this tension of language is not articulated
    within the context of a clearly defined philosophy or theory; rather,
    it is conceived through the poet's own unrelenting attention to
    poiesis—the act of poetic creation itself"—Provided by publisher.
Identifiers: LCCN 2020051725 | ISBN 9781621906230 (hardcover)
Subjects: LCSH: Warren, Robert Penn, 1905–1989—Criticism and
    interpretation.
Classification: LCC PS3545.A748 Z9 2021 | DDC 811/.54—dc23
LC record available at https://lccn.loc.gov/2020051725

CONTENTS

ACKNOWLEDGMENTS

It is a humbling experience to trace the genealogy of influence for a work that has persisted for as many years as this one has. Far from enduring agony from the watchful eyes of any precursors, I have a deep sense of the debt of gratitude I owe to many. As early as my days as a student at the Darlington School, Brad Gioia, E. V. "Doc" Regester, and George Awsumb ignited my love for interdisciplinary learning and affirmed my intellectual curiosity in ways that they were, no doubt, unaware. Don King and Bonnie Lundblad at Montreat-Anderson College patiently honed my abilities in composition and kept in check my youthful pretensions as a writer. At King College—now King University—Craig McDonald, Stephen Woolsey, Linda Mills Woolsey, and Graham Landrum offered me profound examples of scholar-teachers whose love of literature and love for their students shaped my own desires for learning and living. Richard Pratt gave me my first opportunity to work on a real book as one of his many research assistants at Reformed Theological Seminary. And I could not have asked for a better doctoral supervisor and mentor than David Jasper at the University of Glasgow. This work has been shaped, in different ways and to varying degrees, by all of them.

Too many friends have encouraged me along the way to be able to name them all here, but I would be callous not to acknowledge these few here. The constant friendship and encouragement of Scott Fuller for over forty-five years has been a source of deep joy and delight for me. Donald Wilson Bush has challenged my thinking in so many ways over the past thirty years and continues to encourage me to think outside the box. My fellow Glasgow alumnus Andrew McCallion (now at Johns Hopkins University) urged me on more than one occasion to "Finish the damn book!" George Boggs and Wilson Brissett, former students of mine—whose intellectual prowess was apparent long before they ever turned in their final exams and papers—have helped me in their own ways with their intellectual rigor and integrity. My dear friend and faithful pastor, Bill Harrell, unknowingly rekindled my purpose to finish this project and renewed my conviction that this work says something that still needs to be said. Debi Harrell has been a patient reader and an honest sounding board over the final drafts of the manuscript. I would not have been able to complete this on time without her generous help!

I am deeply grateful to my father-in-law, Jim Welch, and my mother-in-law, Barbara Welch, who gave me Warren's *New and Selected Poems 1923–1985* as a Christmas gift in 1986. I am sure they had no idea how important that gift would be. I am thankful for the trust and confidence of my siblings, Joel and Beth Van Dyke, and my brother-in-law Steffan Welch. To my bride and best friend, Lisa, I owe a debt of love for her tireless patience, perseverance, inspiration, and devotion. She hoped for me when I could not hope for myself! To my children, Samuel Van Dyke and Rachel McClain, I acknowledge the sacrifices you have made in different ways over the past year as you have put up with many late nights and with my constant preoccupation with this project! It is hard for me to qualify the loving support and unstoppable confidence of my parents, James and Rosemary Van Dyke. This book is dedicated to the memory of my dear father, who always believed in me and so wanted to see me finish this book. Well, Dad, it's done.

ABBREVIATIONS

APIM	*A Plea in Mitigation*
"APPI"	"A Poem of Pure Imagination"
BD	*Brother to Dragons: A Tale in Verse and Voices*
BD79	*Brother to Dragons: A Tale in Verse and Voices, A New Version*
BL	*Biographia Literaria*
CN	*The Notebooks of Samuel Taylor Coleridge*
CP	*The Collected Poems of Robert Penn Warren*
DP	*Democracy and Poetry*
SL	*Selected Letters of Robert Penn Warren*

INTRODUCTION

One is an artist at the cost of regarding that which all non-artists call "form" as content, as "the matter itself." —Friedrich Nietzsche[1]

It has been over twenty years since I finished the dissertation from which the present work derives. Upon completion of my doctoral studies in 1997 under the supervision of David Jasper in the Center for the Study of Literature and Theology at the University of Glasgow, I had that mixture of elation and sheer exhaustion every doctoral-grantee knows all too well. I had had the luxury of concentrating on one thing for an extended period of time—Robert Penn Warren's wrestling with the impulse to "say the unsayable" throughout his later poetry—but that luxury was soon taken away, leaving me all the more aware of what a privilege it had been. Both the exigencies of life and the demand of the dissertation itself called for a time of rest that has turned out nonetheless to be productive for the present work.

Ideas, like wine, mature over time, gaining more power and effect through their relation to an enlarging cultural and intellectual context. And the most potent of those ideas, like a good wine, persist in new contexts. One of my original concerns in the dissertation was that Warren's work would be forgotten in the context of the postmodern, which was overcoming more and more the modern to which Warren and his work had been relegated. But the brief history of thought since 1997 has only proven the persistence and the potency of Warren's work, especially the poetry composed during the final phase of his career. I am more convinced than ever that the time is now ripe to offer this study as another voice in an ongoing conversation about the poetry of one of the most accomplished "men of letters" in American literature, about the nature of language and articulation, and about the power of poetry to give voice to the unsayable.

While the notion of the unsayable may have been a relatively uncommon idea in the mid-1960s when Warren told the undergraduates at Union College that the work of the poet is to "say the unsayable," it has undoubtedly moved more and more into common parlance in the discourses of politics, psychology, and philosophy, though it is used in a variety of ways. In political commentary, the word "unsayable" is sometimes used to denote what someone has said that was once considered "politically incorrect" or simply what no one else was willing to put into words. In such contexts, the "unsayable" announces what is present but often times cannot be said, highlighting a power structure in which some are considered to be "other" and whose voice is too easily silenced by power. Ivarsson and Isager use it in this way in their 2010 book *Saying the Unsayable: Monarchy and Democracy in Thailand*, an edited volume dealing with the rise and decline of democracy in Thailand. Similarly, Margaret Wente wrote in *The Globe and Mail* in 2010 that Angela Merkel had said the unsayable by declaring multiculturalism in Germany to be an "abject failure" and by declaring that "immigrants should learn to speak German" ("Angela Merkel says the unsayable"). Annie Rogers employs the idea of the unsayable in the context of clinical psychology, relying heavily on the psychoanalytical work of Jacques Lacan and his premise that "the unconscious is structured like language" (*The Unsayable* xiii). She describes her confrontation with "the hidden language of trauma" in victims of childhood abuse and abandonment and observes in these persons a tension between what can be said and what cannot be said as a result of the trauma experienced. In that space, these men and women face a silence with terrible power to evoke what cannot be said—the unsayable.[2] Finally, at the intersections of literature, philosophy, and theology, the notion of the unsayable has been explored as one of the most recalcitrant problems of Western thought. Budick and Iser's 1989 edited volume, *Languages of the Unsayable*, broke new ground in the study of the unsayable, though the work itself responds in large part to the earlier thought of both Heidegger after his linguistic turn and Wittgenstein, who famously remarked in his *Tractatus* (1921), "Whereof one cannot speak, thereof one must be silent" (xii). They provide a helpful summary of the issues raised by the question of the unsayable: "Once we have encountered the limits of the sayable, we must acknowledge the existence of 'unsayable things' and, by means of a language somehow formed on being silent, articulate that which cannot be grasped" (xii). More recently, William Franke has mined the unsayable in the apophatic tradition of theology and philosophy. For him, the tension between the sayable and the unsayable underlies all discourse to such an extent that the whole history of Western thought is a response to the unsayable. "The classical problems of philosophy," he claims, "are thus, in untold ways, all implicated in the problem of the unsayable" ("Varieties and Valences of Unsayability" 496). His 2014 volume, *A Philosophy of the Unsayable*, foregrounds the notion of the unsayable in a way that demonstrates its inescapability in contemporary thought. One direct result of that work is the 2017 volume, *Contemporary Debates in Negative Theology and Philosophy*, which sprang from essays originally presented at a 2016 symposium on Franke's *A Philosophy of the Unsayable*.

At the same time, the past two decades have been crucial for the growth of the Warren corpus and for criticism of his work. Thanks to the tireless work of John Burt, Warren's literary executor, we now have an edition of Warren's collected poems, published by the Louisiana State University Press. Harold Bloom beautifully summarizes the importance of this work: "John Burt's devoted edition gives us the definitive text of all of Warren's poetry, and thus restores an American masterwork, one that will be read, studied, and absorbed, so long as the love for, and understanding of, great poetry survives among us" (*CP* xxiii). We also have the benefit of six volumes of Warren's *Selected Letters* carefully edited by Randy Hendricks, James A. Perkins, and William Bedford Clark. Charlotte Beck has contributed a long-overdue volume on Warren's critical work, in which she surveys seven decades of his critical writing. Gloria L. Cronin and Ben Seigel have edited a new volume of interviews under the title, *Conversations with Robert Penn Warren*.[3] In 2006, Randolph Paul Runyon published *Ghostly Parallels: Robert Penn Warren and the Lyric Poetic Sequence* as a companion piece to his 1990 volume, *The Braided Dream: Robert Penn Warren's Late Poetry*. Mark Royden Winchel edited a 2007 volume, *Robert Penn Warren: Genius Loves Company*, which examines the literary relationships between Warren and many of his contemporaries. Younger scholars have also entered into the conversation during these years, engaging his work in a variety of ways and proving that it continues to be a rich ground for critical reflection.[4]

There is, however, a certain irony in these simultaneous developments in the currency of the unsayable and in the ongoing critical reflection on Warren's poetry. While various critics have highlighted Warren's attention to language, there is a striking absence of attention specifically to his acknowledgement of the unsayable and the way that shaped his struggles with language throughout his poetry but especially in his later work.[5] This is perhaps due to the fact that his poetry is often read only within certain monolithic streams of criticism and appreciation, either within a canonical context of Southern literature or within a certain genealogy of mid-twentieth-century American modernist writers. While there is no doubt a place for reading his work in these contexts, confining any critical reflection to those particular contexts runs the risk of missing a depth of thought and richness of connection within his poetry. All too often, his work has been read under the lamp of an assumed or ascribed reputation, which has left in the dark some of the richest and most pervasive ideas in his work. For so long, Warren's reputation was shaped by his identification by critics as a "Southern writer" or an old "New Critic" or even a "Modernist poet." In *A Plea in Mitigation*, Warren admits, "We can, for example, all remember the orthodoxies that were parroted at us when we were young, and how sometimes it took us years to get at a poet behind the received opinion of him" (10). What is required in order to really get at the poet is the destruction of "the barbed wire entanglements of admiring orthodoxy" (10) that get set up.[6] This is certainly the case with Warren's own work, about which a certain orthodoxy has hardened into place. For some critics, that orthodoxy veers toward what could be described as hagiography, while for other critics the orthodoxy is a summary dismissal of Warren's work as bound up by its social and cultural setting. Each of these orthodoxies presents such a "barbed wire entanglement," which keeps us from reading Warren's work in new ways. The irony is that both of these conflicting orthodoxies arrive at the same conclusion: there really is not anything new to be thought in light of Warren's work. But, as Warren knew so well, history gives us perspective, and a new millennia provides an opportunity to see vital aspects of his poetry and thought without the obstruction of reputation. As he goes on to say in that same essay, reputations always live "in a perilous balance, subject to the shocks of the world and the never-ending revisionism which is the proper academic pursuit" (10). This study is an attempt to engage in that proper pursuit and read his poetry not in light of reputation but as a persistent engagement with the powers and limits of language in which the unsayable opens itself in the moment of articulation.

In *Modern Poetry after Modernism*, James Longenbach makes much the same point when he compares Robert Lowell to T. S. Eliot, describing him as a "poet whose reputation was overwhelming, even stifling during his lifetime—

but a poet who remains vital because other writers could see aspects of him that the reputation had obscured" (17). Warren is another such poet. More than just a remaining presence in the canon of twentieth-century American literature, his poetry and thought have a persisting vitality precisely because aspects of the work that were obscured by the reputation still call for new exploration. In his foreword to *The Collected Poems of Robert Penn Warren*, Bloom acknowledges that his own reading of Warren had been obscured by his reputation. "Until I purchased and read *Incarnations* in 1968, I had thought of Warren's poetry as being admirable but essentially derivative: Eliotic in mode, manner, and argument" (xxiii–xxiv). But Bloom observes a new strength in Warren's poetry from *Incarnations* forward, demonstrated by his wrestling with the sublime and overcoming the shadow of his precursors. In an earlier essay published while Warren was still living, he describes the "shock of my personal conversion" ("Sunset Hawk" 64–65) to Warren's poetry in 1969, after having considered his reputation so long as entangled with Allen Tate and John Crowe Ransom. But, to his credit, Bloom was able to see how Warren's poetry had matured through his wrestling with these literary precursors and had become something more than it had been before. "No final perspective is possible upon a strong poet whose own wars are far from over" ("Sunset Hawk" 59).

Bloom's convictions about Warren's later poetry highlight the way his body of work is usually read. While schematizations vary, critics tend to divide his career into distinct phases marked off by the publication of his selected volumes.[7] The first phase includes his work up to the publication of his first selected volume, *Selected Poems: 1923–1943*. The earliest poetry of this period is marked by the high modernism of T. S. Eliot, whose poetry had so impacted Warren as a student at Vanderbilt, and by the meters and diction of the Metaphysical poets who were revered by Eliot and other modernist poets. Nonetheless, Warren struggles at various points during this early phase with the power of poetic language, sometimes in an effort to find his own distinctive voice or persona but at other times out of the necessity to find a way to speak in the face of life's urgency. That struggle culminates in what is perhaps Warren's most important poem of these early years, "The Ballad of Billie Potts." Published as the first poem in *Selected Poems 1923–1943,* this was the final individual poem that Warren would complete and publish for at least ten years. In it, Warren experiments with his style and voice, dropping the

Metaphysical cadences of seventeenth-century England in favor of the popu-
lar rhythms of the Kentucky backwoods banter. But this lengthy poem also
reveals a growing suspicion about the unavoidable problems of language, as is
suggested by its sustained attention to the problem of naming and the nature
of truth.

Following the publication of his first selected volume, Warren entered a
long hiatus from poetry during which he wrote some of his most important
critical essays and published both his Pulitzer Prize–winning novel, *All the
King's Men* (1946), and his only collection of short stories, *Circus in the Attic*
(1948). He also continued his collaborative work with Cleanth Brooks, publishing *Modern Rhetoric* in 1949. But, the publication of his first book-length
poem, *Brother to Dragons* (1953), announced the beginning of his second phase
of poetic work from *Promises: Poems 1954–1956* to his second selected volume,
Selected Poems: New and Old, 1923–1966. Arguably, Warren wrote some of his
best and worst poetry during these years.[8] While the problems of language
and the struggle for articulation remain in the background throughout much
of this poetry, they are foregrounded in such remarkable poems as "Dragon
Country: To Jacob Boehme," "A Dead Language: Circa 1885," and "Myth on
Mediterranean Beach: Aphrodite as Logos." "Dragon Country," for example,
explores the tension between what may be said by way of explanation in the
face of trauma and what must remain unsaid in powerful silence, introducing
the notion of negativity both linguistically and existentially.

Warren's final phase begins with his 1968 volume, *Incarnations: Poems
1966–1968*, but it is *Audubon: A Vision*, published a year later, that announces
the full force of his concentration upon language and the act of poetic creation. This poem adumbrates several issues raised in *Incarnations* and explores
more intensely the role of the artist, which occupied Warren in his 1946 essay,
"A Poem of Pure Imagination: An Experiment in Reading," and in his 1966
lecture, *A Plea in Mitigation*. *Audubon*—rather than *Incarnations*—sets the
course for Warren's subsequent poetry by raising to a higher degree of self-
consciousness the poet's meditation upon the act of creation and on the tension between the simultaneous problems and possibilities of language. It is
this final phase of poetry that Bloom praises so highly in his foreword to the
Collected Poems. "From 1966 to 1986 Warren wrote much the best poetry composed during those two decades in the United States . . . " (xxiii). Bloom de-
picts this last great phase as a period during which "Warren wrestled with the
angel of the poetic sublime and carried away the victory of a new name" (xxiii).

While these divisions of Warren's body of work can be helpful in isolating different concerns at various points in his writing, they run the risk of obscuring the organic development of his relationship to language over the course of his career. To put it simply, Warren was, from first to last, a poet, and the poetic impulse was never dormant. In 1985, the then-eighty-year-old Warren told Tom Vitale, "The poetry was always primary for me, from the start, from fifteen, sixteen, seventeen on" (Watkins, Hiers, and Weaks 395). His literary life started and finished with poetry, and in between he struggled continually with the act of poetic creation as the archetype of artistic endeavor. This was the great issue that confronted him, regardless of which genre he chose to work in at any given time. At points he was willing to take risks as a writer, trying out new styles and genres, but through all of these he pursued language as the sphere in which he might encounter the world and by which his being in the world might be shaped. This is evident in Warren's first published book, *John Brown: The Making of a Martyr* (1929). Brown, the enigmatic abolitionist anti-hero whose moral struggles capture Warren's attention, set the tone for what was to come in Warren's quest for articulation: a figure caught between his ideals and his longing for redemption and reconciliation on the one hand and his continual confrontation with the exigencies of the world on the other. Within the tension between these two "realities," the figure must find a way to speak without being silenced even by the moment of death. Like Brown, all of Warren's central fictional characters are confronted by some form of this dilemma: from Percy Munn in his first novel, *Night Rider* (1939), to Jack Burden in his Pulitzer Prize–winning *All the King's Men* (1946); from Adam Rosenzweig, in what is arguably his most neglected novel, *Wilderness* (1961), to Jed Tewksbury in the final novel, *A Place to Come To* (1977). Even in the cadence of his narrative voice, Warren's central characters are, in some way, a poet figure, and the dilemma confronted by each is, in the end, an expression of the dilemma faced by the poet: how do I speak?

In his critical work, Warren's analytical impulse also betrayed this central concern, bridging his quest for articulation with his commitment to concrete readings of texts. This is born out in "A Study of John Marston's Satires," his B.Litt. thesis on the Elizabethan satirist written as a Rhodes Scholar at Oxford in 1930.[9] Like John Brown, Marston is a poet figure who cannot deny the inherent tension between the goal of making a final utterance and the fact of the experience of his own fallible speech. In one of Warren's early critical essays, "John Crowe Ransom: A Study in Irony," he takes up these issues in a way that reaches beyond mere formalistic concern for making some statement, even as tentative as it must be, about the role of the poet in the world. Some forty years later, this theme reappears in *Democracy and Poetry* (1974), giving the reader a glimpse of an internal dialogue that had been going on in Warren's thinking for all those years. His major critical essays, especially "A Poem of Pure Imagination" (1946) and *A Plea In Mitigation: Modern Poetry at the End of an Era* (1966)—both of which play a crucial role in the present study—grapple openly with this poetic struggle to speak while confronted with the problems of language itself.

But it was in his poetry that Warren struggled forthrightly with the problematic nature of language and articulation. Even his earliest work indicated the different angles of approach in a struggle that would only be fully realized in his later poetry. In his early uncollected poems, the experience of linguistic powerlessness appears frequently. In "Apologia for Grief" (*CP* 14–15), the speaker frames his own moment in language that ironically captures what so many have experienced in the face of death: "I shall be brief, who have no word / Not fabulous with other tears than mine, / No barbarous tongue you have not heard" (9–11). In "Easter Morning: Crosby Junction" (*CP* 17), written just a year later, in 1925, the inner voice of the narrator counters the loud appeals of the preacher in the intertextual fabric that makes up the poem. The narrator acknowledges a certain suspicion about the power and nature of language when he asks, "How may we sing who have no golden song / How may we speak who have no word to say, / Or pray, or pray—who would so gently pray?" (30–32). "Mr. Dodd's Son" (*CP* 18) captures another moment of grief, eulogizing the life of one who longed for the sea though reared in a land-locked town. But the narrator describes his experience of finally seeing the sea before his death: "He could not speak—as one who suddenly / Hears in the night beyond the coasts of time / Faintly the surges of eternity" (14–16). In "The Return" (*CP* 38), the final section of the seven-part poem "Kentucky Mountain Farm" published in Warren's first published volume of poetry, *Thirty-Six Poems* (1935), the speaker describes the way that a moment in nature intimates the experience of the inner self. "So, backward heart, you have no voice to call / Your image back, the vagrant image again" (13–14). Warren's next volume of poetry, *Eleven Poems on the Same Theme* (1942), contains "End of Season" (*CP* 70), a meditation on a turning moment like so many throughout his later poetry. The narrator describes the wordless encounter between summer lovers who bump into each other in town. The experience of linguistic powerlessness becomes a moment for prescription: "You will have to learn a new language to say what is to say, / But it will never be useful in schoolroom, customs, or café" (23–24). Warren returns again to this experience in "The Mango in the Mango Tree" (*CP* 98–99), the fifth section of his "Mexico is a Foreign Country: Five Studies in Naturalism," published in *Selected Poems 1923–1943*. The poet personifies the mango as a moral agent, bearing guilt associated with some unnamed crime. It may be that Warren envisions the mango as the forbidden fruit in the Garden of Eden in the biblical creation account. At one point the speaker muses, "I do not know the mango's crime / In its far place and different time . . ." (19–20). But the mango has been appointed as an agent of God, given the task of reporting on man's crimes. Toward the end of the poem, the speaker ponders the interdependent complicity of self and nature evidenced by a linguistic curse.

> For, ah, I do not know the word
> That it could hear, or if I've heard
> A breath like *pardon, pardon,* when its stiff lips stirred.
>
> If there were a word that I could give,
> Or if I could only say *forgive,*
> Then we might lift the Babel curse by which we live. . . . (28–33)[10]

At other points in the early poetry, the poet experiences the world speaking in a way that he cannot, an experience Warren describes many years later in "Three Darknesses"(*CP* 529), the first poem in his final selected volume: "Since my idiot childhood the world has been / Trying to tell me something. There is something / Hidden in the dark . . ." (17–19). Again and again, the poems are attuned to the world as a living entity that speaks by its own voice something that the poet cannot speak. But the problem is bigger than his own incapacity of speech; he cannot fully comprehend what it is the world has to say. In many poems, that voice comes through the call of various birds. One of his earliest poems, "Vision" (*CP* 3), mentions the whip-poor-will and the owl, merely hinting at the role played by the birds in later poems.[11] In "The Owl" (*CP* 22), he invokes the owl as an image of impending death in the speaker's memory of some traumatic event. In "Tryst on Vinegar Hill" (*CP* 23), the voice of the whip-poor-will intimates more strongly the language of nature that speaks when we have no language. Speaking of the "Yaller girl and big black boy" who lie "side by side on Vinegar Hill," the narrator notes,

> Just once they hear the tardy whip-poor-will
> To whose uneasy questioning refrain
> They have no ready answer but to lay
> The lip to lip and heart to heart again." (42–45)

In some of these poems, the voice of the world is spoken through the wind. "The Last Metaphor" (*CP* 54–55) is structured around the interplay between the voice of "one fellow" and the voice of the wind, and this fellow recognizes in the wind what he cannot speak with his own voice. As the fellow ventures into the winter landscape contemplating his own mortality, he says to himself:

> "... I go where brown leaves drift
>
> "On streams that reflect but cold the evening,
> Where trees are bare, the rock is gray and bare,
> And scent of the year's declension haunts the air,
> Where only the wind and no tardy bird may sing." (4–8)

After the song of the wind ceases, the narrator says that the fellow hears "the wind's deep diapason" (23), that is, a burst of sound that encompasses a whole range of musical tones and notes. There is something about the nature of its sound that seems to crack the code of mortality in a way that his own musings cannot. The narrator continues after the fellow speaks one last time:

> And hence he made one invocation more,
> Hoping for winds beyond some last horizon
> To shake the tree and so fulfill its season:
> Before he went a final metaphor,
>
> Not passionate this, he gave to the chill air,
> Thinking that when the leaves no more abide
> The stiff trees rear not up in strength and pride
> But lift unto the gradual dark in prayer. (37–44)

The hope for an utterance "beyond some last horizon" yearns for a sense of fulfillment that the fellow cannot attain on his own. But he realizes that this hope is the same sort of prayer uttered by the leafless trees.[12]

The early poems also express a sense of tension through certain phrases crafted to open up an inner experience of anxiety that Warren will frame more openly in light of the unsayable in the later work. Sometimes the tension is present in what is presented to the narrator in the poem by the world itself. In "Eidolon" (*CP* 41), the narrator parallels in the first two stanzas the phrases "by moon, no moon" (4) and "by wind, no wind" (9) to heighten the tension of his childhood memory of the "tongue" (3), the "nocturnal disquiet" (10), and "the fangèd commotion rude" (20) of dogs chasing an unseen phantom that they will never capture. In "Letter to a Friend" (*CP* 51), the narrator contrasts a dream of a world beyond time and necessity with the reality of the world in which we live—one that requires even stuttering courage and hope. He begins by describing the idealized moment remembered in his dream as one of sustained tension in the world: "Our eyes have viewed the burnished vineyards where / No leaf falls, and the grape, unripening, ripes" (1–2). In other poems, Warren captures this experience by demonstrating the poet's struggle to speak. "To a Friend Parting" (*CP* 50–51) expresses the tension as an explicitly linguistic experience: "Recall: the said, unsaid, though chaff the said / And backward blown" (9–10).

By the 1960s, these different themes became intensely focused through the vocabulary of the unsayable. It was during this period that he first speaks openly about the unsayable. His attention to language in his early poetry and to the role it plays in the poet's experience of the world had matured and comes to full fruition in his last great phase of work, beginning with *Audubon: A Vision* (1969). This was not some sort of conversion or transformation in his work. Rather, it was more a change in attitude, comparable to the kind of change he described in his headnote to the typescript draft of *Selected Poems 1923–1943*. "But changes in attitude do not usually come all at once, and when the change is going on one may not even be aware of the nature of the process. The awareness comes later. And even when looking back, one can scarcely lay one's finger on the spot on the calendar and say, 'That was the time'" (*CP* 656–57). To borrow Bloom's metaphor, this gradual change came about as Warren won his struggle with the influence of a modernist critical paradigm in which language functions as a passive tool for description or representation that might circumscribe reality. Language became the matter itself. In the early work, language had not yet been fully problematized; it was still in the service of working out the metaphysical concern for poetic form and the existential confrontation with deterministic naturalism. Language had not been brought into question to the degree that it is in the later poetry, in an open and self-conscious confrontation with what the poet perceives to be the tense but inevitable relationship between the sayable and the unsayable.

Throughout the later poetry, the unresolvable tension between the power of what may be said and the limits of what cannot be said puts the poet at the limits of language where he is able to hear the unsayable speak. His struggle as a poet, however, is not articulated through a clearly defined aesthetic philosophy or literary theory; rather, it is conceived through the poet's own unrelenting attention to *poiesis*, to the act of poetic creation itself. Language is not for Warren simply a linguistic system made up of signifiers detached from that which is signified. Neither does he hold to a mechanical theory of language in which there is one-to-one representational correspondence between word and thing. Whether spoken by a poet or a politician, human language is fallen, fractured, and arbitrary; but instead of abdicating to linguistic paralysis, his poetry envisions something beyond that speaks through the fissures of what is said. This language is a vital power of being that enacts and actuates those things which may not be spoken. Such a vision was shaped to a large extent by Warren's long-running preoccupation and interaction with the thought of Samuel Taylor Coleridge, especially Coleridge's conception of the imagination as a living and "verbal" power. In terms of Coleridge's system, Warren's poetry demonstrates a view of language as the living power and agent by which the imagination functions both in the act of poetic creation and in every enactment of being in the world, that is, the exercise of the conscious will in the creative engagement with the world. Like thinkers such as Rosenzweig and Heidegger, he understands language as that which speaks and declares the condition of our being in the world. His later poetry suggests that the poet may speak only after he has listened to the speaking of language itself, an experience marked by a continual confrontation with the limits of the sayable but driven on by the necessity for some means of articulation within that limit. From Coleridge, Warren adopted and adapted the notion of tension not so much as a formal concept for poetry but as an unavoidable ontological category. The poet yearns for the moment of articulation that both acknowledges the boundaries of the sayable and is empowered by that which lies beyond such boundaries; that is, the unsayable. This yearning manifests throughout his late poetry in "boundary moments," in which the poet confronts in the world around him his own inability to speak, name, or represent what is before him. The poet's quest after the unsayable is therefore filled with tension, which yields a poetry that is impure and open-ended, a poetry that resists closure and totalization through an ongoing questioning of what it means to live in the world. His hope is not that he will be able to say the unsayable finally but that the unsayable will be spoken by the voice of language itself.

This book sets out both to trace the development of these convictions in Warren's poetry—from *Audubon: A Vision* through his final works—and to observe the way specific poems seek to give voice to the unsayable. While there is no doubt a variety of themes and issues woven through the complex layers of his work, I am specifically concerned in this book with his struggle with language as the mark of real maturity in his later poetry. That struggle results from his conviction that the work of the poet is to "say the unsayable," and his later poetry achieves an open meditation upon that conundrum to a degree not seen in his earlier work. In the first chapter, I explore the development of his notion of the unsayable throughout the critical work of the early 1960s, culminating in what is a watershed moment in his thought: the 1966 lecture *A Plea in Mitigation*. Warren demonstrates a high degree of self-consciousness about his own work and seems to wonder if even he can survive the revolution that was taking place. His musings about poetry and the poet harken back to his earlier Coleridge essay, "A Poem of Pure Imagination," which is the subject of the second chapter. Warren's reading of *The Rime of the Ancient Mariner* provides a framework for the first thorough-going expression of his understanding of language and the role of the imagination in the act of poetic creation, which opens the door to his struggles in the later poetry. Warren's linguistic concepts are rooted in and shaped by—but not limited to—Coleridge's own confrontation with the problem of language in his theory of the imagination and the symbol. In chapter three, I explore the way Warren returns to those issues in *Audubon: A Vision,* which recasts the symbolic complex of Coleridge's poem in the figure of John James Audubon and sets the tone and direction of much of his subsequent poetry. Chapter four responds to the concluding imperative of *Audubon,* "Tell me a story of deep delight," and picks up on a theme present in Coleridge's linguistics and central to *Audubon*—the relation between language and the world and the tension between the ways language in the world sometimes withholds and at other times gives itself to the poet. Warren shares Coleridge's conviction that the world is itself a symbolic language where the unsayable may be encountered in the "here" of the poem's moment. A reading of various poems from the late work explores the way the language of the world both withholds and gives as an expression of the concomitant power and limit of language. Chapter five takes up the earlier imperative in *Audubon,* "Tell me the name of the world," identifying the tension of "naming the unnamable" as another linguistic issue raised by *Audubon* but worked out more fully in the later poetry. Warren's poetic musings on the problem of naming parallel questions asked about "the name" in the writing of Heidegger and other thinkers. In the final chapter, I argue that the latest of Warren's poems bring the poet to "boundary moments," where he encounters what may not be presented but is nonetheless present. In many of these moments, the boundary encountered is death itself. By bearing witness to the unpresentable, Warren's poetry enters into the environs of postmodernity in its surrender to the unsayable.

I readily admit my own ongoing admiration for Warren's poetry, but I also must confess a fear that his work will be largely forgotten. Despite Bloom's declaration of Warren's fixed place in the canon of twentieth-century American literature, I have the audacity to believe that Warren's poetry calls for more than that. His poetry bears a quality that resists being put away as an historical artifact. When asked about the influence of Heidegger upon his own work, Jacques Derrida remarked, "Heidegger's texts are still before us; they harbor a future of meaning which will ensure that they are read and reread for centuries" (Kearney, *Dialogues* 110). This futurity marks Heidegger's works as great philosophical texts. "The future of the great philosophies remains obscured and enigmatic, still to be disclosed. Up to now, we have merely scratched the surface" (113). Warren's texts harbor such a future of meaning which calls for a rereading of his poetry. While it would be stingy at best to suggest that the critical writing on Warren's poetry up to this point has "merely scratched the surface," I do believe that something about his poetry remains enigmatic and obscure. There is something yet to be disclosed. Even with the amount of worthy criticism devoted to these texts since the publication of Victor Strandberg's *A Colder Fire* in 1965, there is something about them that urges us to begin again. Derrida says of Heidegger's texts, "No matter how rigorous an analysis I bring to bear on such texts, I am always left with the impression that there is something *more* to be thought" (113–14). The greatness of Warren's poetry is that there is something more to be thought, not simply about the texts themselves but something more in light of his poetry.

Such thought has to begin by returning to Warren's work and asking what it means to say the unsayable. My goal is not to attempt to construct a linguistic philosophy grounded in Warren's ideas; neither is it to attempt an exhaustive reading of all of Warren's later work, such that there would be little left to be said about his poetry. That would be impossible. Rather, I set out to read his later poetry not only in light of several of his essays but also in the context of developments in philosophy over the course of the past century, especially as it pertains to language and the unsayable. Like a great wine, the last thing his poetry needs is a critic whose recommendations can never replace the first noseful of the bouquet, the first splash on the palate, or the first breath after you swallow. The best contribution a critic can make is to act as a host who welcomes to the table those who want to taste. This book, then, is really a plea—a plea both to those who have never read his poetry and to those who have read it for many years. There is a richness to his work and a robust flavor that must be tasted for itself.

CHAPTER ONE

Warren's Apophatic Moment

Only in the rigor of questioning do we come into the vicinity of the unsayable.—Martin Heidegger[1]

Warren's open confrontation with the unsayable in his later poetry began in the tumultuous decade of the 1960s, a period of both personal revolution and literary and cultural upheaval. In his critical work as well as in his poetry, he attempts to come to terms with what he considers to be a time of social and literary crisis resulting in part from questions about the power and limit of language. In this context, he begins to grapple openly with the unsayable and with the nature of his own work as a writer, and he gains a critical vocabulary for the experience of the poet in the moment of creation through his reflection on three seemingly disparate but crucial questions: Who speaks for the oppressed when the lines of racial segregation dissolve? Why do we read fiction? And, what has happened to modernism? In response to each of these, his thought returns again and again to the problem of language and the inability to speak something that presses to be said.

Warren's thinking during this period proves to be an example of what may be called an apophatic moment. In "Franz Rosenzweig and the Emergence of a Postsecular Philosophy of the Unsayable," William Franke describes such a moment in this way: "Periodically in intellectual history, confidence in the *Logos*, in the ability of the word to grasp reality and disclose truth, flags dramatically. Discourses in all disciplines and fields suddenly become dubious and problematic as language enters into generalized crisis and the currency of the word goes bust" (161). During such periods, the experience of linguistic crisis fosters "cultures that can be characterized as 'apophatic,' that is, as veering into widespread worries about the reliability of words and even into wholesale refusal of rational discourse" (161). According to Franke, the persistence of apophatic discourse since the nineteenth century is rooted in the Romantic rebellion against Hegel that runs through the history of German thought. "This suggestion may at first appear paradoxical, since the history of German speculative mysticism, one of the most fertile seedbeds for apophatic thought from Meister Eckhart and Nicholas Cusanus through Jakob Böhme and Silesius Angelus, is oftentimes taken to culminate in Hegel" (163). Rather, he argues, "the whole line of apophatic speculation" may be traced from the Neoplatonism of Plotinus through Eckhart to the work of Friedrich Wilhelm Joseph von Schelling and ultimately comes to full expression in the thought of Franz Rosenzweig, who is, according to Franke, "arguably the preeminent thinker of modern times" (163–64).[2] In Rosenzweig, elements of German Romantic philosophy and Jewish mystical thought merge in a way that opens up the apophatic as the moment in which the unsayable arises in the midst of concrete experience in the world.

Franke's observations offer a remarkable context for understanding developments in Warren's thought and poetry during the 1960s, both of which reflect interest in and influence from the same genealogy of apophaticism traced by Franke. While Warren had been deeply influenced by the Kantian aesthetics of his teacher John Crowe Ransom, his study of Coleridge and *The Rime of the Ancient Mariner* brought him face to face with the German Romanticism of Schelling and its roots in Plotinus, a tradition that had exerted so much power in Coleridge's thinking ("A Poem of Pure Imagination" 403). Warren was also well aware of the mystical tradition stemming from Plotinus and showed particular fascination for the thought of Jacob Boehme (1575–1624), the German mystic to whom Coleridge acknowledged a debt of gratitude as one of the mystics who helped "prevent my mind from being imprisoned within the outline of any single dogmatic system" (*Biographia Literaria* I.152).[3] In 1957, he published the poem, "Dragon Country: To Jacob Boehme" (*CP* 133–34). In a recording of him reading this poem made by the Yale Series of Recorded Poets, Warren says at the beginning, "It's based on a line I encountered many years ago in Law's translation of Boehme."[4] In twelve quatrains, the narrator struggles to make sense of repeated unaccountable acts of violence in his rural community. The attacks themselves are never witnessed, but the inescapable after effects of the ravaging demand some explanation that cannot be fully given in the end. ". . .We are human, and the human heart / Demands language for reality that has no slightest dependence / On desire, or need . . ." (46–48). Warren structures the narrative line of the poem to frame an apophatic moment of linguistic crisis brought about by the violence and rupture caused by the attacks of an unseen dragon upon a community. He continued to work within this genealogy when he published his 1961 novella, *Wilderness*, whose protagonist is a German Jew named Adam Rosenzweig. The narrative traces his idealistic pursuit of justice and action by emigrating to the United States in the midst of the Civil War in order to fight against the South and the evil of slavery. Though he is hampered by a club foot, he has a boot made that gives him the ability to keep in step with the other mercenaries until the same foot betrays him and gives away his limitations. Left on his own, he pursues the battle that he believes will both purify and prove him as a man. Rosenzweig's inability to fight is mirrored in his own linguistic crisis as he struggles to be able to pray in the face of not only the violent ruptures of the war but also his own sense of inadequacy.

Rather than mere coincidence, these texts suggest that Warren was well aware of both the philosophical and mystical traditions and that they shaped his thinking about language, the self, and the world. It should be no surprise, then, that during the 1960s Warren's own confrontation with language and the unsayable reached a new expression. He had made an important step in that direction in "A Poem of Pure Imagination," written some twenty years earlier, when he discusses Coleridge's characterization of the symbol. Warren states, "The symbol affirms the unity of mind in the welter of experience; it is a device for making that welter of experience manageable for the mind—graspable. It represents a focus of being and is not a mere sign, a 'picture-language'" (352). In a footnote to that statement, he clarifies that this is what he understands Suzanne Langer to mean when she speaks of "the 'unspeakable' in the import of the symbol" (404). He quotes from her *Philosophy in a New Key* (1941), in which she states that "an artistic symbol . . . has more than discursive or presentational meaning" (262). There is a vital difference for Langer between what she calls the "material of poetry," which is discursive—the ideas that can be directly stated—and the nondiscursive "product" of poetry, which is its significance that cannot be fully stated or translated. Langer's distinction derives from her reading of Ludwig Wittgenstein and mirrors tensions central to the divide between Analytical and Continental thought in the twentieth century. She would go on to develop these ideas in her 1953 book, *Feeling and Form*.[5] What is significant, though, is the way Warren connects Coleridge's view of the symbol with Langer's notion of the unspeakable in order to clarify the power of poetic language. His brief discussion introduces two ideas that will become fundamental to his later thinking. First, he suggests that the "unspeakable" is tied to the way poetry engages us in our experience. Second, he acknowledges that symbolic "representation" is an ontological phenomenon and not simply a function of correspondence between word and thing.

Warren first mentions the unsayable in his 1962 essay "Why Do We Read Fiction?" His answer to the question is that we as readers are drawn into the conflict of a story because conflict wakes us up and makes us see our surroundings or ourselves as problematic again. In that waking moment, we "feel that surge of energy which is life" (56). Fiction is an "imaginative enactment" that brings to its readers a form of knowledge—knowledge of ourselves and of our world. In language that echoes his study of Coleridge, Warren characterizes this kind of knowledge as "imaginative participation" that permits readers to know "things which we would otherwise never know—including ourselves" (61). Fiction is no less symbolic than poetry for Warren. In Langer's categories, fiction is not discursive but has a significance that is implicit and cannot be translated. As a work of art, it "concerns experiences that are not *formally* amenable to the discursive projection. Such experiences are the rhythms of life, organic, emotional, and mental ... " (*Feeling and Form* 241). It has a significance that connects with our experience as readers. Warren's description of the symbol in "A Poem of Pure Imagination" applies just as much to fiction as it does to poetry: it is "a device for making that welter of experience manageable for the mind—graspable" (352). Or, as he puts it in "Why Do We Read Fiction?": "This fiction is a 'telling' in which we as readers participate and is, therefore, an image of the process by which experience is made manageable" (62).

Fiction casts our experience in a manageable form by creating a logical structure that implies a meaning. "By showing a logical structure," he goes on to say, "it relieves us, for the moment at least, of what we sometimes feel as the greatest and most mysterious threat of life—the threat of the immanent but 'unknowable,' of the urgent but 'unsayable.' ... It says the unsayable" (62). At this point, for Warren, the unsayable is not so much a linguistic concept as a description of that part of the human experience that gives significance and meaning to our lives. By framing the threat in terms of "the urgent but 'unsayable,'" Warren continues to hold on to the notion of a tension that is productive for writer and reader alike. For the writer, the threat is that he will not be able to speak in the face of the unsayable; for the reader, the threat is that the logical structure or the significance of life will never be seen. As will become more obvious later in this chapter, the idea of urgency is significant for Warren. It is what drives and motivates a writer or poet. It defines what he will describe as the prophetic quality of the poet's work, which is more important to him than the aesthetic function. A poet writes because he has something to say, which may be something that no one wants to hear. But in his saying, he is confronted by what remains unsayable. Warren recasts this tension in similar language in "Three Darknesses" (*CP* 529). "There is some logic here to trace, and I / Will try hard to find it. But even as I begin, I / Remember one Sunday morning . . . " (1–3). The speaker is trying to find the logical structure in his experience, but before he can ever state the significance of his experience, he is thrown back upon his memory. Rather than being stated discursively, the only "logic" or meaning that can be found is realized in the concrete reality of human experience, expressed through his memories of one particular Sunday morning in the zoo in Rome.[6]

The unsayable reappears in Warren's 1965 book, *Who Speaks for the Negro?* In his foreword, Warren states that he wrote this book "because I wanted to find out something, first hand, about the people, some of them anyway, who are making the Negro Revolution what it is—one of the dramatic events of the American story" (ix). His use of the word "revolution" to describe the histori- cal phenomena he sought to engage is far from mere metaphor. This was a time of violence during which the social fabric was being torn and language played a complex role both in politics and in shaping identity.[7] But it also becomes apparent that Warren wanted to find something out about himself. This was an intensely personal project for Warren, a personal revolution in which he felt the tearing and reshaping of his own narrative. He acknowledges this in an early section of the first chapter. In language that can only be described as confessional, he writes, "Back in the winter of 1929–30, when I was living in England, I had written an essay on the Negro in the South. I never read that essay after it was published, and the reason was, I presume, that reading it would, I dimly sensed, make me uncomfortable" (10–11).[8] His discomfort may be indicated by the deliberate omission of the title of that earlier essay—"The Briar Patch"—because of its inescapable racist overtones. He admits that his self-conscious defense of a humane segregation—truly "separate but equal"—indicated "an awareness that in the real world I was trying to write about, there existed a segregation that was not humane" (11). Having grown up in southern Kentucky, just north of the Tennessee state line, in the first quarter of the twentieth century, Warren knew the shape and effects of segregation and was led to the conviction that "no segregation was, in the end, humane" (12). When he returned to the South in the 1930s, he soon became convinced that he "could never again write the essay" (12).

Mindful of his own complicity, Warren knows that he cannot be the one to speak for the Negro, despite the implicit irony of typesetting on the book cover. Rather, his use of transcripts of his interviews with African American leaders, interspersed with sections of commentary and reflection, creates an intertextual narrative in which individuals speak for themselves. Warren is more a listener and transcriber who responds to what he hears than an author who creates a reality. That is particularly evident in his interview with Roy Wilkins, who was at that time the president of the NAACP. Warren asks him at one point to respond to Norman Podhoretz's claim in the journal *Commentary* that "assimilation is the only solution of the Negro problem" (148–49). Wilkins says, "I don't know. I don't know that I can put it into words. I've had the feeling that he was trying to say the unsayable. I don't know" (149). Warren then muses:

> But what is the "unsayable"? Is it the thing we think too painful or shameful to admit—that there may be a deep, irremediable, incorrigible, hard germ of prejudice in all of us, a real entity and not something that we can explain away by all the theories of symbolism, or economics, or a shadowy relic of tribal xenophobia, or political manipulation? But if we should admit to such a prejudice, what is the moral of the tale? Would it mean hopelessness or self-torturing guilt? Or is the question always, in immediate terms at least, not that of the extirpation of prejudice but of what to do about it? (149)[9]

Warren does not attempt here to give a comprehensive definition of the unsayable—that would be impossible. Rather, he asks the question in a very specific context. More than just acknowledging the presence of the unsayable, his adoption of the questioning trope emphasizes his recognition that it exceeds explanation or quantification. His aim here is geared more toward understanding. As in "Why Do We Read Fiction?," he links the unsayable to human experience, particularly to the experience of what we perceive to be a threat to the self. There is the implicit threat of what is "too painful or shameful to admit" about ourselves. When the unsayable is framed in such a way, most people recoil from it. The comparison between the experience of Jew and that of the Negro in the context of Warren's book is significant. While not explicitly mentioning the Holocaust, there are parallels in the experience of the African American that can be drawn from the experience of the Jews in Germany. Both suffered a prejudice fueled by powerful rhetoric, while both have survived by an even more powerful narrative of hope. There is a kind of apophaticism in the experience of the Negro as Warren engages with it that resembles what Franke describes as Jewish apophaticism worked out in Rosenzweig's thought. The reality of separation and alienation are powerful in such discourses, yet there is a possibility of something new but unsayable arising from the tension of "unassimilable difference" ("Franz Rosenzweig" 166). In this light, Wilkins's musing about the unsayable becomes even more striking.

In the final chapter of *Who Speaks for the Negro?*, entitled "Conversation Piece," Warren describes the immanent application of relative power by Negro leadership to the various points of vulnerability within the White community. "In other words, in all sorts of subtle and shifting combinations, Negro leadership is committed to playing a most complicated tune on the strings of white desires, and convictions" (409). In language that suggests the inevitable presence of the unsayable, Warren then adds, "And the string the harpist touches most often, sometimes lightly, sometimes with an authoritative *whang*, is the white man's desire to be a just man, or his conviction that he is a just man. For few men are willing to say: *I am unjust*" (409). Such a thing would be too painful or shameful to admit. The unsayable strikes at one's sense of identity and significance but also calls for action or enactment that engages the self. Later in the same chapter, Warren discusses the shocks experienced by the Southerner when he learns that the world does not conform to expectations shaped by prejudice and the assumption of homogeneity within "white culture." "It is not evil that shocks," he says, "it is the unexpected" (425). The unexpected shocks the sense of identity and purpose, both personally and culturally. There were plenty of shocks for the White Southerner to feel during the 1950s and 1960s. Warren then observes:

Long before these recent shocks, the white Southerner, in one dimension of his being, had harbored the scarcely specified memory of a gallantly defeated nationalism, and had felt himself part of a culture waning sadly before the dominant American ethos. He had lived with pieties and defensive impulses no less desperate for being unsaid or unsayable. Now when the world, which even in its decay had seemed stable, begins to crack, he is shaken to the core. He is then inclined to strike blindly back. (425–26)[10]

Warren suggests that the unsayable becomes unavoidable when the structure of the world cracks and what is beyond saying rises to the surface through new possibilities that have been opened up.[11] What he is describing is the apophatic moment for Southern culture, a time in which the accepted discourses no longer hold. In this view, the unsayable means more than simply what is unspoken. There is an immanence and an urgency to it that requires a rethinking of the self in relation to the world. To confront the unsayable will shake one to the core, regardless of race. Such a confrontation was at the heart of the revolution Warren chronicles in *Who Speaks for the Negro?*

In 1966, Warren turned from the social revolution taking place in race relations in America to the literary revolution occurring the same time. In his 1966 Eugenia Dorothy Blount Lamar Lecture delivered at Wesleyan College under the title *A Plea in Mitigation: Modern Poetry at the End of an Era,* Warren writes, "We are witnessing . . . the end of a poetic era, the end of 'modernism,' that school of which the Founding Fathers were Eliot, Pound, and Yeats" (1).[12] Using a narrative line parallel to what he developed in *Who Speaks for the Negro?*, Warren describes the end of this era as the collapse of a regime brought about by the failure of insight, the hardening of principles into orthodoxy, and the institutionalizing of personal styles. While he does not specifically speak about the unsayable in his lecture, Warren nonetheless focuses intensely on the role that language plays in the collapse of modernism and the turn toward a new poetic era. It is a moment of linguistic crisis. To borrow Franke's terms, confidence in the modernist Logos has flagged dramatically. Gone is the assumption that words can be relied upon to grasp reality and disclose truth. It is an apophatic moment in which language becomes less the "given" it had once been for Warren and more the matter itself. In the revolt against the age, Warren says, "The world changes, the tonality of experience changes, and we seek a language adequate to the new experience. Except for an undefined malaise, we may not even know that language no longer conforms to experience" (1). As in both "Why Do We Read Fiction?" and *Who Speaks for the Negro?*, Warren connects language to experience in the world but acknowledges a profound sense of the failure of direct correspondence between language and experience. He seems to be less and less concerned about reference or representation and more captivated by the power of language to articulate the way we relate to the world.[13] The sense of malaise is not caused by language itself but by not knowing "the nature of our experience" (2). In the wake of the fall of the modernist regime, there is a need for a revolution in which one can "discover identity—to locate oneself on the vast and shifting chart of being" (2). Warren understands that this ontological crisis necessarily involves language. He goes on to say:

> When we are disoriented, when we cannot thus locate ourselves, when we no longer find language adequate for defining ourselves, it is natural for us to feel angry with the last age—the age that gave us our recent language and most intimate images, for only its own time and not for eternity. The age did not keep its promises. It dwindled before our eyes. It dwindled even into us, alas—and that is the hardest thing to forgive. (2)

The fall of modernism is marked by a recognition that the language it gave us—its promises to speak the final word that can close the gap between word and thing—does not work, and the effect of that is felt in the formation of identity. It is not that language itself has changed; rather, this moment of crisis highlights the false assumptions about the power and limits of language. Warren acknowledges a growing awareness that language does not always perform the way we think it should. Sometimes it will give adequate images, but at other times it withdraws and holds itself in reserve. The promises about the way language works and may be used not only "dwindled before our eyes" but "dwindled even into us." For Warren, this appears to be an intensely personal crisis. His use of the personal pronoun is not rhetorical. He includes himself here much in the same way as he does in *Who Speaks for the Negro?* How may he continue to speak?

Warren's goal, however, is not merely to acknowledge the fact of modernism's demise; there would be no real value in that. Rather, he is interested in what may be an adequate response to this demise and how that will shape the poetry yet to be written. Instead of adopting what he describes as the reflexive response of rebellion, he sets out to assess the modern age and to look forward to new values that may be discovered in the wake of its collapse. It is clear that he is not out to debunk or negate the work of modernist poets—his own work up to this point is to some degree implicated in the problems of the age. His project here is every bit as personal as his task in *Who Speaks for the Negro?* He is assessing himself and his own work, looking forward to what may emerge in his own poetry as well as in the poetry of the age. The view he takes of the past is rather like that of Heidegger in his assessment of the Western metaphysical tradition—which was in so many ways a very personal goal at the heart of his philosophy. The modernist past must not be abolished or rejected but must be overcome by demonstrating what it had forgotten when it was drawn into the technological and political conflicts of the age. All too often, modern-ist poets inadvertently let science define language in terms of its power and limits, but their attention to language and the urgent need for articulation must be preserved. His goal, therefore, is to arrive at some understanding of the modernist past and how it came to be so that we do not become victims of that age. In order to reach that goal, Warren asks a simple question: "what made modern poetry 'modern'?" (*APIM* 4).

Warren begins to answer that question by pointing out what he considers to be "the most obvious fact about modern poetry . . . that it is an 'alienated art'. . . ." (*APIM* 4). This sense of alienation was forced on it to a large ex-tent by the increasingly technological culture of the late nineteenth and early twentieth centuries as a consequence of the Enlightenment, which shifted the locus of "truth" to science and relegated poetry to mere aesthetics. No longer was the poet the legislator of truth; instead, the poet "was told that he couldn't even be trusted to speak the simple truth; that that was the business of science" (4). This created one of the most palpable tensions in modern-ist aesthetics: the perceived conflict between the artist and the scientist. To whom does truth rightly belong? That conflict was one expression of the de-bates that defined the relationship between the Analytical and Continental traditions in twentieth-century philosophy, especially in the way that each conceptualizes the nature and function of language.[14] While both of these traditions derive from the thought of Kant and Hegel, each leans on a dif-ferent side of tensions already present in these earlier thinkers in order to legitimize the role of philosophy in the modern world. On the one hand,

Analytical philosophy, oriented toward the object, seeks to secure a foundation for the natural sciences as that which is able to explain the world as it is. Language, therefore, is used to describe what is objectively verifiable without any ambiguity which may be brought in by experience. Gottlob Frege represents this attitude within German philosophy, and Bertrand Russell develops similar ideas within Anglo-American philosophy.[15] On the other hand, the Continental tradition, oriented toward the subject, questions the way analytical philosophy limits truth to what can be empirically verified by showing the preconceptual assumptions about what is "given" and demonstrates that the human sciences provide another way of seeking to grasp meaning and truth.[16] Continental philosophy does not deny the validity, even necessity, of using language at times to explain what is there in the world; but it does emphasize that language also provides understanding of the experience of encountering what is presented to us in the world. Edmund Husserl provides an important point of departure in the development of Continental thought, especially in his response to Frege. In his introduction to German philosophy, Bowie presents a succinct explanation that helps to clarify the direction of Warren's developing views of language and the unsayable.

> Husserl's accounts of perception (there is no single definitive version) stress the fact that experience has to be understood in terms of meanings: every kind of awareness involves a relationship between a mode or modes of attention, and material from the world. . . . Seeing indeed involves photons hitting the retina, which can be explained in terms of scientific laws, but the experience of seeing something cannot be explained in such terms, and is both prior to and necessary for scientific explanation. Seeing something means that what is seen presents itself as something significant. . . . (94)

For Warren, poetry is a "mode of attention" that engages the world in a specific way, one that is every bit as true as the more descriptive mode that predominates in science. But as modernist poetry developed in a culture too easily dominated by analytical thought, modernist poets assumed an alienated role. In a world that denied the poet's "prophetic" role because poetry lacked any verifiable scientific rigor, writers tended toward what Warren describes as "an 'essential' poetry which might, by saintly rigor, rise superior to its deprivations" (5). Modernist poetry was marked by a "will to style" which only led to further obscurity; too often it came off simply as listening to the poet talk to himself (5).

The alienation experienced by the poet was only a species, however, of a larger phenomenon. As Warren goes on to argue, modern poetry was an alienated art because it was written in an alienated age which impacted not only poets but all people. Modernity was marked by "the rise of industrialism, financed capitalism, and the great power state . . . ; the sense of community and of human ties was being replaced by anonymous forces; communion seemed to be lost in noise of communication by mass media; the historical sense disappeared into a cynical, or supine, acceptance of the incoherent present" (*APIM* 5).[17] As a result of the loss of community and communion, society had become "a No-Society" or even an "Anti-Society" that threatened any "sense of meaningful relation to other men and to nature" (5). What was at risk, in Warren's estimation, was the loss of the ability to form identity. The development of this alienated age is witnessed in the writing of Baudelaire, Melville, Hardy, and Proust; it can be seen in the work of Marx and Freud. "But the climax came in 1914," Warren says. "The blood-bath of 1914–18 was the dramatic image of the end of the old order, the petering out of history, and the life-story behind all the written stories and poems was in the image of a lonely man etched against the red sky of a historical crisis" (6). Warren makes a similar assessment in *Who Speaks for the Negro?* when he says, "The notion is current that history has failed us, specifically Western history, Western culture, the Judeo-Christian tradition. This notion has been with us a long time, and all our literature of this century, especially since World War I, has been shot through with it, with the sense of a crisis of culture" (440). The First World War authoritatively pronounced the collapse of the old order, and the effect that it had upon poetry, philosophy, and theology shaped the course of all subsequent thought. Warren was not alone in recognizing this collapse, so vividly portrayed in the ravaging of Europe and the West. The demise of the old order had already been announced—almost prophetically—in the ironic critiques of Kierkegaard and in the apocalyptic meditations of Nietzsche. After the turn of the century, Husserl observed what he called the "crisis of European thought" (Spanos, "Martin Heidegger" xi). The same period was a critical time for Heidegger. George Steiner suggests that the two primary influences on Heidegger's development were the appearance of Karl Barth's *Epistle to the Romans* in 1918 and the First World War with the resulting economic debacle of Weimar Germany.[18] Bowie comments that the decisive event in the emergence of Critical Theory "was the First World War and what came after it. The war was initially greeted by some intellectuals . . . as a welcome way out of a supposedly decadent society, but resulted in the horrors of the trenches and the attendant economic, political, and social breakdown" (*German Philosophy* 110). The critique brought by Continental philosophy in response to this social and cultural demise culminated in the mid-sixties, the same period in which Warren declared the end of modernism, and found its most pointed expression in the thinkers such as Jacques Derrida and Emmanuel Levinas, who declared, "For everyone, this century will have witnessed the end of philosophy" (Blanchot 41). In a statement that appears to summarize much of twentieth-century thought, Warren states that, because "the crisis of history, the crisis of culture . . . was an inexpungable element in life," it therefore became the subject of poetry and "of literature in general and of the speculations of philosophers" (6).[19]

Poets responded to this collapse in a variety of ways. Some pursued the presumed safety of aestheticism, submersing themselves in beauty at the expense of moral or social engagement, while others sought to reach back to the past and recapture something that had been lost. Some focused on man's predicament as a lonely animal while others found empowerment through religious yearning or political activism. "Despite all this variety," Warren writes, "the common bond is . . . discernible" (*APIM* 6). A pervasive sense of irony unites the work of modernist writers as they respond to the crisis of history. "Irony, in fact, veins the whole tissue of modernity, and the irony itself compounded the poet's alienation" (7). There was a certain complexity to the irony, though; it was not merely directed against the values of Western civilization—thereby unmasking "the Victorian Gospel of progress"—but was directed against the poet himself. In light of the "unmaskings" of Freud and Marx, there was a "recognition of his otherness" and a "suspicion that his work might be nothing but the twitch of a dying economic order" (8). Warren's insight again anticipates critiques that will be made by poststructuralist thinkers in the years that follow his essay. Issues of alterity and suspicion figure prominently in postmodern thought, especially in thinking about language. The point Warren makes, though, does not look forward but looks back. By owning his alienation and questioning his role in society, the modernist poet adopted a romantic aesthetic and owned the role of the *poète maudit*.

The Romantics, and their 18th century precursors such as Collins and Gray, were experiencing the first tremors and doubts about the poet's role. They, too, had been told that poetry could not attain to truth, that it was a vestigial remnant of the prattling and lalling childhood of the race, that it had no social function. So the poet, with his very existence *qua* poet at stake, plagued the question, and out of the plaguing of the question came such poems as Collins' "Ode to Fear," Wordsworth's *Prelude*, Coleridge's *Ancient Mariner* and "Kubla Khan," Keats' "Ode on a Grecian Urn," and Shelley's "Ode to the West Wind." (9)

The only difference between the Romantic poets and their modernist heirs, in Warren's estimation, is that the issues have simply become more aggravated for the modernist poets which has led to a compounding of his sense of alienation. "The poet was not merely talking *to* himself. Worse, and even more impolitely, he was talking *about* himself" (9).

Warren then comes to a crucial question: did modern poetry succeed? But this may appear to be an odd question as well. Succeed at what? Given the denunciation of a raw scientific world view, how would one begin to quantify the effects of the poetry of an age? For Warren, the measure of success is whether modern poetry found readers. The difficulty of the question is reflected in the complexity of the possible answers. Some would argue that it had "no real audience"—perhaps modernist poets never really wanted an audience, Warren concedes—and that this would mark its failure (9). Some argued that what success was enjoyed was due to the "dubious practices and dark conspiracies" of the New Criticism, which became the propaganda machine of modernist aesthetics (10). Warren actually uses the word "AGITPROP" (10), ironically pointing to the hardline ideology not only of New Criticism but also of its detractors. This is the point at which Warren might be accused of his own "sad self-irony," but it has to be recognized that Warren does not engage in any sort of nostalgia for the New Criticism or for its aesthetic—no more so than he longs for some idealized past in *Who Speaks for the Negro?* He recognizes that the New Critical project is finished and that it is time for something new. The central tenets of New Criticism, which were essentially formalist principles, could no longer be lionized. In the first half of the twentieth century, Formalist criticism developed in two distinct groups, each independent—and apparently unaware—of the other. In Russia, the Moscow Linguistic Circle and the Petrograd Society for the Study of Poetic Language (known by the acronym *OPOYAZ*) formulated a poetics preoccupied with the possibilities of literary structure. Roman Jakobson's work is representative of what became known as Russian Formalism, which viewed poetry essentially as a function of linguistics. This perspective shows a degree of kinship with Ferdinand de Saussure's revolution in linguistic theory in its fundamental distinction between *langue* and *parole*. In England, the Cambridge Critics pursued a similar line of approach, represented especially by I. A. Richards and William Empson. However, the New Criticism, formulated by John Crowe Ransom, Cleanth Brooks, and Warren himself, set out not to create a linguistic philosophy but to delineate a way of reading poetry that both honored the poem as a poem and also elevated it to a form of articulation able to rival the supposed priority of scientific language. Even in *A Plea in Mitigation*, Warren maintains a similar emphasis upon poetry itself, vice theories about poetry. He is still concerned with what poetry is being read and how it is being read.

Mindful that denunciations of New Criticism often assume a unified narrative from critic to critic, Warren contends that "the so-called New Criticism was never monolithic. It was shot through with irremediable tensions and disagreements, both as to methods and values" (*APIM* 11). Even as early as 1957, he had made a similar observation when asked by Eugene Walter about the New Criticism in an interview in the *Paris Review*. With characteristic humor, Warren replies, "Let's name some of them—Richards, Eliot, Tate, Blackmur, Winters, Brooks, Leavis (I guess). How in God's name can you get that gang into the same bed? There's no bed big enough and no blanket would stay tucked" (Watkins and Hiers 34). Warren does acknowledge in *A Plea in Mitigation*, though, that "What gave an impression, sometimes false, of unity in the New Criticism was a special application, in sharp focus, of principles derived from Coleridge—not to mention I. A. Richards, Freud, or Aristotle" (11). Those principles were essentially symbolist and viewed the poem as a literary object which concretizes meaning. By the mid-1960s, the simplicity of such an approach had proved untenable.

> As for what the New Criticism may have done for us, that is now a closed chapter. What was temporarily useful has served its turn and what is permanently sound has been absorbed. What was merely fashionable has become old-fashioned—the formal schematizations, the over-refinement

of terms, the hair-splitting of exegesis, the academic mass production of "certified" critics, the dogmatic hardening. But such things always follow as disciples expound a revelation. We are now waiting for a new revelation. (12)

Warren himself is looking for what is yet to come; but, as he had said earlier, the "new revelation" will not come primarily by theories about poetry but by poetry itself. Warren denies that any "new revelation" is to be found in what he calls "younger poets who are sometimes set invidiously over against the moderns" (13)—a group in which he includes Dylan Thomas, the Beat Poets, Shapiro, Lowell, Jarrell, Frost, and Sandburg. They are each in their own way vitally connected to modernism and "cannot be thought of without reference to the past period" (18). The nature the relationship each has with modernism, though, varies from poet to poet. The Beat poets, for example, "constitute a footnote to modernism, rather than a radical reaction against it" (14), whereas Frost—whose poetry is far more significant than that of the Beats for Warren—"may be said to be much closer to a poet like Eliot or Yeats than to Sandburg" (17). In Warren's estimation, the philosophical weightiness lacking in the Beat poets can be found throughout the poetry of Frost who was "aware of the tensions of the age, and . . . aware of the difficulty of solutions" (17).

Applying the same criteria to the poetry of the new generation as he did to that of the modernist poets, Warren questions whether the "new" poetry is being read. His observation is that there is a "hard core" audience of serious readers who may be holdovers from modernist poetry. But there seems to be an increasing audience which indicates that a "reassessment is under way" (*APIM* 17). Among this audience, there is as much plurality of taste as there is diversity among the poets, reflected in the way readers seek different kinds of satisfaction from poetry. One kind of reader looks for "poetry as art" in order to "feed his love for the richness and variety of life" through the engagement of the imagination "as the great 'as-if' of truth," while another kind needs "poetry as prophecy" to provide "the image of truth as a way to be, see, or live, quite literally with no 'as-if' attached" (18–19). Early in the lecture, Warren raises these concepts as indications of change in the practice of poets and in the taste of readers. "When a new poetic period dawns," he says, "it always dawns with prophetic urgency; it brings with it the possibility of new experience, and is, quite simply and necessarily, a challenge of life" (2). As new poetry becomes more and more established, it loses that sense of urgency and "no longer answers the life-need for defining identity, for establishing equilibrium in change" (3). When this happens, though, some poetry passes through death and is resurrected as "poetry as art." "Poetry as art has entered history, and history demands the great 'as-if' of our imagination. Urgency of involvement is now sacrificed for profundity of vision. At that moment we see, at last, what poetry of an age may survive the 'idea of poetry' fashionable in that age" (3). Near the end of his lecture, he raises these concepts again to establish what he sees as a truth about the work of the poet.

> The individual writer must . . . drive hard at his truth. He must be "committed." In whatever way he can he must drive hard to establish his own precise personal relation with the world and with literature—even at the expense of distorting history and logic more coolly considered. The writer, ultimately, makes his art from such distortion. He cannot be all things to all men, not even to truth. He can strive only to be himself—to himself. As a writer—that is in the moment of writing—he must think of poetry only as prophecy. (19)

Clearly, Warren indicates here that his relationship to his own past and to the commitments of modernism has undergone a reassessment. His own thinking has shifted away from a representational framework to a relational one. Poetry is about articulating a relation to the world, even if such articulation involves distortion. History, in his view, is not an objective, unchangeable "fact" to be presented. Rather, it is about the relation between the self and the world mediated in and through language. Language has the power not only to "represent" but also to distort. And this distortion is merely one indication that the writer cannot say everything. Not only are there things that remain unsaid, but there remains what is itself unsayable. To articulate a relation to the world in the face of this truth requires the commitment of the poet.

Such a view, therefore, illuminates for Warren the difference between reassessing the poets of the previous age and simply repudiating their work. With their own prophetic urgency, they responded to the real crisis of their age and the resulting problems for writers and humanity alike. Warren points out, though, that "the problems of that age are still with us. For a half century we have somehow survived new wars, new revolutions, new depressions, new failures of faith, and the corrosive effects of new knowledge" (*APIM* 19).

Warren sees the parallels between the sense of crisis in the moment in which he wrote—especially the new wars and revolutions of the mid-1960s—and the crisis faced by his modernist fathers. He has a strong sense that the moment in which he wrote was fraught with "new experience," which demanded a "new language" able to open up to his generation "the nature of the experience potential in the new world around us—and know the nature of ourselves" (2). In Warren's estimation, this was a day when all things were new and revolution was necessary "to discover identity—to locate oneself on the vast and shifting chart of being" (2). At such a time, it is necessary to

> ... combat, or find a way to rise above, the dehumanizing forces of our time. One remaining piece of high ground after another is flooded, with little said. It is true that the remnants of a period style tend to blunt perception, and we may feel the nausea of repetition, the nausea of emptiness. It is true that we can overcome that nausea only by opening ourselves to what new experience is available to us in our time and by taking the risks of our time. (19–20)

The only way to overcome that existential nausea is by risking the new experiences available in that new day. So, even if the methods of modernist poets are repudiated and "their programs of salvation" are denied, we cannot "repudiate their insights, or forget the pathos and the 'pinch of glory,' to use Sir Herbert Read's phrase, or their effort" (20). What persists after their strict formalism is given up and their dogmatic doctrines are denounced is their conviction that language is more complex and troublesome than the scientist would have us believe. There is something more to our relation to the world than mere quantification. For the poet, the "risk of our time" is to open himself to language in a new way in order to articulate that relation. What revolution may occur will come through language itself.

In the opening paragraphs of his lecture, Warren had stated his view of what was happening in the wake of modernism's collapse. "Out of the babble of tongues and the darkening of counsel . . . the future gradually emerges. . . . It will emerge from poetry, not from debates about poetry. It may be emerging this very minute, but we do not yet see its shape" (*APIM* 1). He ends his essay with a prophetic declaration that echoes his earlier prediction: "Meanwhile it is well to remember that revolutions in poetry are made by new poems—not by repudiating old ones. Mere repudiation is not revolution. That is, to pursue the political metaphor, merely a servile revolt" (20).

His essay is more than a lengthy observation that a revolt against modernist poetry has happened or an in-depth analysis of its critics. In the moment of turning, Warren looks forward to what may emerge from the rupture that results from the break with the past—and this is what really distinguishes his essay. Warren was not the first to engage in a postmortem on literary modernism. One of Warren's students had made a similar declaration nearly a quarter century earlier. Randall Jarrell wrote in a 1942 essay that modernist poetry had reached "the end of the line" as the "culminating point of romanticism" (81). "Modernism As We Knew It—the most successful and influential body of poetry of this century—is dead. . . . Who could have believed that modernism would collapse so fast?" (81)[20] What distinguishes Warren's assessment from Jarrell's, however, is its timing. Despite his conviction that the future would not emerge from debates about poetry, there was a significant future emerging at that very moment even if he could not fully see its shape. During the same year in which Warren delivered his lecture, literary theory was experiencing a seismic shift from structuralism to poststructuralism, signaled by a conference held at Johns Hopkins University in 1966 that produced the 1970 volume *The Languages of Criticism and the Sciences of Man*.[21] At this conference, Jacques Derrida delivered his groundbreaking essay "Structure, Sign and Play in the Discourse of the Human Sciences," which is intensely aware of the moment in which it is written. Like Warren, Derrida acknowledges that a change is taking place as he looks back on the heritage of phenomenological thought and introduces his distinct form of apophatic thought. In the conclusion of his essay, Derrida writes,

> Here there is a kind of question, let us still call it historical, whose *conception, formation, gestation,* and *labor* we are only catching a glimpse of today. I employ these words, I admit, with a glance toward the operations of childbearing—but also with a glance toward those who, in a society from which I do not exclude myself, turn their eyes away when faced by the as yet unnamable which is proclaiming itself and which can do so, as is necessary whenever a birth is in the offing, only under the species of the nonspecies, in the formless, mute, infant, and terrifying form of monstrosity. (293)

The kind of thinking engendered by Derrida is one that functions by questioning and (ostensibly) not by answering. Yet, through such questioning, "the as yet unnamable which is proclaiming itself" speaks. Derrida went on to develop his discourse of deconstruction and *différance* in the original French editions of *Writing and Difference* (*L'Ecriture et la différance*), *Speech and Phenomena and other Essays in Husserl's Theory of Signs* (*La Voix et le phénomène*), and *Of Grammatology* (*De la grammatologie*), all of which were published in 1967. In many ways, what Derrida announces at the intersection of philosophy and literary theory within the context of Continental thought is parallel to what Warren asserts about the end of literary modernism and the turn toward an unnamed future in the context of Anglo-American poetics. There is no way that Warren could have anticipated the changes that were occurring in literary theory, even though many of his ideas at this point were keeping pace with the broader developments in philosophy and theory. Szczesiul helpfully points out that Warren "does make some provocative comments in this essay that indeed seem to forecast the poststructuralist's intensive critique of language—namely, he begins to foreground the uncertain relationships between language, reality, and the self or 'subject'" (*Racial Politics* 137). Without a doubt, he was well aware of developments in literary theory; as a professor at Yale, he interacted with younger critics like Harold Bloom who were beginning to develop the American remix of deconstruction. In "The Lessons of Theory," Jay Parini notes Warren's awareness of what actually emerged in the years after *A Plea in Mitigation*.

> Not long before he died in 1989, I sat on the porch of my Vermont neighbor, Robert Penn Warren, talking about the early days of the New Criticism. . . . "The older members of the profession thought of us— the New Critics—as revolutionaries," Warren said. "In a way, we were. Deconstruction is already fading fast. It will be absorbed—its insights and techniques repossessed and deployed in new ways." (92–93)

The apparent parallel Warren draws between the New Criticism and deconstruction suggests that he saw each critical approach as revolutionary in its day—each with its own legitimate insights and techniques—but ultimately absorbed by the future that inevitably emerges. As Warren himself emerged into that future, he began to deploy his growing sense of the problematic nature of language in reference both to the formation of the self and to one's relationship with the world.

After his questioning and musing in *Who Speaks for the Negro?* and *A Plea in Mitigation*, Warren did address the unsayable one more time during the mid-1960s when he made perhaps his most direct statement about the poet's relation to the unsayable at a poetry reading and address at Union College. William Kennedy covered the event and published his account under the title, "How a Poet Works," in *The National Observer* in February of 1967. Kennedy concludes his account with a quotation from Warren's remarks that is as important as it is enigmatic. "Most writers are trying to find what they think or feel. They are not simply working from the given, but working toward the given, saying the unsayable, and steadily asking, 'What do I really feel about this?'" (Watkins and Hiers 90).[22] In light the work he had done earlier in the decade, his statement may now be seen as a culmination of his confrontation with language and the unsayable. "Saying the unsayable" is more than merely a linguistic task or a philosophical problem; it is the mission of the poet who is willing to no longer assume that language itself is the given. Working from the given is no longer possible when the foundations have been shaken and all that had been taken as certain is opened up to questioning. The poet must work instead *toward* the given, recognizing that the given is approached through the act of questioning in the midst of concrete experience in the world. Rather than beginning from some statement of which the poem is the outworking, Warren sets out to work toward meaning or significance as it is found in the moment of articulation. And even if the final statement of meaning is endlessly deferred, the poet must continue to speak. As he had said in *A Plea in Mitigation*, the writer must pursue the moment of writing with prophetic urgency, that is, with the "urgent *frisson* of experience" that in the moment "answers the life-need for defining identity" (3). Through his articulation, the poet establishes "his own precise personal relation with the world" (19). In the midst of the social and cultural shifts taking place during the 1960s, he owned the potential shock and threat of the unsayable not merely as an individual or as a White Southerner but more particularly as a poet in what for many writers would have been the twilight years of their careers. How could he continue to speak? His own "pieties and defensive impulses" about language and the way the poet works were called into question, but through the resulting cracks the unsayable appears and begins to figure more prominently in his late poetry.

It is worth asking, though—as Warren himself does in *Who Speaks for the Negro?*—"What is the unsayable?" When Warren uses this term, what does he mean by it? Where does it come from? Can we even really speak about the unsayable? Without a doubt, this notion resists being nailed down. It is easier to speak negatively about the unsayable than positively, which is why the unsayable is so often addressed in the context of negative theology or Kabalism.[23] The unsayable is neither the unsaid that remains dormant whenever I do speak, nor is it the unspeakable that is too horrible to utter, though I may conceive it. For Warren, it becomes apparent that the unsayable is distinctly *unsayable*— what cannot be said and formulated in our language but what shapes and determines all of our speaking.[24] When he speaks of the unsayable, he clearly means something quite different than does the American poet and critic Donald Hall when he addresses the unsayable in his 1993 essay "Poetry: The Unsayable Said." For Hall, the unsayable is an emotional excess in a poem that exceeds the power of paraphrase. "By its art of saying the unsayable, poetry produces a response in excess of the discernable stimulus" (4). Adopting an architectural metaphor, Hall likens the unsayable to a secret room within a house which "conceals itself from reasonable explanation." He adds, "The secret room is something to acknowledge, accept, and honor in a silence of assent; the secret room is where the unsayable gathers, and it is poetry's uniqueness" (4). What distinguishes poetry from prose for him is that poetry is able to add "the secret (unsayable) room of feeling and tone to the sayable story" (6), which is present in prose.[25] For Warren, though, the unsayable is already present and is inescapable—in both fiction (prose) and poetry, for that matter. It is not something that the poet adds. Hall's concluding paragraph parallels some of Warren's convictions about the unsayable, yet it shows the great divergence in Hall's view.

> When we wish to embody in language a complex of feelings or sensations or ideas, we fall into inarticulateness; attempting to speak, in the heat of love or argument, we say nothing or we say what we do not intend. Poets encounter inarticulateness as much as anybody, or maybe more. They are aware of the word's inadequacy because they spend their lives struggling to say the unsayable. . . . The poets we honor most are those who—by studious imagination, by continuous connection to the sensuous body, and by spirit steeped in the practice and learning of language—publish in their work the unsayable said. (9)

Hall's acknowledgement of the inevitable collision with the limits of language echoes Warren's recurring confrontation throughout his later poetry. They both frame the work of the poet in terms of "struggling to say the unsayable." But Hall seems to hold out hope that some poets—the ones we honor most—are those who "publish in their work the unsayable said." This reversal of his terms suggests that he believes that the unsayable can finally be said. Warren takes what might be thought of as a darker view of the poet's work in the face of the unsayable. For him, the poet relentlessly pursues the unsayable until the only moment in which it can be spoken—the apocalyptic moment of death. There is an inescapable agony in this pursuit, something that he learned not only in his own experience as a poet but also from Coleridge's Ancient Mariner who returns from his mysterious journey bound to be repeatedly seized by a "strange power of speech" which fills him with "woeful agony" until his tale is told. The unsayable for Warren is not about feeling but about truth, and truth is the one thing that cannot be finally spoken.

During the 1960s, Warren found himself in the midst of an apophatic culture that had veered into worries about the reliability of language both in literature and philosophy and into an apparent refusal of rational discourse in the public and social spheres. But in the midst of this moment, Warren finds a way of return to language by means of confronting the unsayable. This was not a moment of conversion; there was no open repentance from the literary sins of his youth. But it was a moment of overcoming his past by rethinking his role as poet as well as rethinking his relation to language and to the world. If he was to survive the crisis, he must find a way to continue to speak. Throughout his later poetry, then, Warren explores the limitations and possibilities of language within the act of poetic creation. His pursuit of the unsayable leads from one poem to another, and each poem becomes a moment of articulation. In his early poetry, Warren tended to play the role described by Kevin Vanhoozer as the "poet-teacher," for whom "language is the means for gaining access to reality and truth" (26). But through his confrontation with the literary and social mores of his day, he assumes more and more the role of the "poet-artist," for whom language "has become the problematic and is . . . the new object of contemplation" (26). This pursuit begins in earnest in his 1969 poem *Audubon: A Vision* and is followed through the course of his poetry until his death in 1989. *Audubon*, however, is itself indebted thematically and aesthetically to Coleridge's *Rime of the Ancient Mariner*, which Warren had explored in his 1946 essay, "A Poem of Pure Imagination."

CHAPTER TWO

Coleridge, the Mariner, and the Search for Articulation

I could spend my life very happily studying Coleridge.—Robert Penn Warren[1]

Warren's open confrontation with language and the unsayable in his later poetry resulted from an organic process that began its development in his early days at Vanderbilt. While his thinking was no doubt influenced by fellow modernist poets and critics, it was profoundly shaped by an earlier poet whose presence hovers about all of Warren's work—the English Romantic poet Samuel Taylor Coleridge. Warren appropriated Coleridge's thought in a way that was unique among his contemporaries, plundering Coleridge's work for his own poetic and critical vision. In various interviews, Warren acknowledged his life-long fascination with Coleridge. His admission at age seventy-two that he could very happily spend his life studying Coleridge ought to surprise no one who has read much of Warren's work—fiction or poetry![2] In an early letter written in 1924 to Allen Tate, Warren admits his deference to Coleridge and to the poem that would prove to be seminal for his own work. Speaking of a failed relationship with Catherine Baxter Nichol, Warren hints at his disappointment by describing it as his "Albatross." After a lengthy analysis of his experience, he writes, "Anyway, to borrow a figure from the Ancient Mariner, the body on board may unfortunately but naturally cause me to be pursued by a shadowy figure swimming six fathoms beneath my keel. One accumulates such unwelcome attendants during a visitation in antipodal seas" (*SL* 1:28).[3] William Bedford Clark comments:

Moreover, it is significant that in portraying his moribund relationship with Chink Nichol as his "Albatross," Warren makes a telling nod in the direction of Coleridge's *Rime of the Ancient Mariner,* thus collaterally confirming the interplay between letterly writing and literary production that tended to inform his correspondence at every stage of his career, for Coleridge's poem would in time provide an intertextual foundation for much of Warren's subsequent work. (*SL* 1:9)

Indeed, Warren devoted several years to the *Ancient Mariner,* resulting in what is arguably his most important critical essay, "A Poem of Pure Imagination: An Experiment in Reading."

Originally prepared as the 1945 Bergen Lecture at Yale University while Warren was Consultant in Poetry in the Library of Congress, "A Poem of Pure Imagination" provides a focal point for the development of Warren's thinking about the task of the poet who confronts the limitations of language. This was, in large part, the critical soil out of which grew his later thinking about both language and the act of poetic creation as it brings the unsayable to light. In the essay, he seeks to provide a reading that was consistent with Coleridge's philosophy, especially concerning the act of poetic creation. Warren's resulting meditation on the function of the imagination and the symbol in poetic creation forms the foundation for his thinking about language in the poem. It is no exaggeration, then, to say that this essay shaped his thought in a way unlike any other single influence. The textual history of the essay confirms that this influence took shape over several years. In fact, there is no other essay to which Warren apparently devoted so much time and effort. In 1946, the publishers Reynal and Hitchcock included Warren's essay in an edition of *The Rime of the Ancient Mariner* illustrated by Alexander Calder. Parts III, IV, and V were published in an essay in the Summer 1946 issue of the *Kenyon Review.* The entire essay was then included as the final selection of Warren's 1958 *Selected Essays.* This version of the essay, though, was significantly revised, more so than any other piece in the volume. In the preface, Warren states, "I have lifted some material from the notes into the text, have struck out some notes and added others, and in a few instances, in the hope of greater precision, have changed a formulation" (xiii). His hope for greater precision indicates that the central focus of his essay continued to be vitally related to the central focus of his own work as a poet.

Coleridge's impact is obvious in one of Warren's later poems, included as the "Coda" in his 1981 volume, *Rumor Verified* (*CP* 487). "Fear and Trembling" begins with what is an archetypical moment in Warren's later poetry:

> The sun now angles downward, and southward.
> The summer, that is, approaches its final fulfillment.
> The forest is silent, no wind-stir, bird-note, or word.
> It is time to meditate on what the season has meant. (1–4)

This concrete moment in nature—unstable and turning—is neither timeless nor isolated in space but is actuated in the poet's simultaneous encounter with language and nature. It is a moment of ripeness both at the end of the day and at the turning of the season.[4] Within this moment the speaker posits, "It is time to meditate on what the season has meant." He then continues in the second stanza:

> But what is the meaningful language for such meditation?
> What is a word but wind through the tube of the throat?
> Who defines the relation between the word *sun* and the sun?
> What word has glittered on whitecap? Or lured blossom out? (5–8)

Warren's speaker senses that his own language is inadequate for a meditation upon the meaning of nature's turning. His own words are conspicuously arbitrary—"What is a word but wind . . ."—and so he yearns for a language in which word and thing are co-terminus—"What word has glittered on whitecap?" At the heart of his linguistic struggle is the problem of referentiality. He acknowledges that there is a "relation between the word *sun* and the sun," but who or what defines "*the* relation"? In light of the problem of referentiality, the speaker queries the limits of the meditation of the heart throughout the rest of the poem and probes the linguistic moment in nature: "Walk deeper, foot soundless, into the forest. / Stop, breath bated . . . " (9–10). In the midst of this place where "nothing grieves" (12), the poet asks the question at the heart of his search for articulation: "Can one, in fact, meditate in the heart, rapt and wordless?" (13) In the final stanzas, Warren raises two of the issues at the heart of his linguistic concerns in his later poetry: the desire to find one's voice before the unsayable and the recognition of the outwardness of language.[5] There are also Platonic overtones that appear not only in his study of Coleridge but also at various other points in his poetic corpus. Warren intimates here that, in order to speak, the poet must be able to listen to language in the world and in his own heart. Only at the death of his ambition for a *pure* language will language avail itself in its fallen yet powerful speaking.

The way in which Warren questions language and reference within this poem were informed without doubt by his continued interaction with Coleridge. This is especially the case in the second stanza, which bears a striking similarity to a passage from one of Coleridge's lecture note fragments, contained within the volume *Shakespearean Criticism*. Coleridge states, "The sound *sun*, or the figures *s*, *u*, *n*, are purely arbitrary modes of recalling the object.... But the language of nature is a subordinate *Logos*, that was in the beginning, and was with the thing represented, and was the thing represented" (I.185). In a curious foreshadowing of Saussurian linguistics, Coleridge acknowledges the arbitrariness of the linguistic sign and its reference. In response to this, however, he proposes the notion of the Logos, which was at once aesthetic and theological. In his theory of the Logos—that primary and personal agent of creation and revelation declared at the beginning of John's gospel—the wound of the Fall has split word and thing apart and can only be healed by a living word that defines the reconciled relationship between the two. The Logos is both "with the thing represented" and "was the thing represented," making it the essential symbol for Coleridge. Coleridge draws from this three different ways of approaching language: a purely arbitrary, human language; a more fundamental language of nature; and an essential language contained in the Logos. It was the aesthetic sensibility as well as the theological cast of Coleridge's thinking about language, the imagination, and the symbol that so significantly impacted Warren's thinking.

"A Poem of Pure Imagination" in undoubtedly one of Warren's most widely read critical essays, having received a variety of responses from both critics of Coleridge's poetry and theorists who regard it as a representative text of New Criticism. Among Coleridge scholars, Stephen Prickett, in *Romanticism and Religion,* characterizes it as the "best discussion of the *Ancient Mariner* as an artistic whole . . . " (16). Stanley Cavell states that he knows "of no better discussion of the question of [the killing of the Albatross], and its motive, than Robert Penn Warren's . . . " (194). James C. McKusick goes even further when he describes Warren's essay as "perhaps the single most important essay in the history of Coleridge criticism" ("Symbol" 225). Homer Obed Brown considers the essay to be "one of the finest examples of New Critical explication, while at the same time it places Coleridge's poem in the larger context of his literary, philosophical and theological theory" (238). He goes on to praise Warren's critical foresight, claiming, "Robert Penn Warren set up the issues for future criticism, but what is more, he provided the basis for, indeed a solicitation of further attempts at interpretive totalization, for the necessity of reading it in some sort of integrative and structurally unitary way" (255). Jonathan Arac counters Brown's argument, though, by proposing that Warren's repetition of New Critical presuppositions and exclusion of various parts of Coleridge's own theory pertains to "the whole problem of cultural reproduction" (261), which institutionalized the New Criticism and established textual canons. Arac's comments echo the criticisms leveled by Elder Olson, one of Warren's earliest detractors and a member of the Chicago Critics who sought to repudiate New Criticism through a primarily Aristotelian aesthetic. According to Olson, the essay "seems . . . to be valuable principally as exhibiting what happens to poetry in interpretation, and not particularly valuable as a comment upon the poem" (138). Olson rejects Warren's argument that the poem is symbolic, and maintains that "Warren's interpretation clearly makes the poem what Coleridge calls 'allegory'" (142). William Empson was also among Warren's detractors. Although he found the essay on his second reading to be "better than it seemed in my vague memory of it," Empson still considered Warren's work to be a prime example of Symbolist criticism, which "invites irrationalism" (155–56). More recently, David Perkins has attempted in "The 'Ancient Mariner' and Its Interpreters: Some Versions of Coleridge" to point out what he calls Warren's "New Critical naivete" in his tacit assumption "that his interpretation of the poem would have been Coleridge's also" (432). Perkins argues that "Warren's concepts of symbolism were not drawn from Coleridge but from well-known theories in psychology, anthropology, and the arts and, in the literary milieu, from *symbolisme*, Yeats, Ernst Cassirer, C. S. Lewis, Susanne Langer, and so forth" (433).[6]

Despite either such praises or denunciations of Warren's critical work, the great value of this essay is found not simply in his analysis of the imagination and symbol but in the character of his experimental reading. While Warren's work displays a degree of aptitude in a kind of literary-historical scholarship, this aspect of the essay is eclipsed by his overriding concern for the nature of poetic creation. His essay is about the poet and poetry, and he writes not so much as a critic than as a poet himself, one who has wrestled with language in order to win some articulation and has lived to tell his story bearing the wound of the imagination. As a result, his reading of *The Ancient Mariner* is filled with a high degree of self-consciousness. The poem embodies what he called "the question of the poet to himself," and his essay poses that question to himself in the moment of the act of poetic creation in the poet's confrontation with the unsayable. In *A Plea in Mitigation*, Warren identifies the *Ancient Mariner* as one of several Romantic poems that "plagued the question" (9) of the role of the poet and the relation of poetry and truth. He makes that distinction more sharply in "A Poem of Pure Imagination" by contending that, in its dealing with these issues, it was a central poem among Romantic poetry. *The Ancient Mariner* certainly is not, in his estimation, "one of the 'great, formless poems' which the Romantics are accused of writing, and not a poem which would fit into T. S. Eliot's formula of the dissociated sensibility of the period" (394). Warren takes the poem to be "central and seminal for the poet himself" as well as "central for its age, providing not a comment on an age, but a focus of the being and issues of that age" (394). Warren pinpoints the "focus of the being and the issues of that age" when he states that he considers the poem to be "a document of the very central and crucial issue of the period: the problem of truth and poetry" (380). Although he sees the roots of this issue in the Platonic dialogue *Ion*, Warren claims that this was "directly or indirectly, an obsessive theme for poetry itself" during the Romantic period (380). This was nothing really new; eighteenth-century poets and writers had attempted to establish "a holy alliance between science and religion" (380). But, perhaps the Romantic poets were the first to feel the need of an alliance between poetry and truth precisely because of the cultural milieu in which they wrote. Whereas the link had been assumed, it began to be loosened by the Industrial Revolution and the social and communal changes that began to be felt. Warren states, "There were two truths, and they themselves might very well be in deadly competition: the truth of religion and the truth of science" (381). In this competition, the Romantic poets maintained "that poetry gives truth; or if they were as subtle as Coleridge, they sought to establish an intimate and essential connection between truth and poetry on psychological as well as metaphysical grounds" (381). This issue continued to be a central concern for Warren as well as for New Critics and modernist critics who were the heirs of this Romantic vision in a similar cultural and social milieu. They struggled to create a space in which poetry might speak its truth in the midst of a world that relied upon science alone as a truth-register. Warren, however, sees in the work of Coleridge—as opposed to that of Shelley or Wordsworth—an effort toward reconciliation between all areas of thought: "But the main problem of reconciliation for Coleridge was that between poetry and religion, or morality, for since those were his twin passions, it was necessary for him to develop some vital connection between them if he was to be happy" (381). In a similar way, Warren sought a comparable reconciliation between poetry and the unsayable.

Warren outlines Coleridge's detailed solution to the reconciliation of the poetic and the religious in a way that indicates how he began to come to grips with the struggle to "say the unsayable." As with Coleridge, his struggle with language centered around the problem of representation and reference, or between the relationship of word and thing. He worked with a great awareness of the crisis of modernity: the experience of alienation after the "death of God," in which individuals as well as words and things seem to be irreparably separated. This crisis, however, was the same confrontation with the linguistic consequences of the Fall experienced by Coleridge. As Warren moved away from viewing language as a tool for prying open reality, he confronted the fractured and arbitrary nature of language that opened up a fundamental problem for the poet: what is the nature of the poet's task if language both reveals and hides—or, if like Derrida's *pharmakon,* it both heals and wounds? If, as Jefferson surmises in *Brother to Dragons,* "language betrays," then what is a poet to do?[7] Is there an "adequate" language available? Does "poetic language" transcend these limits, or does it merely incarnate them all the more concretely? Does "poetic structure" coerce the recalcitrance of language into a yielding, subservient instrument? Warren's wrestling with these issues began to take shape in "A Poem of Pure Imagination;" however, his meditations on the poem did not yield firm answers, as much as it clarified the appropriate questions for the poet to ask.

At the end of his essay, Warren states that his purpose is to vindicate what he calls "a discursive reading of the symbol which is the poem" (398). His experimental reading sets out not only "to establish that *The Ancient Mariner* does embody a statement" (337–38) but also "to establish that the statement which the poem does ultimately embody is thoroughly consistent with Coleridge's basic theological and philosophical views as given to us in sober prose" (339).[8] That statement consists in what he identifies—with a self-conscious nod to

Coleridge's definition of the imagination—as the primary and secondary themes of the poem. The primary theme—which is not more important than the secondary but is, according to Warren, "at the threshold of the poem"— is that of the sacramental vision or the "One Life" (348). According to Warren, this identifies "the issue of the fable," or the basic narrative of crime, punishment, repentance, and recognition. The sacramental vision of *The Ancient Mariner* brings to light the metaphysical and theological issues of the mystery of original sin and of the Fall of humanity in Adam, the primary symbol for humanity in Coleridge's thought. The secondary theme of the imagination has to do with "the context of values" that the poem "may be found ultimately to embody" (380). These values undergird the metaphysical nature of the sacramental vision that extends his interpretation of the imagination to the theological notions of the Fall and of original sin found throughout the poem. Warren's professed goal, though, is to define the way in which these two themes undergo a "final symbolic fusion in the poem" (349), because this symbolic fusion reveals something about the nature of poetic creation as Coleridge understood it.

These two themes are "the central and crucial fact" (380) of the poem precisely because symbolic fusion reveals the way Coleridge reconciled the aesthetic and religious dimensions of his thought. This reconciliation, which Warren calls a "precarious solution" to the problem of truth and poetry, "was, of course, one aspect of his doctrine of the creative unity of the mind, which appears and reappears in his work and which is his great central insight and great contribution to modern thought" (382). In order to substantiate his experimental reading, Warren seeks to vindicate Coleridge's poem by extensive reference to Coleridge's own thought, using what sources were available to him in the mid-1940s through the early 1950s.[9] Since that time, however, Coleridge studies have flourished and have produced definitive editions of his works, including five volumes of his *Notebooks* as well as six volumes of his *Marginalia*. In light of these more recently published works, Warren's essay proves to be an even more insightful engagement with Coleridge's theory of the imagination and the symbol than it was when first published. It is this engagement that opens up a way to Warren's later confrontations with language and the unsayable.

Warren begins with the implicit recognition that his reading goes against the grain of previous criticism of *The Ancient Mariner*, yet he clearly assumes that his reading is consistent with Coleridge's aesthetic as a whole. He seeks to vindicate Coleridge's formulation of the imagination from previous interpretations of the poem and strives to show the limitations and problems of those interpretations, primarily those of Griggs and Lowes, for whom "the poem is nothing more than a pleasant but meaningless dream" (340).[10] Warren's objection to both critics is rooted in the priority he places upon the role of the imagination in Coleridge's overall philosophy and in the poem itself. Griggs's reading represents what Warren calls "a brand of hyperaesthetical criticism" (336) of the poem, which he describes as inherent to a theory of "'pure poetry'— some notion that a poem should not 'mean' but 'be,' and that the 'be-ing' of a poem does not 'mean'" (337). Ultimately, *The Ancient Mariner* is, for Griggs, "a journey into the supernatural for the sake of the journey" (340). Warren also rejects Lowes's moralistic criticism of the poem, summarizing his reading of the moral of the poem as, "a man should not have to suffer so much just for shooting a bird" (339). In light of Lowe's assessment that the poem's "inconsequence is the dream's irrelevance," Warren asserts that the author of *The Road to Xanadu* considers it as "an illusion for the sake of illusion" (340). Warren also responds to what he considers to be other fallacious interpretations based upon false critical pretenses. For example, he wants to distinguish what he means by the "theme" of the poem from the idea of "the personal theme," which seems to have held a central position in interpretations of the poem. He cites Kenneth Burke's concern in *The Philosophy of Literary Form* for "the sexual and opium motives" (349) in Coleridge's composition. Furthermore, when considering the nature of the Mariner's act, he strongly rejects both literalist and allegorical readings. He especially cites Gingerich's reading which attributes the Mariner's act to a necessitarian philosophy: "The Mariner does not act but is constantly acted upon, that 'he is pursued by a dark and sinister fate' after having done the deed 'impulsively and wantonly' and presumably under necessity" (356). Warren's skepticism about these readings hinges upon their limited interpretation of Coleridge's theory of the imagination and the symbol. He says of Griggs and Lowes that "they take the word imagination here at their own convenience and not in Coleridge's context and usage" (341).

Warren's discussion of the symbolic fusion of the two themes provides a window on the way Coleridge came to characterize his own struggle with language. These two themes and their fusion are vital to understanding what happens when the poet wrestles with language in order to create a poem. Warren says toward the end of the essay that he has tried "to show, by dwelling on details as well as on the broad, central images, that there is in *The Ancient Mariner* a relatively high degree of expressive integration" (390). He goes on the say, "For I take the poem to be one in which the vital integration is of a high order. . . . It is, in short, a work of 'pure imagination'" (394). By looking for a high degree of "vital integration" in the poem, Warren seeks to apply Coleridge's own aesthetic, as he understands it, to the interpretation of the poem, to take his theory of the imagination and his formulation of the symbol as the most helpful perspective. To look at this poem "in the light of the poet's lifelong preoccupations, we may come to conclude, with Leslie Stephen, that 'the germ of all Coleridge's utterances may be found . . . in the 'Ancient Mariner'" (394). Warren's interpretation of the poem certainly points to Coleridge's utterances about language and its role in his aesthetic theory. As Coleridge's preoccupation with the symbol shaped his own life-long struggle to validate a linguistic theory, so it was this theory that shaped Warren's own coming to terms with the problem of language.

Early in the essay, Warren does acknowledge that he is not primarily "concerned with a detailed exposition of Coleridge's theory, and certainly not with an account of the stages of its growth and clarification" (342). However, a careful reading of his observations as they are developed in both the body of the text and his extensive footnotes does provide something of a skeletal framework, noting several critical moments and influences in the growth of Coleridge's thought. While paying particular attention to Warren's account of the imagination and its function in poetic creation, it is also helpful to explore those "stages of . . . growth and clarification" more closely and in specific relation to the development of Coleridge's linguistic theory. Warren begins his discussion of the imagination by quoting the "key passage" on the imagination from Chapter 13 of the *Biographia Literaria* (1817).

> The IMAGINATION then I consider either as primary, or secondary. The primary imagination I hold to be the living Power and prime Agent of all human Perception, and as a repetition in the finite mind of the eternal act of creation in the infinite I AM. The secondary I consider as an echo of the former, co-existing with the conscious will, yet still as identical with the primary in the *kind* of its agency, and differing only in *degree*, and in the *mode* of its operation. It dissolves, diffuses, dissipates,

in order to re-create; or where this process is rendered impossible, yet still at all events, it struggles to idealize and to unify. (I.304)

Within this chapter, Coleridge begins his exposition of the imagination as a reconciling and completing power by discussing it in light of his attempt to construct a true transcendental philosophy. He begins from the Kantian presupposition that nature is composed of two contrary forces, "the one of which tends to expand infinitely, while the other strives to apprehend or *find* itself in this infinity . . . " (I.297). These forces are not contradictory in the sense that they "must neutralize or reduce each other to inaction" (I.299); following Kant, these are opposites or contraries that are "real without being contradictory" (I.298). If these two forces are contrary without being contradictory, then the problem of transcendental philosophy is "to discover the result or product of two such forces" (I.299). Their relationship necessarily involves what Coleridge calls "one power with its two inherent indestructible yet counteracting forces, and the results or generations to which their interpenetration gives existence, in the living principle and in the process of our own self-consciousness" (I.299).

It becomes evident by the end of this chapter that Coleridge conceives this "one power" to be the imagination, making his clearest distinction between the primary and the secondary imagination as stated in the "key passage" quote above. By means of the primary imagination, we are able to perceive ourselves in the midst of an intelligible world and are able to exercise a conscious will. The exercise of the human will as a finite repetition of the eternal will of God as displayed in the act of creation is central in all of Coleridge's thinking about the imagination and is a key feature in Warren's subsequent thought. The secondary imagination, as an exercise of the creative will to idealize and unify, is an echo of the former and co-exists with the conscious will, differing only in the degree and mode of its activity. In "Appendix C" of *The Statesman's Manual*, Coleridge describes the imagination as that "completing power which unites clearness with depth, the plenitude of the sense with the comprehensibility of the understanding" (69). When the understanding becomes "impregnated" with the imagination, it then "becomes intuitive, and a living power" (69). Apart from this power of the imagination, the understanding would function at the level of fancy alone. Coleridge says in Chapter 9 of the *Biographia* that, as a result of his early relationship with Wordsworth and his reading of Wordsworth's poetry, he came "to suspect . . . that fancy and imagination were two distinct and widely different faculties, instead of being, according to the general belief, either two names with one meaning, or at furthest the lower and higher degree of one and the same power" (I.82). He describes the fancy as "no other than a mode of MEMORY emancipated from the order of time and space; and blended with, and modified by that empirical phenomenon of the will, which we express by the word CHOICE. But equally with the ordinary memory it must receive all its materials ready made from the law of association" (I.305). Rather than being re-creative and unifying, the fancy is merely descriptive. In terms of his later linguistic observations, the fancy seeks to give permanence to things by formulating linguistic abstractions. In the hands of the fancy, language is used simply as a tool.

Understanding the importance of this distinction in Coleridge's philosophy, Warren is committed to preserving its integrity in his reading of *The Ancient Mariner*. He rebuts the argument of several critics who apparently confuse the imagination and the fancy, stating, "Actually, a little reflection instructs us that the word was for Coleridge freighted with a burden of speculation and technical meaning. His theory of the imagination, upon which his whole art-philosophy hinges, 'was primarily the vindication of a particular attitude to life and reality'"(341).[11] In a lengthy footnote, Warren appeals to what he calls "the principle of presumptive coherence in development" (400), arguing against the view that Coleridge arrived at his understanding of the imagination later in his career after his time spent in Germany. He goes on to gloss Coleridge's comment in the *Biographia*: "First, Coleridge says flatly that he had become aware of the special power of the imagination at an early date, his 'twenty-fourth year.' . . . The whole discussion of the origin of the *Lyrical Ballads* makes it clear beyond doubt that the basic conception of the imagination had been arrived at early" (400–01). Indeed, this preoccupation is apparent as early as his 1795 "Lecture on the Slave-Trade," in which Coleridge states,

> To develope the powers of the Creator is our proper employment— and to imitate Creativeness by combination our most exalted and self-satisfying Delight. But we are progressive and must not rest content with present Blessings. Our Almighty Parent hath therefore given to us Imagination that stimulates to the attainment of *real* excellence by the contemplation of splendid Possibilities that still revivifies the dying

motive within us, and fixing our eye on the glittering Summits that rise one above the other in Alpine endlessness still urges us up the ascent of Being, amusing the ruggedness of the road with the beauty and grandeur of the ever-widening Prospect. Such and so noble are the ends for which this restless faculty was given us—but horrible has been its misapplication. (235–36)

Even here, the way Coleridge frames the imagination anticipates his later, more nuanced description of the revivifying power as "a repetition in the finite mind of the eternal act of creation in the infinite I AM." His symbol of the Alpine summits that endlessly rise, one above the other, reveals what he conceives to be the real power of the imagination: it is by means of the imagination that we move "up the ascent of Being" and gain "the ever-widening prospect." His description clearly anticipates both the notion of the imagination as a "living power" and his later conception of language as "living words."[12]

This passage also betrays the theological significance of the imagination for Coleridge, a significance that is not lost on Warren in "A Poem of Pure Imagination." In fact, he takes to task I. A. Richards for "casting into psychological terms what in Coleridge's thought appears often in theological and metaphysical terms . . . ," and argues that even though Coleridge "defended the use of the word *psychological*, he was not content to leave the doctrine of the creativity of mind at the psychological level" (345). Warren describes the theological import of the imagination in terms of the *imago dei*:

There is a God, and the creativity of the human mind, both in terms of the primary and in terms of the secondary imagination, is an analogue of Divine creation and a proof that man is created in God's image. . . . Reason, as opposed to the understanding, is, in Coleridge's system, the organ whereby man achieves the 'intuition and spiritual consciousness of God,' and the imagination operates to read Nature in the light of that consciousness, to read it as a symbol of God. It might be said that reason shows us God, and imagination shows us how Nature participates in God. (345)

Human creativity, for Coleridge, was not merely a psychological phenomenon shaped strictly by sense experience in an empirical world; rather, its roots are embedded in man's creaturely nature, being made in the image of God.

Because of this, the imagination is that innate faculty by which the mind is able to "read" nature as a "symbol of God." Coleridge's insistence upon the innate nature of the imagination—based upon the analogue of the human mind to the divine—defined his understanding of language and distinguished it from the predominant mechanistic and materialistic theories of language in seventeenth- and eighteenth-century philosophy.

As Warren develops his argument in Sections II and III of the essay, he establishes the vital relationship both between the imagination and the symbol in Coleridge's thought and between the primary and secondary themes in Coleridge's poem. Through the course of his analysis, he points out something of Coleridge's intellectual progression, which increasingly defined his aesthetics. He traces his interactions with eighteenth-century philosophers and linguists, but he also rightly highlights Coleridge's indebtedness to the Platonic tradition, acknowledging his relation especially to Plotinus and Jacob Boehme.[13] While he does not systematically develop Coleridge's aesthetic in conversation with these various philosophers, it is nonetheless helpful to pursue in more detail the unmistakable connections between Coleridge's theory of the imagination and symbol and his convictions about the nature of language. These connections prove to be significant for opening up Warren's own developing struggles with language.

Coleridge's earliest reflections on language involved a mixture of his philosophical, theological, and poetic questions. According to Goodson, poetic language was his "originating question": "In the beginning Coleridge was occupied with language in its poetic setting" (48). These reflections on language were shaped by his interaction with the works of Locke, Hartley, and Berkeley and were concerned with problems that the Rationalists and Empiricists sought to solve—such as the relation of thing to thought, the distinction between presentation and representation, and the differences between sensation, perception and feeling.[14] Coleridge was particularly influenced by the differences between the idealism of George Berkeley and the empiricism of John Locke. He adamantly rejected Locke's fundamental repudiation of the rationalist theory of innate notions, which formed the singular presupposition of his *Essay Concerning Human Understanding* (1690).[15] Locke proposed that such a notion was built upon a "universal consent" that "there are certain principles, both *speculative* and *practical* . . . , universally agreed upon by all mankind: which therefore, they argue, must needs be constant impressions which the souls of men receive in their first beings, and which they bring into the world with them, as necessarily and really as they do any of their inherent faculties" (I.2.2). Locke argues, however, that the mind is in its first being a *tabula rasa*, void of these ideas, and contends that principles only enter the mind through the use of reason by means of the senses; as he says, "the foundation of all *our knowledge of corporeal things lies in our senses*" (III.11.23). He states,

> The senses at first let in particular *ideas* and furnish the yet empty cabinet; and the mind by degrees growing familiar with some of them, they are lodged in the memory, and names got to them. Afterwards the mind, proceeding further, abstracts them, and by degrees learns the use of general names. In this manner the mind comes to be furnished with *ideas* and language, the materials about which to exercise its discursive faculty. (I.2.15)

He then goes on to discuss the relationship between language and ideas in Book III, "Of Words." He argues that man has by nature organs that are "so fashioned as to be *fit to frame articulate sounds*, which we call words" (III.1.1), but this is not to say that language is in any way innate. Words signify only ideas in Locke's theory, "those names becoming general which are made to stand for general *ideas*, and those remaining particular where the *ideas* they are used for are particular" (III.1.3). But, if the "whole extent of our knowledge or imagination reaches not beyond our own *ideas*, limited to our own ways of perception" (III.11.23), then language as well as the imagination cannot extend to have any vital interaction with things. Rather, it is an obscure and unclear relation between word and thing which ultimately divides the one from the other. Locke contends that "it is a perverting the use of words, and brings unavoidable obscurity and confusion into their signification, whenever we make them stand for anything but those *ideas* we have in our own minds" (III.2.5).

What Coleridge apparently found untenable in Locke's thought was just this division between word and thing precisely because it violated his commitment to a unified vision able to sustain the identity between word and thing. He, therefore, states in the *Biographia* that he summarily rejected Locke's system because he could not find in it "an abiding place for my reason" (I.141). This statement is significant in light of his linking the imagination with reason. Ultimately, Locke's system could not make a place for the imagination as Coleridge understood it. After his time in Germany, Coleridge continued to express his great concern over the influence of Locke's philosophy. For instance, Coleridge rejected James Mackintosh's views because of the latter's adherence to Locke's notion of the non-innateness of all ideas (*CN* 1.634). In a notebook entry from 1801, Coleridge proposes an "Essay on Locke" in which he would seek to vindicate the power, ability, and role of the creative imagination. According to Coburn, Coleridge believed that the "creative human mind brings what is dim and unrealized into clarity" (*CN* 1.930n), and for Coleridge the work of Shakespeare and of the Bible display this most prominently. It is the living power of the imagination that vivifies and links the act of perception to the creative will. Even in 1807, Coleridge wrote in his notebook, "Time, Space, Duration, Action, Active, Passion, Passive, Activeness, Passiveness, Reaction, Causation, Affinity—here assemble all the Mysteries—known, all is known—unknown, say rather, merely known, all is unintelligible / and yet Locke & the stupid adorers of this that *Fetisch* Earth-clod, take all these for granted . . . " (2.3156).

In rejecting Locke's empiricism, Coleridge entertained for a period the philosophical system of the eighteenth-century English philosopher David Hartley, who espoused the doctrine of association. Associationism, with roots in Aristotelian thought, observes in "the spontaneous movements of thought and the principle of their intellectual mechanism" a "law of association as established in the contemporaneity of the original impressions" and then seeks to center this as "the basis of all true psychology" (*BL* I.91).[16] Nonetheless, Coleridge saw in Hartley's formulation of this doctrine a possible response to the starkness of Locke's position. His interests in this law were naturally drawn by the question of human perception. In Chapters 5 through 9 of the *Biographia*, he recounts the history of the law of association, tracing its development from Aristotle to Hartley. He begins in Chapter 5 by going back to Aristotle in order to find "the fullest and most perfect enunciation of the associative principle" (I.100) and summarizes Aristotle's "general law of association" in this way: "Ideas by having been together acquire a power of recalling each other; or every partial representation awakes the total representation of which it had been a part" (I.102–03). Coleridge is critical of what he calls the "principle of *contemporaneity*, which Aristotle had made the common *condition* of all the laws of association . . . " (I.110). Ultimately, he saw the law of association as "the universal law of the passive *fancy* and *mechanical* memory . . . " (I.103–04), which denies the power of the imagination and the importance of its relationship to human language. He also points to Descartes as another exponent of the law of association who sought

> to establish it as a general law; that contemporaneous impressions, whether images or sensations, recall each other mechanically. On this principle, as a ground work, he built up the whole system of human language, as one continued process of association. . . . As one word may become the general exponent of many, so by association a simple image may represent a whole class. (*BL* I.94–95)

If impressions merely "recall one another mechanically," then the conscious will is denied its role in the act of poetic creation. If language is simply "one continued process of association," between ideas in the mind, then word and thing are still divided. The problem with the Aristotelian and Cartesian formulations—as well as those of Hobbes and Vives—is precisely this rift between subject and object, thought and feeling, word and thing.

In "A Poem of Pure Imagination," Warren points out both Coleridge's early deference to Hartley and his hesitation to completely adopt his thought as a system. Despite his early devotion to Hartley, Coleridge's commitment was mitigated first by his readings in the mystical and theosophical traditions—especially in Plotinus and Boehme—and then later by his reading of Kant and Schelling.[17] This led to his divergence from Hartley's system especially because of its inadequate formulation of the relation between word and thing. Warren quotes a statement made by Coleridge "during the years immediately leading up to the composition of *The Ancient Mariner*: 'I am a complete necessitarian, and I understand the subject almost as well as Hartley himself, but I go farther than Hartley, and believe the corporeality of *thought*, namely that it is motion'"(356).[18] Coleridge understood himself to "go farther than Hartley" precisely in the relationship between idea and thing, or word and thing. In the *Biographia*, he summarizes the Hartleyan associationism and outlines his reasons for eventually rejecting it. His rejection centered upon the system's implications for language. Hartley's theory extended the materialist tradition that had originated in Aristotle's philosophy and had impacted the eighteenth century primarily through Descartes and Hobbes. Coleridge refers at the beginning of Chapter 6 of the *Biographia* to "Hartley's hypothetical vibrations in his hypothetical oscillating ether of the nerves" (I.106) and goes on the explain why such a mechanical system is not only untenable but is not—in his opinion—properly philosophical. Hartley proposed that ideas are vibrations in the mind that correspond to external objects; so, the idea or vibration a is produced by and corresponds to the external object A. If each vibration has a distinct cause, then how could ideas be associated to one another? Coleridge summarizes it this way:

> To understand this, the attentive reader need only be reminded, that the ideas are themselves, in Hartley's system, nothing more than their appropriate configurative vibrations. It is a mere delusion of the fancy to conceive the pre-existence of the ideas, in any chain of association, as so many differently colored billiard-balls in contact, so that when an object, the billiard-stick, strikes the first or white ball, the same motion propagates itself through the red, green, blue, black, etc., and sets the whole in motion. No! we must suppose the very same force, which *constitutes* the white ball, to *constitute* the red or black; or the idea of a circle to *constitute* the idea of a triangle; which is impossible. (I.108)

In his *Observations on Man* (1754), Hartley applied his doctrine of association to language: "Words and Phrases must excite Ideas in us by Association, and they excite Ideas in us by no other means" (Goodson 55). If the only relationship between words and ideas is a law of association that depends upon the notion of contemporaneity, then words and ideas (or things) are still divided from one another.

By 1797, Coleridge had turned to George Berkeley as his favored muse.[19] Warren points out that in a December 1796 letter to John Thelwall, Coleridge says explicitly, "'I am a Berkleyan'" (357). On a number of occasions, he states that he preferred Berkeley's metaphor of perception over Locke's conception of the senses and their relation to ideas. In a notebook entry from 1809, he states his understanding of the difference between the two philosophers: "Berkeley's Idealism may be thus illustrated: Our perceptions are impressions on our own minds standing to the external cause in the relation of the picture on the Canvass to the Painter, rather than in that of the Image in the Mirror to the Object reflected" (*CN* 3.3605 *f120v*). Berkeley's system was rooted in an idealist metaphysic, in which, according to McKusick, "God is an active presence in the visible universe, and the act of perception is nothing other than the apprehension of the ideas by which he manifests himself" (27). What appealed to Coleridge in Berkeley's system is the way it subverts both the materialist and mechanistic views common to the sort of Deism that descended from Locke. Coleridge was drawn to what he considered to be the theological possibilities of Berkeley's notion of "outness" and of his formulation of what he called the Divine Visual Language. He would adopt this notion of outness when formulating his own theory of the symbol. But, Coleridge was also deeply influenced by Berkeley's concept of nature as the Divine Visual Language, in which he surmises that nature is the primary way of communication between God and man—in this way, Berkeley is able to hold that Christian faith may justly be based on sense-experience alone—and that these appearances form a kind of language analogous to human language. McKusick also points out how Berkeley's doctrine provided the means by which Coleridge was able to respond to Hartley: "But Coleridge adopted Berkeley's philosophy for the sake of its idealism, as a way of emancipating himself from the tyranny of Hartleyan associationism, and he does not hesitate to press its conclusions farther than Berkeley ever dared" (29).

Berkeley's philosophy fit with Coleridge's own sacramental or "organic" view of nature and reality, which Warren observes to be so central to *The Ancient Mariner*. Berkeley did hold, however, that *natural* signs were arbitrary, as arbitrary as signs in human language. Coleridge seems to have agreed with this notion of linguistic arbitrariness. In a notebook entry from 1801, he describes his son Hartley playing with stones, and is struck by the analogy to language: "It seems to elucidate the Theory of Language, Hartley, just able to speak a few words, making a fire-place of stones, with stones for fire— four stones—fire-place—two stones—fire— / arbitrary symbols in Imagination . . . " (*CN* 1.918).[20] The arbitrariness to which he refers is the way Hartley assigns different functions to all the same stones, and yet they function powerfully as symbols by means of the child's imagination. Coleridge distinguished, though, between such arbitrary, "human" signs and natural signs because he understood natural signs, as the language of nature, to be far less arbitrary than signs in human language. So, in the lecture fragment, "Genius and Public Taste," Coleridge suggests that, though human language so often functions by purely arbitrary modes, the language of nature is more than arbitrary because it is "a subordinate *Logos*" (*Shakespearean Criticism* 1.185). He was able to make this adjustment to Berkeley's position through his interaction with various texts, not least of which was the first chapter of John's Gospel, which declares that the Logos was in the beginning, was with God, and was God. He also drew upon both his reading of the eighteenth-century English philologist John Horne Tooke and his deep knowledge of the theosophico-metaphysical tradition, particularly in the works of Jacob Boehme and Plotinus.

Prior to leaving for Göttingen in 1798, Coleridge began to interact with the work of Tooke, whom he knew not only as a philologist but also as a political radical. While he may well have been aware of Tooke before he was tried for treason in 1794, it was not until several years later that Coleridge actually met him.[21] It was Tooke's *Epea Pteroenta* or *The Diversions of Purley* (published in two volumes, 1786 and 1805, respectively) that provided an abundance of critical grist for Coleridge's deliberations about language. In that work, Tooke states, "The business of the mind, as far as it concerns Language, appears to me to be very simple. It extends no further than to receive impressions, that is, to have Sensations or Feelings. What are called its operations, are merely the operations of Language" (Goodson 54). Coleridge was drawn to the idea that the functions of the mind are verbal; however, it was Tooke's concept of "wingèd words" that proved especially helpful as he sought a nonmechanistic view of language. His own concept of epea zwonta, or "living words," seems to have been an adaptation of Tooke's notion. In the Fifth Lecture of the 1808 "Lectures on Shakespeare and Milton," Tomalin reports, "Horne Tooke had called his book *Epea Pteroenta*, 'winged words.' In Coleridge's judgment it might have been much more fitly called *Verba Viventia*, or 'living words,' for words are the living products of the living mind and could not be a due medium between the thing and the mind unless they partook of both" (*Shakespearean Criticism* 2.74). What is curious about Coleridge's enthusiasm for Tooke's linguistics, though, is that his position was primarily a materialist one. McKusick points out that Tooke was "the first English philologist to apply Locke's philosophy to the study of language" (33). It was Tooke's indebtedness to the empirical/materialist tradition—as well as his political exploits—that probably led to Coleridge's eventual disavowal of Tooke's position. As late as 1830, Coleridge commented on his debate with Tooke's argument: "Tooke affects to explain the origin and whole philosophy of language by what it is, in fact, only a mere accident of the history of one or two languages" (*Table Talk* 70). What Coleridge calls an "accident" refers to Tooke's emphasis upon etymologies and the ways in which related words break off from one another. Tooke placed this accident at the center of his argument, whereas Coleridge merely found it helpful for explaining the relationships among words. Goodson explains that this "accident, the fulcrum of Tooke's argument, is the supposed loss of the original meanings of the particles of the English language; the term includes for him all the parts of speech except nouns and verbs" (54). Tooke's resulting philology then is a mechanistic one, "effectively reducing the speaker's role in language to bricklaying" (54).[22] It was this mechanistic simplicity, engendered by Locke's division between word and thing, which Coleridge found to be unbearable.

While Coleridge's thought concerning the symbol and imagination sprang from his earliest work, his time in Germany during 1798 and 1799 was clearly a watershed in his critical development and directly impacted his understanding of poetic language and the power of the imagination in the act of creation. In the winter of 1799, Coleridge wrote to Thomas Poole from Germany, commenting on his life as a student there and citing in particular the lectures of Blumenbach and Eichhorn. His greatest fascination, though, was reserved for the lectures of Tychsen, under whom Coleridge studied many northern languages. In Chapter 10 of the *Biographia*, Coleridge says:

> My chief efforts were directed towards a grounded knowledge of the German language and literature. From Professor Tychsen I received as many lessons in the Gothic of Ulphilas as sufficed to make me acquainted with its grammar, and the radical words of most frequent occurrence; and with the occasional assistance of the same philosophical linguist I read through Ottfried's metrical paraphrase of the gospel, and the most important remains of the Theotiscan, or the transitional state of the Teutonic language from the Gothic to the old German of the Swabian period. (I.207–09)

In the same year, Coleridge commented that he considered the older Northern languages to be the best languages for poetry, because these had an ability to express "only prominent ideas with clearness, . . . others but darkly" (*CN* I.383). During this period, then, Coleridge did not elevate his philosophical questions about language over his original enthusiasm for poetry and the imagination; rather, he continued his attempt to blend the two. His exposure during this time to both a different critical tradition and a different poetic tradition in Germany provided a perspective from which he could critique the work of earlier English influences such as Hartley, Berkeley, and Tooke. The full impact of this year revealed itself not in a single burst or a sudden transformation but in the gradual development over the next five to ten years of his notions of the imagination and the symbol.

In the midst of his time in Germany, Coleridge was still attempting to come to terms with Tooke's influence. In a notebook entry from that period, Coleridge wrote, "Mind - min - meinen - mahnen - mahen / vibratory yet progressive motion" (*CN* 1.378). Echoing the Scotist tradition and its sense of concrete language, Coleridge reveals here his great interest in etymologies engendered by Tooke and probably influenced by the teaching of Tychsen. Tooke's emphasis upon etymologies may be seen as a critique of the notion of words as mere vibrations. He reaches back to the Hartleyan law of association which views words as vibrations in the mind corresponding to external objects. He also appears to be probing the nature or limits of linguistic arbitrariness, a concern raised by Berkeley. Given the arbitrariness of signs, Coleridge nonetheless sees an apparent progressive motion in language in which words are related to one another, and he attempts to show by recourse to etymologies how meaning is formed in linguistic difference. By 1800, however, Coleridge saw that both Tooke's and Hartley's systems were lacking; there still existed this radical division between word and thing. Coleridge wrote to William Godwin on 22 September of that year, urging him to return from writing drama to the work of "a *bold* moral thinker." The work which he proposed for Godwin was a bold linguistic project:

> I wish you to write a book on the power of words, and the processes by which human feelings form affinities with them—in short, I wish you to *philosophize* Horn Tooke's System, and to solve the great Questions— whether there be reason to hold, that an action bearing all the *semblance* of pre-designing Consciousness may yet be simply organic, & whether a *series* of such actions is possible—and close on the heels of this question would follow the old 'Is Logic the *Essence* of Thinking?' in other words— Is *thinking* impossible without arbitrary signs? &—how far is the word "arbitrary" a misnomer? Are not words &c parts & germinations of the Plant? And what is the Law of the Growth?—In something of this order I would endeavor to destroy the old antithesis of *Words* & *Things*, elevating, as it were, words into Things, & living Things too. (*CL* 1.625–26)

Coleridge's charge to Godwin makes clear his own commitment to the power of words as "living Things." Their power comes from the exercise of passion within the will, so that these signs, which may be seen as merely arbitrary, are only an integral part of "the Plant." This image captures the organic nature of Coleridge's thinking, especially in his view of language. Thinking is able to realize the thing thought because both the thing and the thought are part of the same plant. For thinking is not possible without words; so, the passion of the will transforms arbitrary signs into the parts and germinations of the plant. Thus, the "old antithesis of *Words* & *Things*" is destroyed because the words are elevated by the will and become a part of the whole of thinking.

Coleridge is anticipating here what, in 1802, he would call "the *verbal* imagination," a phrase that aptly describes his understanding of the relationship between language and the imagination. As he was concerned for the creative power of the mind, Coleridge's understanding of language was linked to his formulation of the imagination. The roots of his understanding of the imagination are most obviously found in the influence of Kant. Although Coleridge wrote during his stay in Germany of his great admiration for Blumenbach, Eichhorn, and Tychsen, his thinking for the rest of his life was carried on under the shadow of Kant. In Chapter 9 of the *Biographia*, after having surveyed his interaction with the doctrine of association from Aristotle to Hartley, Coleridge confessed:

> The writings of the illustrious sage of Königsburg, the founder of the Critical Philosophy, more than any other work, at once invigorated and disciplined my understanding. The originality, the depth and the compression of the thoughts; the novelty and subtlety, yet solidity and importance, of the distinctions; the adamantine chain of logic; . . . [all] took possession of me as with a giant's hand. (I.153)

The preeminence of Kant is apparent as early as 1801. Shortly after writing his four philosophical letters to Josiah Wedgwood in which he outlined his argument with materialism and empiricism, Coleridge wrote to Thomas Poole to inform him that "I have not only completely extricated the notions of time and space; but have overthrown the doctrine of association as taught by Hartley" (*CL* 2.706). Kant would have been attractive to Coleridge's system of thought for a variety of reasons. First, Kant's thinking stands in the Platonic tradition, which would have accorded well with Coleridge's own reading of Plotinus and his own Neoplatonic tendencies. Also, Kant's distinction between the noumenal and the phenomenal realms as contrary but not contradictory entities provided the terms for Coleridge's own unified vision of the imagination as the living and generative power of "multeity in unity," as he states it in the third essay of "On The Principles of Genial Criticism."

Warren justly observes that it is invalid to claim that Coleridge's "concept of the imagination was arrived at after the visit to Germany and the subsequent philosophical crisis. . . . Germany gave Coleridge form and authority, perhaps, but not the basic motivation for his final views" ("APPI" 401). Kant's influence was not the only "form and authority" that Coleridge derived from Germany; the philosophy and aesthetics of the German Romantic philosopher Friedrich Schelling also figured prominently in shaping his thought. In fact, Coleridge seemed to have been caught for many years in a dialogue between Kant and Schelling. Frank Lentricchia suggests that this tension is responsible for what he calls "a contradiction embedded in Coleridge's philosophical identity" ("Coleridge and Emerson" 37). However, it would appear that such a tension—between Schelling's pantheistic, dynamic aesthetic on the one hand and Kant's more systematic, phenomenological views on the other—is exactly what shaped Coleridge's theory of the symbol.

In "A Poem of Pure Imagination," Warren seeks to vindicate Coleridge's theory of the symbol by both distinguishing it from the trope of allegory and relating it to Coleridge's theory of composition as developed in the primary and secondary themes of *The Ancient Mariner*. Aware of Coleridge's concern for precision in terminology, Warren emphasizes that the term "symbol" held a specific import in contradistinction to terms such as "metaphor" or "allegory." He cites "Coleridge's emphasis on diversity within unity" as evidence of this concern for the symbol and contends that failure to realize the centrality of this in "Coleridge's theory of composition has led a number of critics to try to read *The Ancient Mariner* in terms of a two-dimensional allegory" (350). His view of the symbol was born out of his theory of the imagination, which provided a means of breaking down the antithesis between word and thing through the exercise of the conscious will and gave birth to his conception of words as living things. This position was engendered by Kant's notion of a generative tension between contraries that does not negate reason or understanding but provides a basis for true thought. Out of this tension within the imagination, the symbol arises and forms the dynamic core of Coleridge's theory of poetic creation. If one reads *The Ancient Mariner* as a two-dimensional allegory rather than as a poetic symbol, then he severs the work from Coleridge's conception of the imagination. Warren rejects any allegorical reading of the poem, "the sort of reading which gives us such absurdities as the point-to-point equating of the Pilot with the Church and the Pilot's boy with the clergy" (350). According to Warren, "The method of allegory—if by allegory we understand a fixed system of point-to-point equations—is foreign to [Coleridge's] conception of the role of the imagination. . . . Allegory is, to adopt Coleridge's terms, the product of the understanding, *symbol of the imagination*" (351; emphasis mine). By means of definitions, Warren states:

> The symbol serves to *combine* . . . the "poet's heart and intellect." A symbol involves an idea (or ideas) as part of its potential, but it also involves the special complex of feelings associated with that idea, the attitude toward that idea. The symbol affirms the unity of mind in the welter of experience; it is a device for making that welter of experience manageable for the mind—graspable. It represents a focus of being and is not a mere sign, a "picture language." (352)

What distinguishes the symbol from allegory is the notion of arbitrariness. Allegory is based upon a purely arbitrary way of reading that looks for the "mere sign, a 'picture language.'" The symbol, though, cannot be arbitrary. He says that "a symbol implies a body of ideas which may be said to be fused in it," and that, therefore, "the symbol is not arbitrary—not a mere sign— but contains within itself the appeal which makes it serviceable as a symbol" (352). He states this point more strongly a little further on, saying that "the symbol . . . cannot be arbitrary—it has to participate in the unity of which it is representative. And this means that the symbol has a deeper relation to the total structure of meaning than its mechanical place in plot, situation, or discourse" (353).

Warren derives this description of the symbol from a number of Coleridge's own statements. In *The Statesman's Manual*, Coleridge describes the imagination as a "reconciling and mediatory power" that "gives birth to a system of symbols, harmonious in themselves, and consubstantial with the truths, of which they are the conductors" (29). Symbols are rooted in the imagination and, by their nature, have a reconciling and mediating effect. By "reconciling," Coleridge does not propose that two contrary forces are collapsed into one another; rather, by the mediating effect of the imagination these are brought together and held in tension, so that there is a manifest unity in multeity. The imagination is that "one power" that is "inexhaustively re-ebullient" rather than being restful or neutralizing (*BL* I.299–300). The symbol then is the result of these two forces. It is "a *tertium aliquid*, or finite generation. . . . Now this *tertium aliquid* can be no other than an inter-penetration of the coun-teracting powers, partaking of both" (I.300). As a "finite generation" of the imagination, the symbol is a moment of "an inter-penetration of the counter-acting powers, partaking of both." This is what he means when he states that the symbol is consubstantial with the truth it represents. The old antithesis between word and thing is broken down in the concrete "this-ness" of the symbol itself. Mary Ann Perkins helpfully points out that Coleridge "rejected Kant's view of the symbol as representation which cannot put us in touch di-rectly with noumenal reality, only with material for reflection" (47). Rather, Coleridge believed that the symbol could put us in touch with noumenal re-ality by bringing two counteracting forces into contact and holding them in tension, the one partaking of the other. These counteracting forces are con-trary without being contradictory; therefore, the symbol is neither a dialecti-cal synthesis in which the two contraries are subsumed into one another, nor is it sustained antithesis in which one is privileged over the other. According to Coleridge's definition of the symbol in *The Statesman's Manual*, a symbol

> is characterized by a translucence of the Special in the Individual or of the General in the Especial or of the Universal in the General. Above all by the translucence of the Eternal through and in the Temporal. It always partakes of the Reality which it renders intelligible; and while it enunciates the whole, abides itself as a living part in that Unity, of which it is the representative. (30)

This view of the symbol shaped Coleridge's notion of linguistic reference: he cannot radically divide between word and thing because they participate in one another.[23] The symbol is that reconciling and completing moment in which the two counteracting forces—special/individual, general/especial, universal/general, or eternal/temporal—inter-penetrate one another and par-take of one another. This was the power of Ezekiel's vision for Coleridge; the symbols are the "Wheels which Ezekiel beheld" precisely because of the na-ture of the relationship between the wheels and the Spirit. Symbols and the truths "of which they are the *conductors*," "move in conjunction" with one an-other, just as the wheels and the Spirit do in Ezekiel's vision. It is this symbolic moment, fostered by the imagination, that really constitutes the poetic moment and "procure[s] . . . that willing suspension of disbelief *for the moment*, which constitutes poetic faith" (*BL* II.6; emphasis mine).

In light of the development of Coleridge's system of thought, Warren's dual emphasis upon a symbolic reading and a sacramental vision cannot be seen as arbitrary. It is structured by Coleridge's own understanding of the symbol. Warren understood the sacramental language in Coleridge's formulation of the symbol. He says in his definition that the symbols produced by the imagination are *not only* "harmonious in themselves" *but* are "consubstantial with the truths, of which they are the conductors." Coleridge's love for precision of terminology needs to be appreciated here. The symbol is not a moment of transubstantiation but of consubstantiation. The doctrine of transubstantiation holds that the substance of the bread and wine in the Eucharist is changed—transmuted—into the physical substance of the body and the blood of Christ. The substance of the bread and wine is lost in the new substance of the body and blood. Coleridge, however, uses the word "consubstantial." The eucharistic doctrine of consubstantiation was developed by Martin Luther and proposes that the body and blood are a presence together with the bread and wine, that they are with, in, and under the elements. As symbols, the bread and wine are not destroyed but are acknowledged to remain together as one with the truths of which they are the conductors. Coleridge commented on this view in a marginal note in his copy of Charles Butler's *Vindication of "The Book"*:

> The Eucharistic Act as instituted by Christ is a Symbol, i.e.—a part, or particular instance selected as a representative of the whole, of which whole however it is itself an actual, or real part. Now the Sacramentaries degrade the Symbol into a Metaphor, and that too, a Catachresis, while the Romish Superstition makes the Symbol representant, the whole thing represented, and in consequence equally with the former, destroys the *Symbol*. (*Marginalia* I.862)

In other places, Coleridge expresses his agreement with the sacramental views of Bucer, upon whom the renaissance humanism of Erasmus as well as the reformational theology of Luther had a profound effect. Bucer modified both Luther's and Zwingli's eucharistic positions by arguing for a "sacramental union" of the elements with the body and blood of Christ; the elements co-inhere with the body and blood. Bucer was also the primary influence upon the sacramental theology in the English Prayer Book. Coleridge's conviction reflects, then, the influence of the Anglican tradition with which he had a varied relationship. Following Bucer and Anglicanism in the language used in a late notebook entry, he states that identity

> means One containing the power of two as their radical *antecedent*, or as . . . a point *producing* itself into a bi-polar Line but contemplated as anterior to this production, and *containing* the two Poles or Opposites in unevolved cöinherence. . . . Be thing, however, called Identity or Prothesis, this Coinherence of Act and Being is the I AM IN THAT I WILL TO BE, of Moses, the Absolute I AM, and its grammatical correspondent is the VERB SUBSTANTIVE. (*CN* 4.4644)

This sacramental notion of the "Coinherence of Act and Being" finds expression also in the Logos, which Coleridge understood to be the primary and essential symbol and the primary and essential language. It is in his thinking about the Logos that his theory of the symbol coalesces with his understanding of language. Mary Anne Perkins argues persuasively that "the Logos is the unifying factor of Coleridge's 'system' . . . and the key to understanding every area of his thought after 1805" (3). It "connects his theories of language and imagination, his philosophy of nature, his attempt to establish an epistemology based on the constitutive nature of ideas, and his moral philosophy and anthropology" (267). The development of this "unifying factor" must be seen as an essential part of the development of his thinking about the symbol and language.

The central role of the Logos in Coleridge's philosophy places his thinking at the heart of the Western metaphysical tradition.[24] There are clearly elements from Kant in his search for unity and from Schelling in his notion of the mediating power of the Logos; but there are also obvious influences of the mystical tradition and Neoplatonic philosophy. Warren, however, pays particular attention to the Neoplatonic influence on Coleridge, citing especially Plotinus's doctrine of creation as an important source for Coleridge's own thinking. "It is possible that we have in Coleridge's theory of poetic creation a transposition into psychological terms of Plotinus' doctrine of creation" (344). He then quotes a lengthy passage from the *Enneads* (V.I.7: *The Divine Mind*) in which Plotinus describes the monistic vision of Ideas, "veritable Being," and "veritable Essence," out of which physical creation has emanated ("APPI" 344–45). In a later footnote, Warren suggests that "Coleridge's particular doctrine of symbolism . . . seems to be developed under the shadow of Plotinus" (403). Plotinus's description of the universe as "a stately whole, complete within itself, serving at once its own purpose and that of all its parts" is not very far from Coleridge's conception of the Logos as the primary and essential symbol and word, "a stately whole, complete within itself."

The Logos doctrine seems to have taken precedence in Coleridge's thinking between 1803 and 1805. In a notebook entry from November 1803, Coleridge proposes his "*last & great* work" as "The work which I should wish to leave behind me, or to publish late in Life, that On Man, and the probable Destiny of the Human Race" (*CN* 1.1649). He says that this work is to be "followed and illustrated by the Organum vere Organum, & philosophical Romance to explain the whole growth of Language, and for these to be always collecting materials." By 1805, Coleridge seems to be pondering more specifically the role of the Logos in human language. In a notebook entry from that year, Coleridge ponders the "trinity" of the "Platonic Fathers," which he identifies as "God, his Word, and his Wisdom." As to the second element of this trinity, he writes, "Reason, Proportion, communicable Intelligibility intelligent and communicant, the Word—which last expression strikes me as the profoundest and most comprehensive Energy of the human Mind, if indeed it be not in some distinct sense ενεργημα θεοπαραδοτον" (*CN* II.2445). In that same notebook entry, he says that "the moment we conceive the divine energy, that moment we co-conceive the LogoV," so that under the work of the "*Spirit* of *holy Action*," "the redeemed & sanctified become finally themselves Words of the *Word*—even as ~~lou~~ articulate sounds are made by the Reason to represent Forms, in the mind, and Forms are a language of the notions. . . . As he is the Father, even so we in him!" Under the aegis of the Logos, Coleridge brings together his thinking about language and the symbol. His concept of the Logos underwent a transformation from a Neoplatonist tenet rooted in triunity to the Christian notion of the trinity.[25] By 1817, then, Coleridge was able to write in the *Biographia Literaria* his proposed large and systematic work "which I have many years been preparing, on the Productive Logos human and divine; with, and as the introduction to, a full commentary on the Gospel of St. John" (I.136). In other places Coleridge refers to his "magnum opus" under the term *Logosophia*. That he envisions this to be his great and final work in his later years is apparent. This would mean, however, that he had abandoned his earlier goal for his "*last & great* work" to be his study on "the probable Destiny of the Human Race."

Coleridge's thinking about the Logos brought together and gave shape to other concerns, which formed his thinking about the imagination; for example, he sees in the notion of the Logos the possible ground for a symbolic understanding of language. In April of 1805, he wrote,

> In looking at the objects of Nature while I am thinking, as at yonder moon dim-glimmering thro' the dewy window-pane, I seem rather to be seeking as it were *asking*, a symbolical language for something within me that already and forever exists, than observing anything new. Even when that latter is the case, yet still I have always an obscurecure feeling as if that new phænomenon were the dim Awaking of a forgotten or hidden Truth of my inner nature/It is still interesting as a Word, a Symbol! It is <u>Logos</u>, the Creator! (*CN* 2.2546)[26]

His first thoughts about the Logos appear to have been in its creative and re-creative function, which perhaps correlates to his later description of the primary and secondary imagination. In the work of creation, Coleridge conceives of the Logos as the actualizing power of God. For him, "unity is manifested by Opposites" and "all true Opposites tend to unity" (*CN* IV.4513). So, he describes the creation of the physical universe as the "Incorporation of the Logos" by which the "*potentialized* Actual" is polarized into light and darkness and then the created light is polarized into life and warmth. In the "New Creation," though, Coleridge identifies the "Incarnation of the Logos" by the "polarization into divine Life and Light with Faith as the Indifference (John 1)" (*CN* 4.5162). Christ, then, as both incorporated and incarnated Logos, is "the *Verbum* Dei," "the fixed word, the verb in the form of the Substantive, he is *Nomen* Dei" (*CN* 4.4625).

For Coleridge, the Logos is the essential living word and primary symbol, modifying Tooke's notion of "wingèd words" into his own conception of living words. In his *Lectures 1808–1819: On Literature*, Coleridge clearly goes beyond Kantian dualism when he writes that "words are the living products of the living mind & could not be a due medium between the thing and the mind unless they partook of both" (I.273). Like symbols that are the "living products" of the imagination, words are "products of the living mind" and act as a medium only because they partake of both the thing and the mind. In *Aids to Reflection*, he proceeds to say, "For if words are not THINGS, they are LIVING POWERS, by which the things of most importance to mankind are actuated, combined and humanized" (10). Words actuate, even as the Word, the Logos, actuated all the potentialized actual in the work of creation. But this actuation is by means of symbol, for a symbol "*is a sign included in the Idea which it represents*" (*Aids to Reflection* 263n). Thus, language functions by the same means as the symbol. This is made clear in a notebook entry from the summer of 1803: "Language & all *symbols* give *outness* to Thoughts / & this the philosophical essence and purpose of Language" (*CN* 1.1387).[27] All language and symbols give outness to thoughts, though only the Logos, as the primary and essential word, does so without arbitrariness or limit. In 1808, Coleridge wrote, "All minds must think by some *symbols*—the strongest minds possess the most vivid Symbols in the Imagination—yet this ingenerates a *want, poqon, desiderium*, for vividness of Symbol: which something that is *without*, that has the property of *Outness* . . . can alone fully gratify / even that indeed not fully" (*CN* 3.3325). Coleridge borrowed this notion of outness from Berkeley and later described it as "but the feeling of *otherness* (alterity) rendered intuitive, or alterity visually represented" (*Aids to Reflection* 391 n. 26).

Warren begins section V of "A Poem of Pure Imagination" by stating that "the central and crucial fact" of his reading of *The Ancient Mariner* is "the fusion of the primary and secondary themes" (380), which reflects what Warren considered to be the way that Coleridge reconciled the aesthetic and the theological in his thought. "His solution was, of course, one of detail and not part of the great synthesis of which he dreamed. For the age presented complications which could not, apparently, be resolved into such a system" (381–82). According to Warren, "The precarious solution which Coleridge attained was, of course, one aspect of his doctrine of the creative unity of the mind, which appears and reappears in his work and which is his great central insight and great contribution to modern thought" (382). It is this doctrine that encompasses his thinking about the imagination and the symbol, the Logos and language. In his effort to abolish "the opposition between thought and feeling," Coleridge saw in the act of poetic creation a moment of unified perception. Warren summarizes Coleridge's conclusion "that the truth is implicit *in the poetic act as such, that the moral concern and the aesthetic concern are aspects of the same activity, the creative activity, and that this activity is expressive of the whole mind*" (382). With regard to the imagination, he is expanding here upon Coleridge's definition of the secondary imagination and notes that the distinction between primary and secondary imagination is a distinction between the unconscious and the conscious will. The secondary imagination is an exercise of the creative and conscious will, drawing upon both passion and joy. With regard to the symbol, Warren sees the moment of the poetic act as a symbolic moment, which in Coleridge's words "always partakes of the Reality which it renders intelligible." The poetic moment is a living part of the whole which it enunciates, thus it "is expressive of the whole mind."

Such a summary of Coleridge's solution to the problem of reconciling poetry and religion addresses more than just the issue of *The Ancient Mariner*. In fact, Warren states that his "argument is that *The Ancient Mariner* is, first, written *out of* this general belief, and second, written *about* this general belief" (382). In this way, he reads the poem as a symbol that partakes of the whole reality that it seeks to render intelligible. Warren describes the way in which the poem is written out of this general belief about poetic creation by identifying what he calls little fables of the creative process.[28] In this way, he contends that the poem is "in general, about the unity of mind and the final unity of values, and in particular about poetry itself" (383). The first fable of the creative process is the moment of the blessing of the water snakes, which Warren describes as "the very turning point of the poem." When the Mariner blesses the snakes "unaware," Warren observes an instance of poetic genius, quoting from "On Poesy," in which Coleridge's states that "There is in genius an unconscious activity; nay, that is the genius in the man of genius" (384). According to Warren, then, this moment within the poem suggests "that the writing of a poem is simply a specialized example of a general process which leads to salvation" (384), as instanced by the Mariner's beginning the voyage home only after composing his poem of blessing. However, Warren identifies in the instance of the Mariner's return home what he calls the "doubtful doubleness of the imagination" (386). The fable of the Mariner reveals that the power of the imagination rests in its holding in tension "its two inherent indestructible yet counteracting forces" (*BL* I.299). Warren summarizes in this way: "So we have here a peculiar and paradoxical situation: the poem is a poem in which the poetic imagination appears in a regenerative and healing capacity, but in the end the hero, who has, presumably, been healed, appears in one of his guises as the *poète maudit*. So we learn that the imagination does not only bless, for even as it blesses it lays on a curse" (386).

Warren does observe another fable of the creative process at the end of the poem, and this is "perhaps a fuller statement of Coleridge's conception of the poet, the man with the power which comes unbidden and which is an 'agony' until it finds words." (387). This other fable at the end is the ongoing tale of the poet, the ongoing agony of the doubleness of his position. The power that comes unbidden to the poet "wells up from the unconscious but is the result of a moral experience, and in its product, the poem, the 'tale' told by the Mariner, will 'teach'—for that is the word the Mariner uses. It is a paradoxical process" (387). In the final section of his essay, Warren meditates further on this paradoxical situation of the poet and the nature of the symbolic blessing and curse that he bears. Warren suggests that "the creation of a poem is as much a process of discovery as a process of making" (395). This does not mean that the poetic process is in itself irrational. "What comes unbidden from the depths at the moment of creation may be the result of the most conscious and narrowly rational effort in the past" (396). Warren says that ultimately what "the poet is trying to discover ... is what kind of poem he can make. And the only thing he, in the ordinary sense, may 'intend' is to make a poem" (396). And once the poem is made, it partakes of the reality that it renders intelligible. Thus the power of the imagination, rendered even in its doubleness, gives rise to a power within the poem itself. In *The Ancient Mariner*, "the vividness of the presentation and the symbolic coherence may do their work—as blessing sprang to the Mariner's lips—unawares. For the good poem may work something of its spell even upon readers who are critically inarticulate" (398). Or, as Warren put it earlier in the essay, "we may say that the reader does not interpret the poem but the poem interprets the reader. We may say that the poem is the light and not the thing seen by the light. The poem is the light by which the reader may view and review all the areas of experience with which he is acquainted"(347). As the light, poetry is able to reconcile "by its symbolical reading of experience ... the self-devisive [*sic*] internecine malices which arise at the superficial level on which we conduct most of our living" (399).

Nevertheless, the paradox between blessing and curse remains for the poet. As an integral part of his search for a reconciling language, it is at the core of Coleridge's understanding of the relationship between religion and poetry, as Warren points out. Jasper has also observed this coalescing of the religious and the linguistic in Coleridge: "His approach to words and language is profoundly significant of his sense of the religious experience, and thus it behoves the critic to attend to the literary and narrative techniques of *The Ancient*

Mariner which contribute to its total effect and sense, and which link it with the whole corpus of Coleridge's writings on religion, even to the prose of his last years"("The Two Worlds" 135–36). Within the whole corpus of Coleridge's writings—not just in his distinctly religious articles—this paradox is specifically what remains after all his years of pondering the question of language. It is not inconsistent with his long-standing argument with Locke or with his varied deference to Tooke. As Coleridge sought for a language in which the division between word and thing could be destroyed, in which words became not simply things but living things and living powers, he moved toward the inevitability of the doubleness of language itself. For Coleridge was well aware of the arbitrariness of human language and of the fractured nature of our utterances. But there remained for him a unified language—idealized in the Logos—in which word and thing, or name and nature, were one. According to Fulford, "Coleridge was embracing linguistic breakdown in order to dramatize the fact that the rules of ordinary language were conventional and fallible and to wrest from that dramatization a glimpse of a linguistic unity beyond such rules and such breakdowns" (41). Thus, he continues, "Coleridge had made the extreme of linguistic arbitrariness into a mark of the passage of spiritual knowledge" (41). It might even be said that the symbolic tension between the sayable and the unsayable lay at the heart of his theological understanding. The symbol is the moment of paradox in which unity and fracture are held together, paradoxically and sacramentally consubstantial with one another. There is a symbolic relationship between the sayable and the unsayable, a tension between the two that is productive without destroying either one. These two forces are contrary without being contradictory.

Warren himself expressed this paradox of the poet with regard to language as the effort to "say the unsayable." He was well aware of the agony of the poet, that agony which seeks words able to unify in the midst of fracture and collapse but cannot be finally found. It is this paradoxical situation of the poet resulting from the doubleness of language itself that Warren explores in his late poetry. Even as early as *Promises: Poems 1954–1956*, Warren is probing the nature of language in his poem "Dragon Country: To Jacob Boehme" (*CP* 133–34). Warren's dedication of this poem to that mystic whom Coleridge so admired and who contributed heavily to Coleridge's theological aesthetics could not have been arbitrarily chosen. In fact, the mention of Boehme highlights the central issue in this poem: the search for a language that transcends our finite and unstable words. In this mythical narrative, a small rural community is ravaged by an unseen dragon whose absent presence is seen only in traces of its power. The dragon is for many a curse: it destroys a hog pen, it kills a teamster, it devours all of a man save a boot with part of the leg left inside. And yet the dragon is also a paradoxical blessing: it is the "Necessity of truth [which] had trodden the land" and leaves "the fearful glimmer of joy, like a spoor" (51–52). The dragon itself is never seen, only the traces of its presence. The dragon is that sort of negativity which Budick and Iser describe as being "traceable only through its impact" (xiii). "You followed the track of disrepair, / Ruined fence, blood-smear, brush broken, but came, in the end, to a place / With weed unbent, leaf calm, and nothing, nothing, was there" (18–20). The dragon is a living power that bears that quality of doubleness: it acts for both good and ill. It does not bring either good or ill; it brings about both in a powerful paradox which actuates being in the world. Such a doubleness is the doubleness of language. However, the absent presence of the dragon also draws out the incessant longing for a pure language: "We are human, and the human heart / Demands language for reality that has no slightest dependence / On desire, or need. Now in church they pray only that evil depart" (46–48). Warren's demand here is the demand of the poet: the yearning for that language that will finally speak "reality." However, he does not seem to realize here, as he does in his later poetry, that if the unsayable were finally spoken its consequences could be unspeakable. As it is, the gift of the "fearful glimmer of joy, like a spoor," granted within our fallen language, is what the poet must learn to cherish.

Warren returns most obviously and powerfully to the issues raised in his study of *The Ancient Mariner* in his 1969 poem, *Audubon: A Vision*. The issues of poetic creation, the place of the poet, and the nature of language itself are all developed in this pivotal poem in a way that adumbrates the themes expounded from Coleridge. He does not simply rewrite Coleridge's poem by recasting the same narrative structure into a new context and into new terms. While there are similarities in the narrative plot, *Audubon* stands on its own structurally and stylistically. It is not immediately analogous to the Mariner myth; there is no strict one-to-one correspondence between the terms of the two poems. Rather, he recasts the symbol itself in his own exploration of the thematic concerns relating to the imagination and to language. In this way, Coleridge's aesthetic provides the ground upon which we may read Warren's later poetry.

CHAPTER THREE

The Mariner and the Hunter

The language of poetry, then, is a language of silences, is itself constituted by traces, by words that cannot fully embrace the dynamics of being.—Richard Jackson[1]

At the end of a decade marked by repeated confrontations with the unsayable in his social and literary criticism, Warren penned what is arguably his lengthiest and most forthright poetic meditation upon the nature and power of the imagination in relation to language as it shapes and modifies our experience in the world. In his 1969 multi-poemed poem *Audubon: A Vision* (*CP* 251–67), he articulates in seven sections and nearly four hundred lines a specifically poetic vision shaped under the influence of Coleridge's own linguistically-oriented formulation of the imagination and the symbol. Like *The Rime of the Ancient Mariner*, Warren's poem is preoccupied with the precarious position of the poet and with the double-edged act of poetic creation. While critics have emphasized the historical, biographical, and psychological aspects of this poem, *Audubon* must be considered a poem about poetry and the act of poetic creation. Language has become the matter itself. In this way, *Audubon* is his own contribution to that canon of poems he lists in *A Plea In Mitigation* that "plagued the question" of the poet's role and the nature of poetry (8–9), and as such it rivals those Romantic works in its own significance. Warren returns to the two vital themes explored in "A Poem of Pure Imagination" and provides his own fusion of the sacramental vision and the imagination as he explores the nature of poetic creation. Here Warren deals with the play of tension within the symbolic understanding and with the agency of passion in what Coleridge called the "verbal imagination." He entertains the possibility of a poetry that does not represent the world but shapes and illuminates it so that the poet and the reader alike might continue to walk in the world and even love it. In this illuminating capacity, the poem moves toward the perspective that conceives of language as a living and disclosive pattern of difference. The poet makes his way along the precarious and unstable way of language in order to approach an understanding of being in the world.

Warren began work on *Audubon* in the 1940s, just prior to and during his year as Consultant in Poetry at the Library of Congress.[2] He became enthralled with the life of the early nineteenth-century naturalist and artist while reading "a whole range of subliterary genres" (Watkins, Hiers, and Weaks 333), including journals and memoirs, in preparation for his 1949 novel, *World Enough and Time*. After reading his journals, Warren began drafting a poem based on Audubon's life, but he could not finish it. He told Peter Stitt in 1977 that "it was a trap; I couldn't find the frame for it, the narrative line. I did write quite a bit, but it wouldn't come together, so I set it aside and forgot about it" (Watkins, Hiers, and Weaks 244). Warren also dealt with Audubon in his 1944 essay "Love and Separateness in Eudora Welty," in which he examines Welty's short fiction.[3] In Welty's story "A Still Moment," Audubon is one of three central characters who "stand for a still moment and watch a white heron feeding" (161). According to Warren, Audubon is the only one of the three who "can innocently accept nature" by loving the bird "and so escape from [his] own curse as did . . . the Ancient Mariner" (162). The irony of such love, though, is that in order to know the bird he must shoot it. "But having killed the bird, he knows that the best he can make of it now in a painting would be a dead thing. . . . " (162). Warren goes on to state, "He loves the bird, innocently, in its fullness of being. But he must subject this love to knowledge; he must kill the bird if he is to commemorate its beauty, if he is to establish his communion with other men in terms of the bird's beauty. There is in the situation an irony of limit and contamination" (162). Warren's assessment of Audubon in Welty's story, though, is subtly but importantly different from his own rendering of the artist in *Audubon: A Vision*. There is a clue to this differentiating factor in his reference to the Ancient Mariner within this essay. According to Blotner, Warren set aside his earliest efforts on the Audubon poem in order to pursue his lecture on *The Ancient Mariner,* which was scheduled to be presented in April of 1945 (212, 216). It would appear that this work on Coleridge provided two crucial factors for Warren's later work on his own poem. First, it provided the frame and narrative line that was missing in his earlier efforts. While Warren makes a brief thematic connection between the Ancient Mariner and the Audubon of Welty's story, he does not explore in that essay the specific implications of killing the bird for the narrative line of Audubon's story. Second, Warren's analysis of Coleridge's notion of the imagination supplied a way for the dead birds to become living things through the act of re-creation. Warren specifically confronts in *Audubon* the secondary imagination that struggles to idealize and unify in the work of dissolving, diffusing, and dissipating. His conception of the imagination in this poem is both vital and verbal.

Critics of Warren's poetry understand the significance of *Audubon* in the larger body of his work, though they situate that significance in very different ways. Anthony Szczesiul aptly points out that critics "generally seem to agree that *Audubon: A Vision* is a watershed moment in Warren's career as a poet" ("Robert Penn Warren's *Audubon*" 3).[4] While James Justus recognizes the broad influence of *The Ancient Mariner* on Warren's work as a whole, he does not see any shaping influence that Coleridge's work might have had on *Audubon*. He identifies the Mariner's tale as one of Warren's recurring themes in both his fiction and poetry, but does not discuss that in his reading of *Audubon*. Instead, he is concerned with the structure of the poem and with the comparisons and contrasts between Warren's Audubon and the Audubon of history and biography.[5] Victor Strandberg sees movement in *Audubon* toward a more consciously developed mysticism, tracing connections to Warren's idea of "the osmosis of being" introduced in his 1955 essay, "Knowledge and the Image of Man." Like Justus, he acknowledges Coleridge's significant influence on Warren's work, but he argues that the purpose of *Audubon* is to transmit a "new dimension of beauty" (250) springing from a yearning for knowledge. This gives the poem both a new style and an increased emotional intensity. T. R. Hummer offers a moralistic reading of the poem, relying heavily on the work of Joseph Campbell and C. G. Jung, whereas Daniel Duane reads *Audubon* in light of "Warren's life-long critique of American idealism," describing the poem as "Warren's most dense and ironic meditation on nature and the frontier" (25). John Burt explores what he observes to be the "two closely related problems" of the poem, the first being "the problem of discovering a character who is able to approach an experience of primary significance . . . but who . . . is not consumed and destroyed by that experience" (92). If the first problem is one of content, then the second is "a formal one," in which

"Warren seeks to define in the snapshot method a poetic form that can be at the same time strong and articulate, that can combine the power of the ballad and the intelligibility of the commentary" (93). Calvin Bedient does not make any connection between *Audubon* and Coleridge, though he does argue that Warren's "greatness as a writer began with his determination to concentrate on poetry as the extreme resource of language-knowledge, language-being" and this greatness "began with *Audubon: A Vision*" (3). Instead of following through the implications of his statement, Bedient's discussion of language only goes so far as to analyze the formal elements of the poetry, such as the syntactical "characteristic configurations, [or] linear voiceprints" (34). Most significantly, he abandons in his analysis of *Audubon* any real concern for the nature of language.[6]

Taken together, these critics leave unanswered some very important, even necessary, questions. If, as Bedient asserts, *Audubon* does reveal a concentration upon poetry as the extreme resource of language-being, then how does it do so? What are the implications of such a statement for understanding the poem itself? Also, does *Audubon* only reveal a new style for Warren, as if language were merely "a substantial medium, an object to be shaped according to an established system of stylistic forms and models" (Bruns 49)? Or, is there a more obvious struggle within the poem with the nature of language, shaped under the influence of Coleridge's own linguistically-oriented formulation of the imagination and the symbol? If language has, indeed, become the matter itself in Warren's poetry, then what kind of a reading does a poem such as *Audubon: A Vision* invite? Following Warren's lead, *Audubon* must be read as a poem about writing poetry.[7] It is an exploration of writing in the moment of poetic creation and of the struggle to articulate a world and even a definable self, concerns that appear again and again throughout Warren's later poetry.

From its opening lines, *Audubon* presents the image of an artist who struggles to articulate his place in the world through the power of his imagination. Audubon continually seeks to discover his relation to the world through his creative impulse. His desire is not simply to represent what is in the world but is rather to recreate and illuminate an understanding of being in the world. Such an illumination is the very articulation for which he yearns. His identity is marked by the very "passion" through which he experiences both the blessing and the curse of the imagination. Like the Mariner, he knows the agony of telling his tale. Warren establishes Audubon as the *poète maudit* even in his first epigraph, taken from Psalm 56:8: "Thou tellest my wanderings: put thou my tears into thy bottle: are they not in thy book?" (251) The poem tells of the wanderings of the artist in the world and of the tears that come from both the joy and the agony of artistic creation. But, it also suggests that there is a "book" that is a silent and unsayable text behind and beyond all of the poet's utterances. The work of the poet is not simply to tell but to listen to the voice of that book which "tellest [his] wanderings."

These intertwined questions of identity, vocation, and being appear in the first section, "Was Not the Lost Dauphin," and introduce the themes and issues that recur throughout the other sections of the poem. Warren begins,

> Was not the lost dauphin, though handsome was only
> Base-born and not even able
> To make a decent living, was only
> Himself, Jean Jacques, and his passion—what
> Is man but his passion? (I[A].1–5)

Warren immediately puts to rest the uncertainty of Audubon's origin, which he summarizes in the head note to the poem: he was not the son of a sea captain and his first wife—as his father had instructed him from his childhood—but was in fact the son of a slave-dealer and his mistress, though he was raised in France by his father's estranged wife. The most fantastic legend regarding his origin was "that he was the lost Dauphin of France, the son of the feckless Louis XVI and Marie Antoinette" (*CP* 253). The whole question of Audubon's identity highlights the tension that generates the central character of the poem. These opening lines suggest the precarious position of the poet and establish the specific and recurring motif of Audubon as the *poète maudit*. In "A Poem of Pure Imagination," Warren describes "the paradox of the situation of the poet" which was "a central fact for Coleridge and his age" (387). Being base-born, Audubon is in a paradoxical situation as an outcast and an outsider who dwells "beyond the circle of respectable society" ("APPI" 388). He belongs neither among the highest levels of society nor among even the decent. His situation is similar to what Shelley describes in one of his letters quoted by Warren: "Imagine my despair of good, imagine how it is possible that one of weak and sensitive nature as mine can run further the gauntlet through this hellish society of men" ("APPI" 387). Warren confirms Audubon as such a poet figure in section V, "The Sound of That Wind," when he writes:

Below the salt, in rich houses, he sat, and knew insult.
In the lobbies and couloirs of greatness he dangled,
And was not unacquainted with contumely.

Wrote: "My Lovely Miss Pirrie of Oackley Passed by Me
          this Morning, but did not remember how beautifull
          I had rendered her face once by Painting it
          at her Request with Pastelles."

Wrote: ". . . but thanks to My humble talents I can run
          the gantlet throu this World without her help." ([A].16–24)

The *poète maudit* undergoes the ordeal of human society like one being un-justly punished. For Shelley and Audubon alike, it is a gauntlet that must be run, understanding the cost in human relationships. In contrast to finding communion among human society, Audubon experiences a communion with the natural world in which he dwells and through which he wanders. Several times throughout the poem, the narrator remarks that he continued to walk in the world, and this walking forms a narrative thread through the various images of Audubon.[8]

As an outsider and a wanderer, Audubon is only himself, "Jean Jacques and his passion" (I[A].4). By this combination of name and passion, Warren confirms Audubon's function as a poet, as one who yearns to make his name and his passion co-terminus in himself. His name alone cannot provide his identity but must be combined with his prevailing passion for understanding and articulation.[9] For Coleridge, passion rather than passivity is what distin-guishes both true poetry and the genuine poet. While he sometimes uses the word to refer to the base emotions of mankind, he more often writes of passion in the context of the imagination, describing it as that part of the creative will by which experience is united and modified.[10] Passion is what discloses the character of the imagination. When Coleridge describes the nature of poetry in Chapter 14 of the *Biographia*, he does so with special reference to the dis-tinguishing mark of poetic genius.

What is poetry? is so nearly the same question with, what is a poet? that the answer to the one is involved in the solution of the other. For it is a distinction resulting from the poetic genius itself, which sustains and modifies the images, thoughts, and emotions of the poet's own mind.

The poet, described in *ideal* perfection, brings the whole soul of man into activity, with the subordination of its faculties to each other, according to their relative worth and dignity. He diffuses a tone, and spirit of unity, that blends, and (as it were) *fuses*, each into each, by that synthetic and magical power, to which we have exclusively appropriated the name of imagination. (II.15–16)

True poetry and poetic genius are marked by the power of the imagination, which modifies images and diffuses unity so that there is a fusion of the creative will with all the other faculties of the soul. Coleridge goes on to suggest in Chapter 15, however, that passion is the real proof of this poetic genius, pointing to Shakespeare's *Venus and Adonis* as the greatest example of such genius.

It has been before observed, that images however beautiful, though faithfully copied from nature, and as accurately represented in words, do not of themselves characterize the poet. They become proofs of original genius only as far as they are modified by a predominant passion; or by associated thoughts or images awakened by that passion; or when they have the effect of reducing multitude to unity, or succession to an instant; or lastly, when a human and intellectual life is transferred to them from the poet's own spirit. . . . (II.23)

The work of the poet is not simply to copy from nature by attempting to represent in words what his mind perceives. Rather, the poet imitates, and imitation for Coleridge means "the union of Disparate Things" (*CN* 3.4397 ƒ50v). The genius of the poet lies in his ability to modify these images according to a predominant passion. Coleridge held that passion works to fuse in a way comparable to the imagination, stating as early as 1804 that "all Passion unifies as it were by natural fusion" (*CN* 2.2012 ƒ41v).[11] In 1811, Coleridge also attributed this fusing power to the imagination, writing in his notebook of "the worth & dignity of poetic Imagination, of the fusing power, that fixing unfixes & while it melts & bedims the Image, still leaves in the Soul its living meaning" (*CN* 3.4066). When he considers both the defects and beauties of Wordsworth's poetry in Chapter 22 of the *Biographia*, Coleridge clearly sees a genuine unity when he speaks of "the blending, fusing power of Imagination and Passion" (II.150), ascribing to both a single power which reconciles and unites. In the fourth of his "Lectures on Shakespeare and Milton" presented in 1811–1812,

Coleridge renders more vividly the relationship between the imagination and passion in this work of fusion:

> That gift of true Imagination, that capability of reducing a multitude into unity of effect, or by strong passion to modify series of thoughts into one predominant thought or feeling—those were faculties which might be cultivated and improved, but could not be acquired. Only such a man as possessed them deserved the title of *poeta* who *nascitur non fit*—he was that child of Nature, and not the creature of his own efforts. (*Shakespearean Criticism* 2.63)

Passion provides a sort of agency for the imagination. It is by means of the passion that the imagination is able to reduce a multitude into a unity of effect. The agency of the passion connects it to Coleridge's thinking about the symbol and about language. The symbol-making activity of the imagination is generated by the predominant passion of the poet. Furthermore, the poet's passion enlivens his understanding of language as living words by which the antithesis between word and thing is destroyed.

Coleridge's emphasis upon the role of passion in the work of the poet provides an important clarification of Warren's use of the term in the first section of *Audubon*. Above all, it establishes Audubon's role at the outset as a poet whose activity centers on the imagination and language. Warren confirms this when he moves from Audubon's passion into the world in which Audubon walked. This world is not a world of representation, but is the world shaped by Audubon's own imagination. The scene that Warren presents is not copied from nature; rather, the image presented is modified by Audubon's predominant passion so that the reader sees only as Audubon sees.

> Saw,
> Eastward and over the cypress swamp, the dawn,
> Redder than meat, break;
> And the large bird,
> Long neck outthrust, wings crooked to scull air, moved
> In a slow calligraphy, crank, flat, and black against
> The color of God's blood spilt, as though
> Pulled by a string.
>
> Saw,
> It proceed across the inflamed distance. (I[A].5–13)

Warren introduces in these lines the two primary themes of the poem that mirror the two themes he explored in his analysis of *The Ancient Mariner*. First, the color of the dawn sky as being the "color of God's blood spilt" suggests the theme of the sacramental view of the universe. In "A Poem of Pure Imagination," Warren states that Coleridge's notion of the imagination is rooted in his understanding of the *imago dei*, by which "the world of Nature is to be read by the mind as a symbol of Divinity" (345). This creaturely imagination "operates to read Nature . . . as a symbol of God. It might be said that reason shows us God, and imagination shows us how Nature participates in God" (346). Warren develops the second and related theme of *Audubon* in the image of the heron moving across the sky, suggesting that nature may be read by the imagination because it forms a text and has a voice that declares itself. Warren does not use simile in these lines to describe the motion of the bird. Rather, like the Windhover of Gerard Manley Hopkins, the language actuates the experience in such a way that the experience cannot be divided from the language itself.[12] The bird's motion is not *like* a slow calligraphy; rather, that motion *is* a calligraphy, written in black ink. Warren's language here is strikingly similar to his symbol of the Logos in "Myth on Mediterranean Beach: Aphrodite as Logos" (*CP* 228–30), published only two years before *Audubon*. That poem begins with a similar motion and image:

> From left to right, she leads the eye
> Across the blaze-brightness of sea and sky
>
> That is the background of her transit.
>
> Commanded thus, from left to right,
> As by a line of print on that bright
>
> Blankness, the eye will follow, but
>
> There is no line, the eye follows only
> That one word moving, it moves in lonely
>
> And absolute arrogance across the blank
>
> Page of the world, the word burns, she is
> The word, all faces turn. . . . (1–11)

As in *Audubon*, language has become more than figure of speech. It is consubstantial with what it says, without making any claims to some extra-verbal reality.

By this power of language, there is a re-creation of experience. Audubon's eye is commanded by the heron as it moves across the sky, as "the eye" in this earlier poem is commanded by the image of Aphrodite. Whereas the image in "Myth on Mediterranean Beach" is clearly that of reading a line of print superimposed upon the blank page of the world, in *Audubon* the image is that of writing. Even as Aphrodite is the word in this earlier poem, so the heron that Audubon watches is the word that writes itself upon this other page of the dawn sky. His "eyes [are] fixed on the bird" as he sees "it proceed across the inflamed distance." The concern of the poet is not representation but the shaping and modifying power of the imagination. Audubon's passion shapes what he sees so that by his imagination the bird is the word.

By its modifying and fusing effect, Audubon's passion opens to him the knowledge of the world after which he yearns. But it is not simply a knowledge of identity; rather, the imagination perceives difference and seeks to bring that "multitude into unity of effect," as Coleridge said. The second half of this opening section highlights a knowledge by difference by introducing a necessary tension in Audubon's experience.

> Moccasins set in hoar frost, eyes fixed on the bird,
> Thought: "On that sky it is black."
> Thought: "In my mind it is white."
> Thinking: "*Ardea occidentalis*, heron, the great one."
>
> Dawn: his heart shook in the tension of the world.
>
> Dawn: and what is your passion? (I[A].14–19)

Audubon processes his experience in the moment of perception as an artist. Although he perceives the heron to be black against the sky, in his mind it is white. The difference between this "black" and "white" is not simply the distinction between the knowing subject and the perceived object. The difference here is between Audubon's report of his perception and the report of his imagination. The imagination does not simply reflect what the mind perceives. Rather, it modifies the image so that the bird not only becomes "white" but is named, "*Ardea occidentalis*, heron, great one." Warren establishes here a formal pattern that he uses throughout the rest of the poem by setting up the recurring tension between black and white. He returns to this this pattern at several points in the poem, often using a chiastic structure to make the tension concrete. This linguistic tension is at the center of the poet's imagination.

The shaping power of the imagination—and not the reflective power of the fancy—distinguishes Audubon as an artist/poet. In "The Two Worlds of Coleridge's 'The Rime of the Ancient Mariner,'" David Jasper comments on Coleridge's notion of the imagination in a way that helps clarify the importance of this power for Audubon.

> The artist, abandoning the minimal role of holding up a mirror to nature, shapes the world as he experiences it, in metaphor and symbol his art a self-expression, illuminating and not merely reflecting. As it "dissolves, diffuses, dissipates, in order to recreate," the imagination is a symbolising activity, the symbol focusing and shaping through the very particularity of an event or object the eternal "ideas" which underlie it and of which it is a part. (127)

The shaping power is central to the "vision" of the poem. It opens up a way of understanding the world, a way to see the tension of the world and to embrace that tension rather than attempting to move beyond or around it. It is a vision of the poet's struggle after knowledge—a yearning toward unity—but that knowledge is characterized by the tension of the world. Audubon's passion is his need to understand the nature of that tension. Warren repeatedly highlights this throughout the poem both thematically and formally. And as a poet figure, Audubon is seeking authentic utterance, the kind of utterance rooted in the "woful agony" that grasped the Ancient Mariner and was the impetus for the tale that he told. Returning again and again, the agony burns within the poet, and yet it provides the "strange power of speech" (*The Rime of the Ancient Mariner* 56).

For the poet, the experience of linguistic tension lies at the root of the problem of articulation. It is the tension between the power of language and its limit, between the unsayable and the said. The poet cannot avoid this inherent tension but must embrace it, recognizing within it a parallel between the doubleness of the imagination and of language. Warren describes the working of the imagination in "A Poem of Pure Imagination" in this way:

> So we have here a peculiar and paradoxical situation: the poem is a poem in which the poetic imagination appears in a regenerative and healing capacity, but in the end the hero, who has, presumably, been healed, appears in one of his guises as the *poète maudit*. So we learn that the imagination does not only bless, for even as it blesses it lays on a curse. (386)

The paradox of the poem and of the poet is the simultaneous doubleness of the imagination and of language. The doubleness of the imagination is expressed in the way that it both blesses by regenerating the understanding and curses by failing to give complete knowledge. Warren goes on to observe, "Though the Mariner brings the word which is salvation, he cannot quite save himself and taste the full joy of the fellowship he advertises" (386). Though he brings the word to others, he experiences an agony within himself because the imagination and language can only function within this tension. For Audubon, the heron is both black and white; it is both the heron of the dawn sky and the heron of his imagination. One demands the other, even as the two are held in tension. Furthermore, though the poet may search for adequate words to articulate his vision, they will never completely suffice. His passion will never be satisfied, the agony never quenched. This is what Warren calls the "paradox of the situation of the poet," because the poet is "the man with the power which comes unbidden and which is an 'agony' until it finds words" (387).

As Audubon continues to walk in the world, he bears in himself the very blessing and curse that distinguishes the imagination and language. On the one hand, by pursuing his passion, he led a "blessed" life." In "The Sign Whereby He Knew" (IV), Warren writes:

His life, at the end, seemed—even the anguish—simple.
Simple, at least, in that it had to be,
Simply, what it was, as he was,
In the end, himself and not what
He had known he ought to be. The blessedness! ([A].1–5)

By virtue of his imagination and his passion, Audubon knew the blessedness of being "Himself, Jean Jacques, and his passion" (I[A].4), rather than what he knew he ought to have been. Rather than keeping store, dandling babies and getting rich, Audubon knew the blessedness of seeing "from the forest pond, already dark, the great trumpeter swan / Rise, in clangor, and fight up the steep air where, / In the height of last light, it glimmered, like white flame" (IV[C].5–7). By pursuing his passion, he "saw the Indian, and felt the splendor of God" (V[A].13). On the other hand, the artist learns that the imagination cannot sustain such blessing. In section IV, Warren describes the blessedness of hearing the world declare itself in a voice that speaks of joy. But with such blessing comes a crucial question: "Why / Therefore, is truth is the only thing that cannot / Be spoken?" (IV[E].5–6) The immediate answer is, "It can only be enacted" (IV[E].7). Audubon also experienced the curse of the imagination and language through its failure or regress. He had seen and loved the great heron and the swan, yet he remained something of an enigma to himself: "he did not know / What he was. Thought: 'I do not know my own name" (IV[E].10–11). This inability to speak the name that provides identity is a characteristic of the linguistic tension that gives voice to the unsayable, as Warren will explore in many of his later poems.[13] At the end of his life, Audubon knew the effects of this curse:

> And in the end, entered into his earned house,
> And slept in a bed, and with Lucy.
>
> But the fiddle
> Soon lay on the shelf untouched, the mouthpiece
> Of the flute was dry, and his brushes.
>
> His mind
> Was darkened, and his last joy
> Was in the lullaby they sang him, in Spanish, at sunset.
>
> He died, and was mourned, who had loved the world. (V[A].35–41)

Though he had known the glory of the imagination and understood the glimmering power of a sustaining passion, Audubon was in the end abandoned by imagination, and his mind was darkened. But, in section VI of the poem, entitled "Love and Knowledge," Warren returns to the effect of Audubon's passion. He killed the birds "at surprising distances" (11) and held them in his hands with "his head bowed low, / But not in grief" (12–13). He then adds, "He put them where they are, and there we see them: / In our imagination" (14–15).

By fusing the theme of the imagination with the theme of the sacramental vision, Warren establishes Audubon's experience as that of the poet who confronts the tension of the world and the problem of articulation. In his reading of *The Ancient Mariner*, Warren identifies the Mariner's crime of shooting the albatross as the heart of the overarching fable that enacts the sacramental vision and understands this as a re-enactment of the mystery of the Fall. In *Audubon*, he casts the poet as a Mariner-like figure who must confront his own crime of shooting birds in the same context of the Fall. Warren does this through two prominent images or narrative moments. In the first, the sacramental vision is intimated through the necessary act of shooting birds in order to know and to paint them, the irony of which hearkens back to the doubleness of the imagination and discloses the struggle with language in the act of poetic creation. In the second, Warren develops this theme through a parallel—and equally necessary—narrative in the long second section of the poem, which is the real turning point for Audubon in his own fable. Both of these involve the notion of crime as it relates to the Fall: Audubon commits a crime upon nature in the first image, which paradoxically leads to redemption, and in the second he is the victim of crime, acted upon by another person.

Audubon's apparent crime of shooting birds is an interesting reversal of the Mariner's crime because he kills the creatures so that he might know them and in turn illuminate our imagination. In the third section of "A Poem of Pure Imagination," Warren probes the nature of the Mariner's transgression, rejecting any reading of the crime that views it simply from a moralistic perspective. Warren insists that it be read as a symbol that "re-enacts the mystery of the Fall" (360) and supports this reading by tracing out Coleridge's understanding of the doctrine of original sin and of the Fall, concluding that Coleridge could not intellectualize these matters but could only accept them as an unavoidable mystery. He quotes from Coleridge's *Table Talk*: "A Fall of some sort or other—the creation, as it were, of the nonabsolute—is the fundamental postulate of the moral history of Man. Without this hypothesis, Man is unintelligible; with it, every phenomenon is explicable. The mystery itself is too profound for human insight" (359). If Coleridge held that the Fall is necessary to our understanding of the nature of man, he also maintained that it is necessary to our understanding the whole of creation. In *Confessions of An Inquiring Spirit*, he states, "Not only Man, but, says St. Paul, the whole creation is included in the consequences of the Fall" (Letter I). He also held that the mind of man bore those consequences in an obvious way. In *Aids to Reflection,* he states that the myth of the Fall "speaks to the Catechumen & to the Adept.—To the Catechumen it states the simple Fact, viz. that Man fell and falls thro' the separation and the insubordination of the Fancy, the Appetance, & the discursive Intellect from the Faith or practical Reason" (261 n. 40). The effect of the Fall was the distortion of reason, and man continues to fall by elevating the fancy above the imagination. The mystery of the Fall for Coleridge, however, is that it appears not only to have resulted in a curse but also to have prepared paradoxically for a blessing. Man is unintelligible without the Fall, but he receives his imagination through the Fall. And, for Coleridge, it is by means of the imagination that the fallen creature yearns toward a healing of the wound of the Fall.

Warren interprets the act of the Mariner as an act of sin that is original in the will of the sinner himself and is without prior determination. He states:

> The bolt whizzes from the crossbow and the bird falls and all comment that the Mariner has no proper dramatic motive or is the child of necessity or is innocent of everything except a little wantonness is completely irrelevant, for we are confronting the mystery of the corruption of the will, the mystery which is the beginning of the "moral history of Man." ("APPI" 359–60)

The corruption of the will, Warren says, is mysterious precisely because of its lack of motivation and its perversity. This "is exactly the significant thing about the Mariner's act" and the thing that "flies in the face of the Aristotelian doctrine of *hamartia*" (360). As a re-enactment of the Fall, it reveals a condition of the will that is "'out of time,' and . . . is the result of no single human motive" (360). The Mariner's crime results from the abstraction of the will, and, according to Coleridge, the will in abstraction "becomes Satanic pride and rebellious self-idolatry" that characterize "the mighty hunters of mankind, from Nimrod to Bonaparte" (360).[14] Warren observes that this peculiar phrase blends "the hunting of beasts and the hunting of man" and "takes us straight to the crime of the Mariner" (360). Against the "literal-minded readers" who can only see a lot of moralistic bother over a bird, Warren explains that "this bird is more than a bird" (360–61). In his reading, "the hunting of the bird becomes the hunting of man" and the crime becomes "symbolically a murder" (360) and a motiveless one at that. In this way, the poem maintains its symbolic reference to the Fall. Warren concludes:

> The poet's problem, then, was to provide an act which, on the one hand, would not accent the issue of probability or shockingly distract from the symbolic significance, but which, on the other hand, would be adequately criminal to justify the consequences. And the necessary criminality is established, we have seen, in two ways: (1) by making the gravity of the act depend on the state of the will which prompts it, and (2) by symbolically defining the bird as a "Christian soul," as "pious," etc. (361)

Warren goes on to argue a third way of conceiving the criminality of the Mariner's act, one that is concerned for the deeper religious symbolism of a "sacramental conception of the universe" (362). From this perspective, the importance of the Mariner's act is that "the crime against Nature" becomes "a crime against God" when he hails the bird "'in God's name'" (362). When the cross is removed from the Mariner's neck and is replaced by the dead albatross, there is a transference from the creature of God to God himself. "And the death of the creature of God, like the death of the Son of God, will, in its own way, work for vision and salvation" (362). But the Mariner's crime goes hand in hand with his regeneration, which is revealed in the moment of blessing the sea snakes. "In the end," Warren says, "he accepts the sacramental view of the universe, and his will is released from its state of 'utmost abstraction' and gains the state of 'immanence' in wisdom and love" (365).

While Audubon commits a similar crime when he kills the birds that he will then paint, his act is diffused and re-created by Warren's secondary imagination in his own poem. Like the Mariner, Audubon commits a crime against nature: he shoots birds. But Audubon's act does not appear to be motiveless under a will in a state of utmost abstraction. Audubon's crime is clearly motivated by his passion for true knowledge of the world and of the "Birds of North America" (V[A].4). Warren states in the sixth section of the poem that this passion for knowledge is one name for love. Yet, he "slew" the birds, "at surprising distances, with his gun" (VI.11). Warren commented on this paradoxical situation in 1977: "Audubon was the greatest slayer of birds that ever lived: he destroyed beauty in order to create beauty and whet his understanding. Love is knowledge" (Watkins, Hiers, and Weaks 244). This paradoxical character of Audubon's act reveals precisely how it re-enacts in its own way the mystery of the Fall and reveals the doubleness of the imagination necessitated by the Fall in the context of Warren's poem. Audubon yearns for an immediate and real knowledge that would heal the wound of the Fall, yet this knowledge is not available to him. This is the same paradoxical situation in which the poet finds himself when striving for the unsayable. Warren writes in V[C]:

For everything there is a season.

But there is the dream
Of a season past all seasons.

In such a dream the wild-grape cluster,
High-hung, exposed in the gold light,
Unripening, ripens. (1–6)

Audubon longs for that season past all seasons, but this can only be described by the language of tension and paradox: in that season the wild grape cluster "unripening, ripens." His knowledge is always marked by the tension of the world. Like truth, which is "the only thing that cannot / Be spoken" (IV[E].5–6), this knowledge of what is beyond knowing may only be approached through the enactment of Audubon's art.

Warren further qualifies Audubon's act by framing it as a crime against the self. The slaying of birds is more than a criminal act against nature, even as the Mariner's act is more than the killing of a bird. Whereas the hunting of the bird becomes the hunting of man in *The Ancient Mariner*, the hunting of the bird becomes the hunting of the self in *Audubon: A Vision*. In IV[A], Warren writes,

The blessedness!—

To wake in some dawn and see,
As though down a rifle barrel, lined up
Like sights, the self that was, the self that is, and there,
Far off but in range, completing that alignment, your fate.

Hold your breath, let the trigger-squeeze be slow and steady.

The quarry lifts, in the halo of gold leaves, its noble head.

This is not a dimension of Time. (5–12)

Warren likens the hunt to the way Audubon ultimately resolved the issue of his identity. As when he hunted birds, Audubon sought a particular quarry—the self. But there is an elusiveness to this hunt. Only in a timeless dimension could he awake in that dawn when "the self that was" and "the self that is" actually line up with his fate. But, in the "blessedness" of the imagination, the self may be re-made through this act of self-immolation. The slow and steady squeeze of the trigger enacts a sacramental moment because the death of the self leads to vision. Section VI affirms that Audubon's crime against nature is motivated by knowledge—he slays in order to know. The crime against the self is motivated by the same yearning for knowledge. He wants to know that self which can be finally known beyond the tension of the world. Warren told Peter Stitt that as he worked on the poem he "began to see [Audubon] as a certain kind of man, a man who has finally learned to accept his fate" (Watkins, Hiers, and Weaks 244). However, before he can accept his fate, Audubon must slay the self in an act of the will.[15] Rather than being an instance of the will in utmost abstraction—as Warren suggested the act of the Mariner was— here, we have an instance of the will in its immanence. It is redeemed from utmost abstraction by the desire for wisdom and love.[16] By his recognition of a sacramental union with nature, Audubon does not display what Coleridge describes in *The Statesman's Manual* as that "fearful resolve to find in [himself] alone the one absolute motive of action, under which all other motives from within and from without must be either subordinated or crushed" (65). Rather, his heart shakes with the passion to understand his connection with the natural realm, which alone can provide the overarching motive in the act of poetic creation.

Audubon's crime against nature and the self is not the only way that the theme of the sacramental vision is developed. Warren also highlights this theme by showing how thin the membrane is between Audubon and the natural world. In the second part of the first section, Audubon watches a bear on an autumn afternoon as it prepares for its long winter's nap:

October: and the bear,
Daft in the honey-light, yawns.

The bear's tongue, pink as a baby's, out-crisps to the curled tip,
It bleeds the black blood of the blueberry.

The teeth are more importantly white
Than has ever been imagined.

The bear feels his own fat
Sweeten, like a drowse, deep to the bone.

Bemused, above the fume of ruined blueberries,
The last bee hums.

The wings, like mica, glint
In the sunlight.

He leans on his gun. Thinks
How thin is the membrane between himself and the world. (1–14)

This meditation looks back to the blood-red sky of dawn across which the heron
flew through its own sacramental image of the "black blood of the blueberry,"
even as it further illuminates the tension of the world in which Audubon's
heart shook. It also highlights the tension by extending the contrast between
"the black blood" and the white teeth of the bear, "more importantly white /
Than has ever been imagined." The tension is experienced between what he
perceives and what he knows in his mind but cannot fully conceive. These lines
also look forward to the longest and most narrative section of the poem, "The
Dream He Never Knew the End Of," in which Audubon is given shelter for a
night in a woman's wilderness cabin and is threatened during the night with
his own murder by the woman and her sons. Through the experience of his
confrontation, he will learn how close the connection is between himself and
humanity. If in the first section he learned that this membrane signifies both
a division and a union between himself and nature, Audubon learns in his
encounter with the woman that there is no membrane to separate him from
the tension of the human filth and human hope that he finds in this cabin in
the woods. The first section of the poem emphasizes the glorious aspects of
the tension of the world, but here in the second that tension is shown in all of
its gritty and grimy aspects. If the poet—whether Audubon or Warren—can
frame a definition of joy, it must be a definition that confronts this tension and
embraces it. Such a confrontation is necessary to any poetic vision that seeks
a true knowledge of the world and yearns for that moment of articulation.

The second section begins at the end of a day, seemingly following on from
the dawn and the sunlight mentioned in the first section.

Shank-end of day, spit of snow, the call,
A crow, sweet in distance, then sudden
The clearing: among stumps, ruined cornstalks yet standing, the spot
Like a wound rubbed raw in the vast pelt of the forest. There
Is the cabin, a huddle of logs with no calculation or craft:
The human filth, the human hope. (II[A].1–6)

Warren makes several thematic connections with the first section, most importantly by introduction the call of the crow, "sweet in distance." Whereas

Audubon was able to read the calligraphy of the heron in the dawn sky, here he is able to discern a call from the crow that announces the clearing upon which Audubon apparently stumbles. The image of the clearing is used to develop the notion of nature as sacrament by the way it is described: "a wound rubbed raw in the vast pelt of the forest." The wound suggests that some criminal act has been inflicted upon the forest because Warren uses specifically an animate description: it is a wound in a pelt, the hide of an animal. The crime against the forest appears to be without motive, but it betrays the effects of humanity's presence and labor: the cabin stands among the tree stumps and the ruined cornstalks as a sign of the tension between "the human filth" and "the human hope." It is a fallen scene, devoid of glory or beauty. The smoke coming out of the "mud-and-stick chimney" (7) drains down the roof "like sputum" (9). As Audubon approaches the clearing and the cabin, he stands and thinks about the scene before him, as he did in the first section. In his imagination, he already knows "the stench of that lair beyond / The door-puncheons" (16–17). These physical signs, however, only anticipate the confrontation with fallen humanity that Audubon will face inside the cabin.

The woman who inhabits the cabin is something of a foil to Audubon.[17] She and her voice, which is played against Audubon's thoughts throughout the section, are the embodiment of the tension between the "human filth, the human hope." In both her physical appearance and her voice, there is at once a beauty—or power—and a repulsing crudity. These two are never reconciled, and Audubon must accept both the beauty and the horror: she simply "is what she is" (II[J].14). This sustained tension not only lends to the woman a certain authenticity but also reveals the power of language whose energy resides in its own unresolved tension between linguistic despair and linguistic hope. It is clear that this union of opposites, this multeity in unity, is the basis of the woman's powerful beauty. Her power is also intimated by the way that her image is fused with the image of a bird. In II[A], the woman's voice is paralleled with the call of the crow. The first line ends with "the call" of the crow, and the last line ends with "the voice" of her response to Audubon's greeting. This fusion is heightened when Warren introduces the woman in II[C]; the physical description has a certain ambivalence about it, as appropriate for the crow that invokes this section as for the woman who is being introduced. Her face hangs like a crow in mid-air. It is "Large, / Raw-hewn, strong-beaked" and her eyes, "dark, glint as from the unspecifiable / Darkness of a cave" (II[C].1–2, 6–7). Only after sustaining this description for six lines is this creature defined as "a woman." This combination of images confirms the symbolic role and significance of the woman in the larger vision of the poem. The blending of the woman's image with the imagery of birds affirms that Audubon's encounter in this section is not separate from his paradoxical activity of slaying birds in order to create beauty. The threat to his own life and the subsequent death of the woman and her sons correspond to the crime against the self and the crime against nature. By extending the sacramental vision through the crime against humanity, this narrative reiterates the notion of an atoning sacrificial death. Just as the death of the birds worked to bring about a sort of redemption, so the woman's death in the place of Audubon provides for the him the fullness of this sacramental vision so that, in his own way, he might bless "them unaware" (*The Rime of the Ancient Mariner* 285). And if this moment of blessing is the turning point of Coleridge's poem (as Warren saw it to be), then it would appear to have similar significance in *Audubon*.

Audubon first recognizes the beauty of the woman in II[D], when he takes out his pocket watch and it glows in the firelight.

> It is gold, it lives in his hand in the firelight, and the woman's
> Hand reaches out. She wants it. She hangs it about her neck.
>
> And near it the great hands hover delicately
> As though it might fall, they quiver like moth-wings, her eyes
> Are fixed downward, as though in shyness, on that gleam, and her face
> Is sweet in an outrage of sweetness, so that
> His gut twists cold. He cannot bear what he sees.
>
> Her body sways like a willow in spring wind. Like a girl. (10–17)

This moment of beauty follows a particular instance of the woman's crudity in which she laughed at "the Indian," who is also staying there for the night, for having wounded his eye with his own arrow. But the glittering of the gold watch in the firelight transforms her not only from a woman into a girl but from a crow into a moth. The description of the motion of her hands and body is radically different from descriptions in the rest of this section. Her "hands hover delicately" and "quiver like moth-wings." Her eyes, which were described as dark and glinting "as from the unspecifiable / Darkness of a cave," now are shy and are a part of the "outrage of sweetness" which has come over her face. "Her body sways like a willow in spring wind," but ten lines later she "hulks by the fire" (II[D].27).[18] This irreconcilable beauty and horror nauseates Audubon so that he "cannot bear what he sees." He cannot bear to find in this woman the beauty that he so readily sees in the heron or the crow or the jay, a beauty that captures his passion and his love. It is the power of this tension that proves to be a threat to Audubon as much as the threat of his own murder by the woman and her sons.

In parts E through H, Warren tells the story of the attempt on Audubon's life, thwarted only by the sudden entrance of three travelers. Audubon's re-action to the imminent threat of his murder, however, reveals his sense of complicity. The moment of threat is not only something he knows from an ar-chetypal fairytale told to him as a child but also the substance of a childhood dream. This is the dream to which the title of this section refers, the dream that Audubon has had before and knows well. But he never knows the ending of this dream. When faced with the threat, Audubon is frozen in passivity by "a lassitude / [which] Sweetens his limbs" (II[G].4–5). Rather than fighting back, he lies in wait for the end of the dream. His reaction recalls the bear in I[B], which "feels his own fat / Sweeten, like a drowse, deep to the bone" (7–8). Though Audubon "knows / What he must do" (II[G].2–3), he cannot do it. And he does not understand his inaction: "He cannot think what guilt un-mans him, or / Why he should find the punishment so precious" (10–11). The guilt that unmans him is an awareness of his complicity that unites him to this woman and to the tension of the world, which is why, at the apparent moment of his death, he can only respond, "Oh, oh, the world! / Tell me the name of the world" (12–13). If he could know the ending of the dream, then he would know what is beyond knowing and would be able to speak the name of the world. This knowledge would only come with his death, and he would then not be able to act upon it. Though he may not speak truth while he is alive, it may nonetheless be enacted in what Warren later describes as "the dream become . . . action" (IV[E].8). Being in the world—participating in the tension and "the secret order of the world" (II[L].8)—requires asking questions rather than speaking the answer:

> He thinks: "What has been denied me?"
> Thinks: "There is never an answer."
>
> Thinks: "The question is the only answer."
>
> He yearns to be able to frame a definition of joy. (II[L].9–12)

The ultimate answer or meaning that Audubon looks for is continually deferred, so he must continue to ask questions. Warren confirms this deferral of meaning in his "Afterthought" to *Being Here*: "Here, as in life, meaning is, I should say, often more fruitfully found in the question asked than in any answer given" (*CP* 441). The definition of joy that Audubon yearns for must be a definition made up of questions, of silences and traces that "cannot fully embrace the dynamics of being" (Jackson, "The Generous Time" 24). In the tension of the world, the poet must continue to yearn.

When Audubon is saved by the three travelers who burst into the scene, his role in the narrative shifts from victim to witness. Although he was denied knowledge of the ending of his own dream, he witnesses the fulfillment of "the dream that, lifelong, [the woman] had dreamed toward" (II[K].7). As with his own dream, the fulfillment of the woman's dream only comes with her execution together with her sons. The hanging scene enlarges the imagery introduced in the first section and consummates the theme of the sacramental vision. In the first section, in which Audubon saw the bird "Eastward and over the cypress swamp" (I[A].6), the sacramental imagery of "God's blood spilt" colors the dawn sky. In the second section, when dawn comes, it is gray and "Eastward, low over the forest, the sun is nothing / But a circular blur of no irradiation ... " (II[J].2–3). Through the image of the woman Warren formally portrays the tension between white and black, which in the first section revealed the imaginative passion of Audubon.

> And in the gray light of morning, he sees her face. Under
> The tumbled darkness of hair, the face
> Is white. Out of that whiteness
> The dark eyes stare at nothing, or at
> The nothingness that the gray sky, like Time, is, for
> There is no Time, and the face
> Is, he suddenly sees, beautiful as stone, and
>
> So becomes aware that he is in the manly state. (II[J].15–22)

On a rhetorical level, Warren uses chiasmus to structure the tension that is imaginatively portrayed in the woman's face. On another level, though, he makes it clear that the language is the tension: "white" and "dark" are not referential terms but are the tension within which Audubon recognizes the beauty of the woman's face. The language creates the experience. At the moment of recognition, Audubon "becomes aware that he is in the manly state." Rather than being a gratuitous sexual innuendo, Warren's reference to the "manly state"—Audubon has an erection—counters Audubon's earlier failure to understand what guilt unmanned him while he awaited the inflicting of the fatal wound from the woman.[19] And yet this recognition of beauty takes on the form of blessing. This is made clear in II[K], in which Warren describes the hanging:

> The affair was not quick: both sons long jerking and farting, but she,
> From the first, without motion, frozen
> In a rage of will, an ecstasy of iron, as though
> This was the dream that, lifelong, she had dreamed toward.
>
>   The face,
> Eyes a-glare, jaws clenched, now glowing black with congestion
> Like a plum, had achieved,
> It seemed to him, a new dimension of beauty. (4–10)

The beauty that he perceives is the woman's will, which becomes salvific in a will-to-be. Her face takes on the bloody color of the blueberries in I[B] and in this self-sacrament, he sees "a new dimension of beauty." In her death, the woman achieves a certain wisdom, by virtue of which Audubon himself gains a fuller understanding of this sacramental vision. The fusion of the crime against nature with the crime against humanity is sealed when the crow reappears in the final line of this section to come "to rest on a rigid shoulder."

The sacramental vision of life has specific implications for the poet's understanding of language. According to this vision, nature ceases to be an inanimate object which is passively available to the poet's scrutiny. In *Audubon*, nature becomes an active participant in the sacramental vision, even becoming the sacrament itself at times. The poet, then, ceases to be the only speaker and becomes a participant through listening. Heidegger makes the same claim. According to Steiner:

> For Heidegger, . . . the human person and self-consciousness are *not* the center, the assessors of existence. Man is only a privileged listener and respondent to existence. The vital relation to otherness is not, as for Cartesian and positive rationalism, one of "grasping" and pragmatic use. It is a relation of audition. We are trying "to listen to the voice of

Being." It is, or ought to be, a relation of extreme responsibility, custodi-anship, answerability to and for. Of this answerability, the thinker and the poet ... are at once the carriers and the trustees. (31–32)

As the poet listens to the world, he is ultimately listening to being itself, and the act of poetic creation becomes an act of answerability in which the poet offers his testimony. The sacramental vision lays bare, then, not only the ten-sion of the world but also the tension between speaking and listening, declara-tion and silence, the sayable and the unsayable. Language is no longer simply a given, nor is it a lifeless substance to be shaped; rather, it is a living power. So the moment of poetic creation—Warren's overt concern in his study of Coleridge and his underlying concern in *Audubon*—is a sacramental moment. Poetic creation is a process of discovery, and in the moment of creation the poem comes "unbidden from the depths" just as the Mariner's blessing comes "unaware." The sacramental nature of this moment qualifies the type of speak-ing that is involved in creating the poem: it is a sort of prayer that is watchful and humble in its approach.[20]

This concern for "saying the unsayable," as the poet works toward the given within the tension of the world, recurs throughout *Audubon*. It does so pri-marily through the voice of the world, by which the world declares itself. This voice is heard through the call of the birds throughout the poem. In Section I[A], the heron is identified as moving across the dawn sky in a "slow calligra-phy." What does it write upon the sky? It does not write its own name within the world—either "*ardea occidentalis*" or "heron, the great one." It writes its presence, which opens within Audubon's mind the possibility of a knowl-edge of both the bird's presence and its absence. The world repeatedly calls to Audubon and leads him toward moments of understanding as he continues to walk in the world. The second section of the poem is bracketed by the call of the crow, which at first implicitly draws Audubon toward his passion and in the end explicitly alerts Audubon to his new-found vision. Within that same section, Audubon also encounters the voice of the world when he hears it break the silence once again in the whisper of the stone. In the darkness of the night, he

hears

Like the whisper and whish of silk, that other
Sound, like a sound of sleep, but he does not
Know what it is. (II[E].10–13)

As the woman prepares to murder Audubon, she sharpens her knife on the stone, wetted by her own spit. "The spit is what softens like silk the passage of steel / On the fine-grained stone. It whispers" (18–19). But this whisper alerts him, warning him of his doom. It speaks the tale, which is "the dream he had in childhood but never / Knew the end of, only / The scream" (II[F].8–10). At the end of this second section, Audubon stands alone in the clearing, staring at the face of the woman after she is hanged. He thinks, "I must go," but he could not stop staring at the face; then, "Far off, in the forest and falling snow, / A crow was calling" (II[M].11–12). When the voice of the world sounds, he "stirs, knowing now / He will not be here when snow / Drifts into the open door of the cabin . . ." (12–14).

As the poet, Audubon listens to this voice of the world, which speaks in a language that he may hear but may not fully understand. This language is far more primordial than the approximating and unstable language of human intercourse. This voice of the world speaks the language of being, and the poet patiently waits and listens for the voice. This is what the poet listens for in IV[D]:

> Listen! Stand very still and,
> Far off, where shadow
> Is undappled, you may hear
>
> The tusked boar grumble in his ivy-slick. (1–4)

Here the poet demands the reader to participate with him in listening to the voice of the world. IV[D] continues: "Afterward, there is silence until / The jay, sudden as conscience, calls" (5–6). It is this call of the world, in the midst of the silence, that the poet hears. And it is in the tension between the silence and the call that the poet stands. The possibility of the world "presence-ing" itself is drawn out by the concomitant possibility of the world "absence-ing" itself in silence. IV[E] goes on to describe this tension:

> The world declares itself. That voice
> Is vaulted in—oh, arch on arch—redundancy of joy, its end
> Is its beginning, necessity
> Blooms like a rose. Why,
>
> Therefore, is truth the only thing that cannot
> Be spoken?

It can only be enacted, and that in dream,
Or in the dream become, as though unconsciously, action, . . . (1–8)

The poet waits upon the voice of the world and is inspired by its language. He acknowledges, however, the presence of the unsayable in those things which may not be spoken. The poet dwells in this tension of the world declaring itself, and yet there are things which may not be spoken by man.

Having listened to the voice of the world, though, the poet can only create through the exercise of the creative will by which it "dissolves, diffuses, dissipates in order to recreate" (*BL* I.304). The imagination is not passive but is vital, Coleridge says. In Warren's aesthetic, it is an act of violence that re-enacts the mystery of the Fall, but this violence leads to imagination, knowledge, and even love. So, Audubon's act of slaying these birds—through whom the voice of the world is heard—symbolizes the act of poetic creation. Just as he slays beauty in order to create beauty, the poet slays language by feigning mastery over it, dissolving, diffusing, and dissipating it in the act of creation. However, this imaginative activity ultimately collapses in on itself, and the poet's mastery over language breaks down so that truth may not be spoken. It must be enacted in the on-going work of creativity and collapse.

Audubon ends with this image of the poet as listener and makes a sort of plea that forms an epigraph for all of Warren's subsequent poetry. Section VII, "Tell Me a Story," tells a story and issues the call for a certain story to be told. In subsection A, Warren speaks of a time in boyhood when he heard the voice of the world as the "great geese hoot northward" (3). This forms a sort of bookend to the first section in which Audubon sees the great heron in the dawn sky; here, however, the speaker can only hear the goose in that "first dark" after sunset (2). What Audubon understood to be his great passion as he felt his heart shake in the tension of the world, the speaker here does not understand: "I did not know what was happening in my heart" (6). The speaker's reference to the season as being that "season before the elderberry blooms" (7) recalls the tension in V[C] between "For everything there is a season" and "But there is the dream / Of a season past all seasons" (1–3). In this tension, there is a wisdom to be learned by the poet, a wisdom which the world seems to know and declares to the poet who is willing to listen: "It was the season before the elderberry blooms, / Therefore they were going north. / The sound was passing northward" (VII[A].7–9). Part of the wisdom imparted is that dream of "a season past all seasons," a season that never ends yet is always at its fullness. This is a season that lies beyond the effect of the Fall, a season in which the wound of the Fall and the tension of the world have been reconciled. And it is a season not out of time but the season at the fullness of Time.

In the second subsection, Warren calls for the telling of this story which is intimated in subsection A.

Tell me a story.

In this century, and moment, of mania,
Tell me a story.

Make it a story of great distances, and starlight.

The name of the story will be Time,
But you must not pronounce its name.

Tell me a story of deep delight. (1–7)

A benign imperative, "Tell me a story" contains both a tone of urgency and a sense of yearning as it expresses the passion of the poet for the tension of the world. Part of this passion is his own sense of urgent need for a word or story that will provide some understanding of being in the world. This urgency is evident in the second section of the poem, in which the poet cries out, "Tell me the name of the world" (II[G].13), and later states that Audubon "yearns to be able to frame a definition of joy" (II[L].12). This same yearning finds utterance in IV[E], in the prayerful supplication, "Tell us, dear God—tell us the sign / Whereby we may know the time has come" (14–15). This yearning to know the name of the world and to be able to frame a definition of joy both point toward the imperative in this final section of the poem, which calls for that story whose name is Time. The poet senses the necessity of a story, both diachronically—"In this century..." —and synchronically— "and moment, of mania...." And, between this diachrony and synchrony, between "century" and "moment," the story blooms out of language. This tale is intimately related to the world; it is made up of the world: "Make it a story of great distances and starlight." And though the name of the story is known—"The name of the story will be Time,"—this name may not be pronounced. Like truth, the name may not be spoken because it absents itself as soon as it is pronounced or spoken. While the story may be named, it cannot be encompassed by the pronouncing of that name. The name can only approximate the reality of lived experience within the world; but at the same time, it calls this experience into being. The name of the story is not abstracted from the content of the story, which is the world. While Warren shares Augustine's "thirst to know the power and nature of Time," there is for him no Augustinian notion of time in distinction from eternity, a tension that Augustine discusses in Chapter 11 of the Confessions.[21] Rather, like Heidegger, Warren sees time as something we live. "We do not live 'in time' as if the latter were some independent, abstract flow external to our being. We 'live time'" (Steiner 78). Time and being may not be abstracted from one another, for it is only within time that man can find his identity. So, as long as the name of the story is not pronounced or spoken, it remains a vital presence, and the story remains a "deep delight."

This last section of the poem is one of Warren's "threshold moments," which Richard Jackson describes in "The Generous Time: Robert Penn Warren and the Phenomenology of the Moment." Jackson compares Warren's view of the moment to Heidegger's thinking about poetry and being: "Rather than a statically centered, purely referential moment, a moment of clear origins, there is instead the moment of traces, or rebeginnings in the shadows of the abyss" (21). This moment at the end of *Audubon* is not at all "a statically centered" conclusion or resolution in which the poet states the "moral" or "meaning" of the poem. Rather, it is a moment of beginning that calls forth a sense of what Heidegger in *Being and Time* describes as "anticipatory resoluteness," characterized by a "waiting towards" (388) what is beyond the poem. As Derrida says of Edmond Jabès's poetry, "One emerges from the book only within the book" ("Edward Jabès" 76). Such a perspective is not unfamiliar to this poem. When Warren quotes Psalm 56:8 as one of the epigraphs, he seems to suggest that the wanderings of the poet are already written in the book, which in Warren's vision is the text of the world. It is fitting then to view this final section as Warren's epigraph to all the poetry that follows *Audubon*. This later poetry that contemplates language and the unsayable in the poet's experience of the tension of the world is the telling of that story whose name is Time. But the poetry is careful to "not pronounce its name." It cannot circumnavigate time's expansiveness just as it can never fathom the depths of language. Rather, this later poetry probes possibilities and asks its readers the question of being.[22]

CHAPTER FOUR

Participation and the Voice of the World

Language remains, after all, expressive of an orientation to a real world within which it effectively works and articulates and objectifies all things, including itself. But the sense of that reality is affected: it becomes a relation to something else beyond itself that language cannot encompass.—William Franke[1]

I n a January 1977 letter to Louis D. Rubin, Jr., Warren responds to the critic's assessment of his poetry and career in a chapter to be published the next year in *The Wary Fugitives*. While he admits that he has no quarrels with Rubin's work, he does take issue at one point in a way that suggests he does not want to be locked into his reputation as a Fugitive poet. Apparently concerned by the lack of attention given to his later poetry in Rubin's analysis, Warren says with characteristic wit that his "only (slight) dissatisfaction is that I feel the work of the post *Audubon* period, in both poetry and in my forthcoming novel, is my best and I don't like to be hurried into my grave" (*SL* 5:341).[2] It is striking that, after forty years of prolific poetic labor, Warren considers the poetry of what would be his final phase to be his best. He clearly has a sense of sustained vigor in the poetry, shaped by a distinct power that he would continue to explore for another eight years until his final published volume in 1985. The source of that vigor and power is found in large part within the aesthetic vision of *Audubon,* which calls for both reader and poet alike to listen intently to the ways the world declares itself. In Section IV of *Audubon,* the narrator proclaims, "The world declares itself. That voice / Is vaulted in— oh, arch on arch—redundancy of joy, . . ." ([E].1–2). Audubon himself continues to walk in the world because he loves the world and desires to understand "the secret order of the world" (II[L].8) as it declares itself. But the poet, too, walks in the world and in the narrator's own voice states the imperative of the final section, "Tell me a story" (VII[B].1). He, too, longs to know the story that only the world itself can declare. This is why it must be "a story of great distances, and starlight" (4) and "a story of deep delight" (7).

The poetry of what Warren called "the post *Audubon* period" is indeed a story of great distances, starlight, and deep delight. He repeatedly situates the context of the poems within both spatial and temporal distance, often highlighted by the presence of stars. But there is also a certain ontological distance within the poems as he pursues what it means to be in the world. Being, as a present reality, is encountered in the relationship between the present moment and the memories of the past. But within that tension, there is deep delight to be found that is neither simple nor simplistic. Really, it is not so much that the poet finds delight as much as there are moments when delight seems to find him as he listens to the voice of the world. This gives the poet a certain sense of urgency to tell his own story, as Warren indicates in "How to Tell a Love Story" from *Now and Then: Poems 1976–1978* (CP 365).

> There is a story that I must tell, but
> The feeling in my chest is too tight, and innocence
> Crawls through the tangles of fear, leaving,
> Dry and translucent, only its old skin behind like
> A garter snake's annual discard in the ground juniper. If only
>
> I could say just the first word with breath
> As sweet as a babe's and with no history.... (1–7)

What the mature poet finds is that telling his story is no easy thing. Something pushes back against his sense of urgency. What may have once been an innocent thing for him is now marked by tension and even fear, recognizing that even "just the first word" is beyond him. In the place of that innocence is "only its old skin," left behind as a trace of the presence of the unsayable. He cannot speak that first, timeless word, innocent of experience or history. The paradox is that, even if the poet could speak it, we could not understand such a word as having any meaning. We do not live in an innocent world, free of experience or history, but one full of complicity and tension. This is the world Warren relentlessly engages throughout his later poetry and is repeatedly drawn into by the voice of the world itself. Preoccupied by the possibility of the relation of the self to the world, he is more and more captivated by the ways in which this relation happens, to some degree, *in* language. Such a relation can exist because the "world declares itself" first and the poet responds. Language is the primary means of such engagement between the world and the self. Rather than finding immediate access or final answers in this engagement, Warren experiences an inescapable doubleness in language in the way the voice of the world sometimes withholds itself and at other times freely gives of itself. As a poet, he finds himself continually encountering both the limit and power of language.[3]

As he probes the limit and power of language, Warren is at the same time probing the nature of being itself. There is a very real sense in the later poetry that "man finds the proper abode of his existence in language," as Heidegger suggests in "The Nature of Language" (57). The poet's confrontation with language discloses something real—the limits and character of our existence or being. Being is, for Warren, always situated concretely within the world. It is always being in the world, or "Being Here," as he titled his 1977–1980 collection of poetry. The concrete character of being in the world clarifies Warren's understanding of language as concrete utterance within the actualities of the world. As a result, language is never rarefied into linguistics or into a clear philosophy of language—this is not what he understood to be the purpose of poetry. When Warren says at one point in *Democracy and Poetry* that "the end of poetry is to be poetry . . ." (42), he is not resorting to a notion of "pure poetry" or to some form of the "art for art's sake" argument. Rather, he argues that before it can serve any sort of diagnostic or therapeutic ends, poetry must bring the poet and the reader alike into an encounter with the language of the world. The unique property of poetry is to listen to the voice of being and to give utterance to this source in all its vitality.

In order to listen to the voice of the world, the poet cannot be abstracted from the concrete realities of being but must participate in the world. In this way, the later poetry incorporates Warren's thought about the sacramental notion of participation which he consistently explored from even his earliest poetry but was shaped profoundly by his reading of Coleridge and expressed in the vision of *Audubon*. This kind of participation involves an engagement with being that seeks not to reconcile the irremediable elements of existence but to hold in tension the simultaneous glory and terror of being in the world—and that can only happen by engaging with language and the world. Such a view of Warren's notion of participation runs counter to that proposed by Koppelman when he writes, "Participation in nature—not because nature is a shadow of the divine, but because nature itself is imbued with divinity—is the aim of Warren's late poetry and is . . . what distinguishes his aesthetic as sacramental, or more broadly stated, spiritual" (119). The later poetry does indeed aim for participation in or with nature, but not because it is "imbued with divinity." Rather, "participation in nature" is necessary simply if one is to understand what it means to be in the world. In Warren's vision, both humanity and nature are fraught with irreconcilable and inescapable tensions. Far from being divine, the world groans and aches and, like the self, is limited and changeable. While nature does hold a certain power in Warren's vision, it cannot provide in itself the ultimate unity of experience and knowledge toward which the poet is inexorably drawn. Though the heart may long for such unity, there is no way of circumnavigating the tension of the world.

In an interview with Peter Stitt in 1977, Warren denied that he had any spiritual essence to invest in nature, much less any divinity. Stitt compared Warren's love for the things of this world to that of Richard Wilbur, who "indicates that love by investing physical objects with an implicit spiritual essence." Warren's response, in which he denies any such spiritual investment, is significant.

> I am a creature of this world, but I am also a yearner, I suppose. I would call this temperament rather than theology—I haven't got any gospel. That is, I feel an immanence of meaning in things, but I have no meaning to put there that is interesting or beautiful. I think I put it as close as I could in a poem called "Masts at Dawn"—"We must try / To Love so well the world that we may believe, in the end, in God." I am a man of temperament in the modern world who hasn't got any religion. Dante almost got me at one stage, but then I suddenly realized, "My God, Dante's a good Protestant—he was! Where have I gone?" My poem reverses the whole thing, you see: I would rather start with the world. (Watkins, Hiers, and Weaks 243)

Rather than investing the things of the world in all of their immanence with a spiritual, or transcendent, essence, Warren finds meaning—or meanings—implicit in the things themselves. By starting with the world, he enters into the inescapable sphere of the self's being, where the poet must confront language. As "a creature of this world," he cannot gain any position outside of the world from which he might put an interesting or beautiful meaning into the things of the world. He thirsts instead to understand the meaning of things as they present themselves to him. He seeks to understand the temporality of their being and wants to be able to speak in response to their manifestation. Warren's understanding, though, is often framed in the context of the biblical narrative of the fall and does not shy away from the language of redemption. While denying any real theological commitment, he nonetheless has a clear sense that the poet and the world share a fallen condition that longs for some fulfilment or reparation. As a result, both the poet's understanding and his ability to articulate are limited because they partake of the very contrariness and tension which he observes in such a fallen world. If there is any immanent meaning to be found in the world, it will only be within this tension, which generates meaning in the midst of contrariness. Rather than superimposing this as a stylistic trope, however, he repeatedly encounters such tension within the world as it presents itself to the poet who has an ear to hear and an eye to see.

While the notion of tension is not new to Warren's later poetry, it developed from what had been a vital formal principle in the work of the New Critics into a more consciously ontological principle. As heirs of the Metaphysical poets, the New Critics valued wit, irony, and paradox as the most subtle and powerful formal elements of poetry and held that meaning is generated by poetic structure. In his own 1942 essay "Pure and Impure Poetry," Warren speaks of tension in terms of the structure of the poem.[4] "There is the tension between the rhythm of the poem and the rhythm of speech" (24). He says that "the poet is like the jujitsu expert; he wins by utilizing the resistance of his opponent—the materials of the poem. . . . [A poem] is a motion toward a point of rest, but if it is not a resisted motion, it is a motion of no consequence" (24). For him, impure poetry is marked by tension as it resists the urge to speak in certainties and readily employs the devices of irony and paradox so that the poetic vision can "survive . . . the complexities and contradictions of experience" (26). Warren's long-time collaborator Cleanth Brooks claimed in his seminal work, *The Well Wrought Urn,* that the language of paradox is "the language appropriate and inevitable to poetry" (3). Writing in the context of modernism's "straw man" battles between science and poetry, Brooks argues that paradox is what highlights the uniqueness of language within poetry by heightening the tension between connotation and denotation. As another heir of Coleridge, he sees a symbolic function of language in poetry. "The poem is an instance of the doctrine which it asserts; it is both the assertion and the realization of the assertion" (17). This is what he means when he claims that "the poem itself is the well-wrought urn . . ." (17). Meaning is generated within the form of the poem. He rejects the idea that a poet could avoid paradox and use more "direct methods" of speech because these would "enfeeble and distort what is to be said" into mere "facts" devoid of irony and wonder (17–18). Brooks makes it clear, though, that paradox is necessary because of the nature of language itself. He approaches the unsayable when he acknowledges, "But the poet has no one term. Even if he had a polysyllabic technical term, the term would not provide the solution for his problem. He must work by contradiction and qualification" (9). The poet may desire the final word, but that is what may not be spoken. Warren takes hold of this tension in his later poetry, moving away from a formalist assumption and toward a more consciously ontological presupposition. Meaning is generated by the tension of the world, not simply by a specifically poetic use of language. The tension in the poem is not artificially created by the poet; rather, it arises from the tension of being itself, which dwells within language.

Warren's concern for "the immanence of meaning in things" in the world and for the way that this meaning is generated displays an important similarity to the phenomenological approach worked out by Heidegger in his early thought. Rooted broadly in the Platonic and Kantian traditions, Warren's aesthetic seems to follow what Heidegger called in *Being and Time* the maxim of phenomenology: "To the things themselves!" (50) Heidegger held that a true phenomenology must set out not so much to define the objects with which it deals but to seek a way of meeting things as they manifest themselves within the horizon of time. He stated in *Being and Time* that phenomenology "does not characterize the what of the objects of philosophical research as subject-matter, but rather the *how* of that research" (50). According to Richard Palmer, Heidegger proposes that "the mind does not project a meaning onto the phenomenon; rather, what appears is an ontological manifesting of the thing itself" (*Hermeneutics* 128). In a similar way, Warren's concern for "an immanence of meaning in things" rejects the projection of meaning onto the things in the world and seeks to apprehend the way that the world declares itself in its ontological manifestation. Such a course follows a path parallel to the phenomenological method, which Palmer describes as "letting things become manifest as what they are, without forcing our own categories on them . . . it is not we who point to things; rather, things show themselves to us" (128).

In his later essays and lectures, Heidegger expands his conception of the phenomenological method to incorporate notions of discontinuity and separateness in his thinking about language. In "Language" (1959), he makes his claims about the power of language explicit:

> Language speaks. Its speaking bids the dif-ference to come which ex-propriates world and things into the simple onefold of their intimacy.
> Language speaks.
> Man speaks in that he responds to language. This responding is a hearing. It hears because it listens to the command of stillness. (210)

Warren's poetry engages the same phenomena; language speaks so that we might understand the manifestation of the things in the world. If the poet is to understand the immanence of meaning in things, then he must begin to listen to language itself. In response to its speaking, the poet then may speak by the "verbal imagination," which shapes and modifies his experience of things that manifest themselves in the tension of the world. It is not the poet who points to language, who calls language into being; rather it is language that declares itself to the poet and gives him his being as a poet or artist. Any true experience with language must consist in language making itself manifest to the poet and the reader rather than in any attempt to coerce language into the poet's own service. In three lectures delivered in 1957 and 1958 and published under the title "The Nature of Language," Heidegger set out to probe "a possibility of undergoing an experience with language," specifically an experience that "is not of our own making; to undergo here means that we endure it, suffer it, receive it as it strikes us and submit to it." When we undergo an experience with language, "language itself brings itself to language" (59). But, when does this happen?

> . . . Curiously enough, when we cannot find the right word for something that concerns us, carries us away, oppresses or encourages us. Then we leave unspoken what we have in mind and, without rightly giving it thought, undergo moments in which language itself has distantly and fleetingly touched us with its essential being.

But when the issue is to put into language something which has never yet been spoken, then everything depends on whether language gives or withholds the appropriate word. Such is the case of the poet. (59)

Heidegger's conception of moments in which we are "distantly and fleetingly touched" by language illuminates a reading of Warren's later poetry, in which undergoing an experience with language brings the poet within the sphere of the sayable and the unsayable in the world.

Warren's engagement with the tension of the world, then, must by understood as opening himself to the "possibility of undergoing an experience with language." His concern for being in the world cannot be abstracted from his preoccupation with the power and limit of language. Both the world and language are the givens toward which the poet must work as he seeks the language necessary in the moment of articulation, a language that will finally reconcile the irreconcilable. Every attempt to idealize his own language, however, brings the poet back to the realization that there can be no finally reconciled language either in himself or in nature. Every attempt brings him face to face with the unsayable. What Warren considered to be "meaning"—that is, any conceptual understanding that enables the poet and reader to confront the complexities of the world without being consumed by that experience—is found not in abstract, isolated images, or statements, but in concrete instances of the voice of the world expressly giving or withholding itself as the poet seeks to make an utterance.[5] The poet confronts the essential being of language precisely when he cannot find the right word in himself or in the world, just as he does when he cannot understand the word that the world speaks to him. Frequently, the poetic narrators hear a voice but cannot understand the language being spoken by that voice. The question the poet asks is, "What Is the Voice That Speaks?" (CP 420). At other times, the world declares itself in a way that supplies a word that the poet himself cannot speak. Situated in this tension between the limit and the power of language, the poet confronts the unsayable.

Throughout his later poetry, Warren explores the ways that language speaks within the tension of the world, understanding that as a poet his own articulation depends on language to give or withhold. Even as he observed the blessing and cursing quality of the imagination in *The Ancient Mariner*, he experiences a similar doubleness in his confrontation with language and the unsayable.

In a number of these poems, he encounters on the one hand the curse of language in the way that it withholds itself. Language manifests its fragmentary nature as a casualty of the Fall and its inability to redeem itself. Even in the voice of the world, language withholds itself and the poet cannot find in that voice the appropriate word. In other poems, however, Warren demonstrates the blessing of language when the voice of the world becomes the word that speaks our joy or our experience, precisely when the poet has no language in himself. The world forms not simply a text that may be read but a language that is not finally or fully available to the poet. It is in this place, between the limitations of language and its power, that the language of nature betrays the fundamental tension of the world: it is a realm of great delight that is nonetheless fragmented and fractured. This is the sphere of being in which the poet listens to the voice of the world and hears the voice of being.

In "The Enclave" from *Or Else: Poem/Poems 1968–1974*, Warren draws near to the way that meaning trickles out from the fissure of this tension of the world (*CP* 300–01).[6] The first stanza announces the tension between silence and saying that generates the poem.

> Out of the silence, the saying. Into
> The silence, the said. Thus
> Silence, in timelessness, gives forth
> Time, and receives it again, and I lie.... (1–4)

From the blankness of the page, the poem begins, the black print rising from the white page. Out of the silence of the page, the poem speaks. But the poem ends and returns to the silence of the white page. It is in this tension between the silence and the said that the poem itself exists. Its being gives voice to the being of language. But the silence out of which the poem speaks is not merely a problem of spatial composition. It is a matter of time itself, for silence "gives forth / Time...." Even in the final poem of *Or Else*, entitled "A Problem in Spatial Composition," Warren finds that spatial and temporal concerns are not removed from one another (*CP* 321–22). In the first part of this poem, the speaker ponders the view of the forest visible from a "high window," his vision is interrupted by the upper lintel of the window, which "Confirms what the heart knows: *beyond* is *forever*..." (1, 11). In the second part, he observes through the window the upward thrust of "the stub / Of a great tree, gaunt-blasted and black..." (2–3). Then a hawk enters the composition, "glides...,"

"Hangs . . . ," and finally "Makes contact" (10, 15, 16) with the tree, which "stabs . . . at the infinite saffron of sky" (7). The spatial composition seems complete when "The hawk perches on the topmost, indicative tip of / The bough's sharp black and skinny jag skyward" (17–18), but this is where the problem of time enters the picture. The poem concludes in a single-line set off by itself in the third part, "The hawk, in an eyeblink, is gone." The problem in spatial composition is that it is never only spatial; it is also always temporal, for this is the basic tension of the world. So in "The Enclave," silence and timelessness are identified with one another, and the said is linked to time: "Silence, in timelessness, gives forth / Time, and receives it again. . . " (3–4). The "said" is not an object but a moment in time, spoken out of timelessness in time. Time and the saying are like the river to which Coleridge refers in a footnote in *The Statesman's Manual*, quoting from Plutarch:

> For it is impossible to step into the same river twice, according to Heraclitus, nor is it possible to grasp twice any mortal substance in a permanent state, but in the suddenness and swiftness of its change it scatters and comes together again, or, rather, not again or later but at the same moment it takes shape and dissolves, it comes and goes, so that that which is generated from it never achieves being because the process of generation never ceases or is overcome. (20)[7]

Within the tension present in the poetic moment, there is both a scattering and a coming together, a simultaneous shaping and dissolving, a coming and a going between the silence and the saying. The moment never achieves the fullness of being in itself, just as the poem can never be an isolated, sealed-off entity. Rather, it is only in the between, in the relationship of one moment to the next, between the elements of the poem itself, and between one poem and the next, that meaning is generated.

The second stanza of "The Enclave" draws a parallel between the darkness and the cock-crow. The narrator situates himself within the tension between time and timelessness:

> . . . I lie
> In darkness and hear the wind off the sea heave.
> Off the sea, it uncoils. Landward, it leans,
> And at the first cock-crow, snatches that cry

From the cock's throat, the cry,
In the dark, like gold blood flung, is scattered.... (4–9)

In the darkness, the cry is raised, even as the word is spoken out of the silence. But the wind "snatches that cry" and "In the dark, like gold blood flung, is scattered." The cry is thrown back into the darkness, which receives it again. This second stanza is not simply poetry as mimesis in which Warren copies from nature a scene as accurately as possible; nor is it purely metaphorical in that Warren is simply making a comparison between this moment and the first stanza. Rather, the moment here partakes of the reality of which it speaks. This is an instance of the tension of the world out of which meaning is found. The cock-crow and the word both fall back into the silent darkness, but in the moment of speaking, between silence and darkness, the utterance is made, coming and going in the simultaneous moment. This tension highlights the crisis of the poet in the third stanza.

... How

May I know that true nature of Time, if
Deep now in darkness that glittering enclave
I dream, hangs? It shines. Another
Wind blows there, the sea-cliffs,
Far in that blue wind, swing. Wind

Lifts the brightening of hair. (9–15)

If time never stands still, if it never may be reified into a static picture, then how can the poet know "the true nature of Time ... ?" Warren is asking two questions here: First, how can he know Time if this is the case, and, second, may he know Time's true nature? Is it possible? The emphasis seems to fall upon the second of the two questions, and the poem rhetorically symbolizes the answer to the question. The true nature of time is that it can never be known. Time is like truth, which, as Warren submits in *Audubon*, may not be spoken but may only be enacted. Time and Truth, in their absoluteness, cannot be spoken or known, but must be lived in the tension of the ever-changing moment. The dream of the enclave "hangs" motionless and shines in the midst of the darkness, but its glittering beauty is snatched by the wind just as the cock-crow is scattered in the darkness. Even the dream is not insulated from the true nature of time. Coleridge comments in the same passage of *The Statesman's Manual* on the inability of the human mind to give permanence to things, just as Warren meditates on the impermanence of the dream. Coleridge writes, "The human understanding musing on many things, snatches at truth, but is frustrated and disheartened by the fluctuating nature of its objects; its conclusions therefore are timid and uncertain, and it hath no way of giving permanence to things by reducing them to abstractions" (20). The meaning that is generated by the tension of the world, then, is timid and uncertain; it cannot be a reductive abstraction by which the poet seeks to give permanence to things. It is a meaning tied to the concreteness of the world in which it dwells. Within his encounter with the tension of the world, Warren consistently confronts instances of language withholding what Heidegger calls "the appropriate word" ("The Nature of Language" 59). In "Language Barrier" from *Being Here: Poetry 1977–1980*, the voice of the world manifests what is withheld to the poet in his own language (*CP* 420–21). The poem begins with an archetypal moment in Warren's later work: the reader and poet alike are brought to a verge from which we overhear nature declaring itself, and both are silent before it.

> Snow-glitter, snow-gleam, all snow-peaks
> Scream joy to the sun. Green
> Far below lies, shelved where a great *cirque* is blue, bluest
> Of waters, face upward to sky-flaming blue. Then
> The shelf falters, fails, and downward becomes
>
> Torment and tangle of stone.... (1–6)

This is a jagged world in which mountains, sun, sky, and snow all converge in a clash of joy; but the encounter carries within itself both blessing and cursing for the poet. The snow-peaks "scream joy to the sun" above the green of the forest, the blue of the "bluest waters," and the "torment and tangle of stone." All the elements of this world in the poem are held together in a tension which somehow speaks joy. It is a scene of distinct grandeur and beauty, but that grandeur is found as much in the voice of the world that speaks as in the beauty of the scene frozen in time. The poet's knowledge of this voice is only available to him through difference, that is, through a knowledge of separateness that brings to light his sense of alienation within this world. While the poet hears the voice of the world, there is a still a barrier that he cannot overcome, which leads to the questions of the second stanza:

> . . . Alone, alone,
> What grandeur here speaks? The world
> Is the language we cannot utter.
> Is it a language we can even hear? (7–10)

He is confronted by the voice that "Is the language we cannot utter." He cannot understand, however, what the voice says: "Is it a language we can even hear?"

"Language Barrier" makes clear that the poet's experience in the world finds language withholding itself in two ways. On the one hand, the poet hears and sometimes even understands a voice that speaks a language that is not available to him—a language that he may not utter. On the other hand, the poet is confronted by a voice that speaks a word that he cannot understand. All he can know is that he cannot finally know what the world is speaking. The relationship between these two is similar to the relationship between *langue* and *parole* in Saussurean linguistics. The world forms its own *langue* or language system, which is both a text and a speaking voice. But the language that the world utters is a language that the self cannot possess. The self must listen intently to this language or read this text; it may not speak its words. On another level, the world makes concrete utterance, or *parole*, and the poet questions whether he can even comprehend the speech of the world. These two manifestations of language withholding itself are not divided or opposed in any way to one another; the one is realized in the other. According to Hawkes, "The nature of the *langue* lies beyond, and determines, the nature of each manifestation of *parole*, yet it has no concrete existence of its own, except in the piecemeal manifestations that speech affords" (*Structuralism and Semiotics* 21). The remainder of the poem intimates that while the *langue* of the world remains beyond the grasp of the poet, he can nonetheless hear the *parole* of the world within the horizon of time and within the tension of the world. In the midst of a wakeful night, the poet asks, "What, / Long ago, did the world try to say?" (14–15). Having pondered whether he can even hear the language of the world, the poet offers that we may hear its manifestations as "we hear now / The creatures of gardens and lowlands" (19–20), even if we cannot understand what the world and its creatures are trying to say.

Warren's allusion to the "creatures of gardens and lowlands" recalls "The

Mango on the Mango Tree," the final poem of his *Selected Poems 1923–1943* (*CP* 98). This early poem explores a similar sort of language barrier in the context of a distinctly postlapsarian world in which both the poet and nature long for a final word that could "lift the Babel curse by which we live" (33). The mango and the speaker are bound by a common guilt, perhaps recalling the fruit used by the serpent in the garden to tempt Eve and bringing about the Fall. But, mango and man are nonetheless divided from one another. As another self, the mango looks at the speaker just as he looks at it. The two spy on one another, and each "pours his tale into the Great Schismatic's ear" (15). In the naturalistic vision of the poem, the speaker declares that God has ordained this alienation between the self and nature: "For God well works the Roman plan, / Divide and rule, mango and man . . . " (16–17). Even still, the speaker has a yearning for redemption, a hope for a sacrament in which word and action might meet:

> For, ah, I do not know the word
> That it could hear, or if I've heard
> A breath like *pardon, pardon,* when its stiff lips stirred.
>
> If there were a word that I could give,
> Or if I could only say *forgive,*
> Then we might lift the Babel curse by which we live. . . . (28–33)

Both the poet and the mango have need of a word that will enact a final pardon of such cosmic guilt. The poet yearns for the sufficient word, the redemptive word that will "lift the Babel curse" and speak *pardon,* but he either does not know that word or the word itself does not exist. The language barrier here is not simply a limitation of diction; rather, it is an inherent limitation of our power to enact the words that we might speak.

Warren expands his pursuit of the language that we may not utter—the *langue* of the world—in a number of poems concerned with the nature of truth. The way that language withholds itself in the speaking voice of the world is essentially related in Warren's vision to the way truth also withholds itself so that, while it may be approached, it may never be named. Warren explores the relationship between the voice of the world and truth in "What Is the Voice That Speaks?" which immediately precedes "Language Barrier" in *Being Here* (*CP* 420). The title is repeated as the opening words of the first line, in response to which Warren catalogs a variety of sources for the voice:

the "tongue / Of laurel leaf" (1–2), the "split tongue of *coluber constrictor*— / Black racer to you" (5–6), the "blind man" (8), the "great owl" (11), the "wolf-howl" (13), "my mother" (15), the voice of the lover, and finally "I" (18). Each one of these voices is a manifestation of the voice of the world—or the voice of being—that speaks. All of them are also collectively the voice that speaks, but each and all are limited in what they may speak, whether the laurel leaf or the "I" of the narrator's own voice. In response to the variety of voices that speak, the poet asks, "What tongue knows the name of Truth? Or Truth to come? / All we can do is strive to learn the cost of experience" (23–24). Just as "Language Barrier" proposes that the world is a language that we cannot utter, this poem reckons that the human heart is ultimately unable to name Truth but is bound inescapably to experience within the tension of the world. Rather than finding a unified language that will answer the Truth-question, we must seek to enact truth, to live truth in the tension of experience.

Truth is often what the poet can perceive but precisely what he may not speak. So how does the poet speak? Warren pursues that question in "Truth" (*CP* 415), in which he links utterance to concrete experience within the world.

Truth is what you cannot tell.
Truth is for the grave.
Truth is only the flowing shadow cast
By the wind-tossed elm
When sun is bright and grass well groomed.

Truth is the downy feather
You blow from your lips to shine in sunlight. (1–7)

The absolute nature of Truth manifests in the sentiment that it absolutely may not be spoken. Instead, Truth is revealed in fleeting moments of nonabsolute time. Truth is the shadow and the downy feather that flow and float in the midst of the bright sunlight. These lines are reminiscent of Coleridge's statement in *The Statesman's Manual* that the mind only "snatches at truth, but is frustrated . . . by the fluctuating nature of it objects . . ." (20). As a result, "its conclusions . . . are timid and uncertain, and it hath no way of giving permanence to things by reducing them to abstractions . . ." (20). Warren refuses to reduce Truth to an abstraction that might be told or uttered. Instead, Truth comes in snatches within the experience of the world.

Rather than giving permanence to truth, Warren says that, like a mirage, "its shape is unclear in shadow or brightness" (10). We might expect Warren to propose that the shape of truth—even a truth lived in experience—is more clear in the brightness of the sun; but here truth is unclear in both shadow and brightness. Its utterance is both a "whisper" we strain to hear and a "scream" from which we flee (11–12). He does state positively, though, that Truth is a trick, a curse, and a joke, all of which suggest a certain degree of deception. We want to be able to speak of Truth in an absolute way, but in the end cannot. Warren's allusion to "the curse laid upon us in the Garden" (14)—the Garden of Eden at the point of the Fall—suggests that it is the absolute or unsayable quality of truth that was the curse laid upon us. What was known in fullness before the Fall may now only be enacted within the tension of the world. Warren does not deny that there is truth, but in a fallen world, it may not be named. By "the Serpent's joke," Warren suggests the temptation to grasp Truth in its absoluteness and so to become like God (15). In the final stanza, Warren returns to the notion that "Truth is for the grave:"

> Truth is the long soliloquy
> Of the dead all their long night.
> Truth is what would be told by the dead
> If they could hold conversation
> With the living and thus fulfill obligation to us.
>
> Their accumulated wisdom must be immense. (18–23)

Here, as in other poems, death is seen as the fullness of experience, as the moment in which there is an absolute knowledge and a simultaneous apocalypse of the self.[8] In that moment, the self is dissolved, diffused, and dissipated, though reshaped into something other than what it once was. Warren avoids the vocabulary of Christian theology, which might speak of some glorification or transformation at the point of death; there is, however, this deep sense of a radical change in which the dead and the living are divided by this immense wisdom. For this reason, though the dead might tell the truth, they may not "hold conversation" with the living. Death is the neighborhood of Truth and the dead dwell in what Heidegger would call nearness to one another, facing one another and completing one another.[9]

Warren develops the relationship between the nature of truth and the withholding of language in "A Way to Love God," the opening poem of his short

1975 collection, *Can I See Arcturus from Where I Stand?* (*CP* 325). The poem begins by observing "the shadow of truth":

> Here is the shadow of truth, for only the shadow is true.
> And the line where the incoming swell from the sunset Pacific
> First leans and staggers to break will tell all you need to know
> About submarine geography, and your father's death rattle
> Provides all biographical data required for the *Who's Who* of the dead.
>
> I cannot recall what I started to tell you.... (1–6)

As in "Truth," Warren suggests that truth is never available as the "thing-in-itself," but that we may only catch a glimpse of the shadow of truth. In our experience, only the shadow, unclear as a whisper, is truth. But, if only the shadow of truth is true, then where may the shadow be seen? *Here*, Warren says, in the world and in the poem itself. Warren subverts both the notion that poetry contains truth and the conviction that the poet is the speaker of truth. In the poem the poet can only observe the shadow of truth. Warren also turns to the world, which provides all that you need to know or will be required to know about this shadow of truth. Each of the subsequent sections of the poem marks experiences in the world that are confrontations with the apophatic moment. Through shadows, echoes, and death, the voice of truth speaks and points to a way to love God. Each section interrupts the other: "I cannot recall ..." (6), "I do not recall ..." (14), "But I had forgotten ..." (26). The shadow of truth slips away and recedes like the unified word that may never be uttered. But, within the discontinuity of this experience, Warren highlights a certain subtle continuity in a line set off by itself in the text: "Everything seems an echo of something else" (21). Each experience is a shadow of truth, whether it be the midnight moan of the mountains who "remember . . . that there is something they cannot remember" (11), or the "hairiness of stars" (16) in the midst of the silence, or the sheep huddling together in a midnight mist, who "Stared into nothingness" (30). Within this poetic vision, truth must be seen within each moment in itself, so that "You would think that nothing would ever again happen" (36). Snatching at the shadow of truth, he suggests, "That is a way to love God" (37). It may be that a way to love God is to know and understand the basic contrariness of the world—grasping the continuity within discontinuity—and to perceive that this is the shadow of truth. And though

Truth, like the language of the world, may not be uttered, it must be pursued in the continuous walk within the tension of the world.

Warren characterizes the withholding quality of language in other poems by describing the voice of the world as a code. This is explicit in "Breaking the Code," one his later uncollected poems originally published in the *Southern Review* in 1983 (*CP* 617).

> The world around us speaks in code,
> Or maybe something like the old Indian sign
> Language of the Great Plains—all with a load
> Of joy and/or despair. And in all of which you must resign
> Yourself to ambiguity, or error. The road
> Markers are often missing, or defaced. Is
> The message the veery tries at dusk to communicate benign?
> Does the first flake of snow from a sky yet blue
> Mean *that* or *this*?
> Is the Owl's question—*"Who?—Who?"*—
> Addressed to your conscience, and you?
>
> In dawn light does the scroll-mark of wind-swirl in night snow,
> Or later the bleeding icicle tip from the eaves,
> Tell you a truth you yearn to know—
> Or is it merely an index of the planet's tilt?
> And what of the beech's last high leaves
> Of hammered gold, or glint of sunlit gilt? (1–17)

As in *Audubon*, the narrator has an unambiguous conviction that the world speaks in a structured way that is continuous with our existence within the world, but his understanding of what is spoken is indeterminate. It is a "code" or "something like the old Indian / sign language of the Great Plains . . ." (2–3). The things declare themselves and bring themselves to light in an unmistakable way, but the self cannot hear or comprehend what is said. It is the self that struggles under a certain ambiguity or error as it seeks to understand the meaning of the sign language or the code of the world. Does the world speak with a load of joy and despair, or does it speak with a load or joy or despair? The self can only respond by saying that it hears both, and in this tension there is necessary ambiguity. What complicates understanding though is that "The road / Markers are often missing, or defaced" (5–6). The language of the world is not in and of itself complete, so you never know whether "the message the veery tries at dusk to / communicate [is] benign" or not (7). Even if "the world means only itself," as the speaker posits in "Riddle in the Garden" (*CP* 225–26), the world does not necessarily declare its own meaning, and the poet does not have a meaning to put there. He can only ask, "Does the first flake of snow from a sky yet blue / Mean *that* or *this*" (8–9)? But our own experience in the world complicates this situation so that the speaker concludes, "It is hard to break the code in our little time and space" (32). Within the tension of the world—that is, between time and space, between time and timelessness, between presence and absence, between the silence and the saying—we will never crack the code so that we might understand the final message that the world speaks.

The coded message sometimes appears as a persistent whisper within nature, as in "Summer Rain in Mountains" from *Rumor Verified: Poems 1979–1980* (*CP* 466). The narrator watches as a "dark curtain of rain sweeps slowly over the sunlit mountain" (1), and there is a "whisper . . . moving through the wide air" (11) of the afternoon, which reminds him that he cannot remember something. That something could be "a nameless apprehension" (18), like the dog's tail that wakes you with its thumping the floor at the foot of your bed as you try to sleep. Then,

> . . . The wild
>
> Thought seizes you that this may be a code. It may be a secret warning.
> A friend is addressing you now. You miss the words. You
>
> Apologize, smile. The rain hammers the roof . . . (21–24).

The whisper of the world reminds the speaker of a nameless apprehension that persists like a code, which may be a secret warning, but he may never break that code in order to know. The rain storm passes, the "sun / Emerges like God's calm blessedness . . . " (28–29), and "You pull yourself together. A drink helps" (33). The code remains, but there is no meaning to put there. This tension becomes more explicit in "Code Book Lost" (*CP* 360) from *Now and Then: Poems 1976–1978*, in which the poet demands that there must be some meaning in the world's declaration.

What does the veery say, at dusk in shad-thicket?
There must be some meaning, or why should your heart stop,

As though, in the dark depth of water, Time held its breath,
While the message spins on like a spool of silk thread fallen?

. . . .

What meaning, when at the unexpected street corner,
You meet some hope long forgotten, and your old heart,

Like neon in shore-fog, or distance, glows dimly again?
Will you waver, or clench stoic teeth and move on?

Have you thought as you walk, late, late, the streets of a town
Of all dreams being dreamed in dark houses? What do they signify?

Yes, message on message, like wind or water, in light or in dark,
The whole world pours at us. But the code book, somehow, is lost.
   (1–4, 15–22)

In language that seems to anticipate his later musing in "Breaking the Code," Warren questions the voice of the unsayable in the multisyllabic call of the veery in the evening light. That voice brings to bear the weight of import in the world's persistent declaration. The message "spins on like a spool of silk thread fallen" (4). But the poet has no way of deciphering the messages that he is able to hear. He has no key to crack the code. There is an unavoidable sense that meaning is communicated by the experience of the tension of the world, but that meaning cannot be reduced to a propositional statement. It is a matter of stopping to consider all that is signified by our being in the world. But, the poet must ultimately relinquish himself to the unavoidable tension: "Yes, message on message, like wind or water, in light or in dark, / The whole world pours at us. But the code book, somehow, is lost" (21–22). Though he yearns for language of his own that he might be able to finally comprehend his being in the world, language as the unsayable withholds itself.

Because he wrestles with the unsayable itself, Warren not only encounters the withholding of language but also engages the ways in which language gives itself when the poet reaches the limits of the sayable. He finds that the world speaks a language that he yearns for but may not speak—even if paradoxically that language sometimes speaks through his own writing. When the poet sets forth the poem in language, he brings the poem into the light of language. In "The Origin of the Work of Art," Heidegger claims that "the poet . . . uses the word—not, however, like ordinary speakers and writers who have to use them up, but rather in such a way that the word only now becomes and remains truly a word" (48). It is by virtue of this giving quality of language that the poet is able to question being. In "The Whole Question" (*CP* 566), the speaker begins with the bold suggestion, "You'll have to rethink the whole question" (1), and makes clear by the end of the poem that he is dealing with the question of "what is real" (25).[10] This demands reconsideration is of the ultimate issues of life and identity—that is, being itself. What does it mean to be? The answer to the question, though, is just over the horizon, like the tortoise of Zeno's paradox to which Warren refers in the last two stanzas of "Paradox" (*CP* 328–29):

> Yes, far away and long ago,
> In another land, on another shore,
> That race you won—even as it was lost,
> For if I caught you, one moment more,
> You had fled my grasp, up and to go
>
> With glowing pace and the smile that mocks
> Pursuit down whatever shore reflects
> Our flickering passage through the years,
> As we enact our more complex
> Version of Zeno's paradox. (11–20)

The trap of the paradox in "The Whole Question" is "a matter of language . . ." (26). Being constantly recedes, yet it speaks from the silence. So, the poem concludes with a hopeful burst of desire that the words might yet give of themselves: " . . . You / May yet find a new one in which experience overlaps / Words. Or find some words that make the Truth come true" (26–28). If there is a language in which experience and words overlap and in which words are able to enact truth, it must be spoken by the voice of the world. What this language gives is not a totalized utterance or an absolute statement, but the word that we may not speak for ourselves. A word we may understand and perceive in the speaking voice of the world. Only by virtue of this giving character of language can the poet and reader alike truly speak. As Heidegger says in "The Nature of Language," we who live within the horizon of this world "can speak only as we respond to language" (107). The poet finds that language speaks what the human heart cannot express in itself; it is a vicarious speaking. That which speaks is the unsayable. By virtue of the way that language gives, the poet is then able to speak within the contraries of the world.

Within the voice of the world, the poet is able to hear the very word to which he is unable to give utterance. In a number of poems, Warren presents speakers or participants who are unable to give utterance to the experience in which they find themselves; in this situation, though, the world speaks the "unwordable word" that they are not able to find or to sustain. This appears prominently in a late poem, "Last Walk of Season" (*CP* 559), in which the speaker and a partner climb a mountain in the late afternoon, late in the summer, and late in life. As they walk, the gurgling of the stream of rain water in the ruts of the old logging road "Is the only voice we hear" (10). But, bearing burdens of their own, "We do not ask / What burden that music bears" (10–11). The speaker admits that their only wish "is to think of nothing but happiness" (12) and "The world's great emptiness" (13). And their great desire is to participate in that world, to participate "as part of that one / Existence" (27–28). Within this recognition of being bound with the world, the speaker asks, "Can it be that the world is but the great word / That speaks the meaning of our joy?" (21–22). This is the ultimate union to which this poem points, rather than the union of the speaker with his partner, or of the "last light / ... with the soft-shadowed land" (31–32). In this union between world and word, symbolized in the convergence of summer and autumn, the poet finds the source of the heart's own delight. Language speaks the word that the speaker cannot say. This is echoed in the motion of "happiness" between the speaker and the partner when "Scarcely in consciousness, a hand finds, on stone, a hand" (30). The moment of the poem opens the giving quality of language so that the poet is able to approach the unsayable.

Warren pursues this theme of participation in the word of the world in "Star Fall" (*CP* 351–52). In terms of the narrative of the poem, Warren returns to the vivid scenes of *Promises* in the old Mediterranean fortress overlooking the sea. Though he hearkens back to "that far land, and time" (1), the poem is a present experience in a moment of fullness: "There we, now at midnight, lay" (5). But the poem itself is not a faraway time, but is now, and it is not simply there, but it becomes here. As in "Last Walk of the Season," the sound of water provides the only audible voice: " ... the only sound to our ears / Was the slap and hiss far below ... " (9–10). And, as in the former poem, the speaker and a partner lie next to one another, each engrossed in the moment of the world's speaking. Warren probes the nature of our participation not simply with nature but with one another. The third stanza begins, "We did not lie close, and for hours / The only contact was fingers, and motionless they" (12–13). But the union envisaged is not simply between man and woman or sea and land, but between our communication and the voice of the world. Warren draws together even more explicitly his concern for language and being, apparently suggesting something similar to Heidegger's statement that the being of language is the language of being. He ponders:

> For what communication
> Is needed if each alone
> Is sunk and absorbed into
> The mass and matrix of Being that defines
> Identity of all? (14–18)[11]

The communication mediated by human language is fragmented and failing before the voice of the world. What privilege can human language demand when Being itself is a language and communicates what the human voice may not articulate? Warren is not denying the necessity for communication but is rather redefining—or, reshaping—an understanding of the nature of communication itself, moving it beyond a strict system of signs and signification. In the final sections of the poem, he turns to this defining "matrix of Being":

> We lay in the moonless night,
> Felt earth beneath us swing,
> Watched the falling stars of the season. They fell
> Like sparks in a shadowy, huge smithy, with
> The clang of the hammer unheard.
>
> Far off in the sea's matching midnight,
> The fishing lights marked their unfabled constellations.
>
> We found nothing to say, for what can a voice say when
> The world is a voice, no ear needing?
>
> We lay watching the stars as they fell. (19–28)

Rather than isolating the two from one another, the "matrix of being" provides a kind of communion in which element echoes element. The stars are not reflected in the sea as if one provides a mirror image of the other. Rather, the lights of the fishing boats, hung in the midst of their own midnight, echo the light of the stars. The stars in the moonless night fall "Like sparks in a shadowy, huge smithy" (22) just as the lights of the fishing boats mark their own "unfabled constellations" (25). In light of this communication, what can the human heart find to say? "We found nothing to say . . . " (26). This "nothing," though, is a vital presence within the poem. "Nothing" does not denote an emptiness that is a dead-end but suggests that place from which the poet might listen to the voice and the world and that place from which he might begin to speak.[12] This contact between the poet's voice and the voice of the world is the contact to which the poet moves. Human language appears inadequate before the voice of the world which speaks what the human voice may not say. This communication, or communion, moves beyond the understanding of words as strictly linguistic signs to be read or heard. The voice of the world is a voice "no ear needing." The final line of the poem utters the communication that the language of the world gives: "We lay watching stars as they fell" (28).

"August Moon" (*CP* 396) echoes these other poems in its preoccupation with stars and in its concern for the nature of communication, but here he specifically ponders the nature of growth and age in light of the infinity of being. The moon of the title announces to the speaker his being bounded by time within the world.

> Gold like a half-slice of orange
> Fished from a stiff Old-Fashioned, the moon
> Lolls on the sky that goes deeper blue
> By the tick of the watch. Or
> Lolls like a real brass button half-buttoned
> On the blue flannel sleeve
> Of an expensive seagoing blue blazer. (1–7)

He then turns to the stars which "Slowly . . . , in a gradual / Eczema of glory, gain definition" (8–9). The world does not count the years as the speaker is tempted to do; the world moves on in its slow way of defining itself. So, the poet asks, "What kind of world is this we walk in?" to which he replies, "It makes no sense . . ." (10–11). With an urgent desire to make sense of the world, the narrator must continue to walk on in the tension of this apparent disparity.

Anyway, while night
Hardens into its infinite being,
We walk down the woods-lane, dreaming
There's an inward means of
Communication with
That world whose darkling susurration
Might—if only we were lucky—be
Deciphered. (16–23)

The poet dreams that there might be within himself some means of communication with the world and a way of deciphering the language of the world in its
own inexorable rhythm. But a dream is not simply some illusion in Warren's
aesthetics, as he learned in his study of *The Rime of the Ancient Mariner* and
as he expresses in *Audubon*. The dream is a specific way of enacting the truth.
So his dreaming here is a means of envisaging what is in reality true, though
he can only see the shadow of truth. Occasionally, the "darkling susurration"
of the world can be deciphered in glimpses of the world's being, and there is
a means of communication that moves beyond human words or speech. As
the poet ponders what it means to count years, the world moves on, and "the
great owl in distance" (39) utters his call and rescues the poet from "what they
say" (38) (the reasons given for counting the years) by urging him to walk on.
The poem concludes:

The moon is lost in tree-darkness.
Stars show now only
In the pale path between treetops.
The track of white gravel leads forward in darkness.

I advise you to hold hands as you walk,
And speak not a word. (42–47)

The forward movement of the "track of white gravel" into the darkness is
the very means of communication the poet sought. It is not a static perspective from which one may count the years but the dynamic motion of living
the years, within which there is a means of communication beyond that of
human words. This is the deciphering of the world's darkling susurration, before which the human heart must "speak not a word," for "what can a voice say
when / The world is a voice, no ear needing" ("Star-Fall" 26–27)?

In a number of poems, Warren not only contemplates the way in which the world is a voice speaking a word that says what we cannot say, but also considers the way in which the world itself is that word spoken. It is not simply that the world speaks a language that is unsayable to the poet. The world is the wordless language that gives of itself so that we might find meaning in "the secret order of the world," as he says in *Audubon*. As such, it gives of itself, defining human language rather than human language establishing the system of reference among the various elements of the world. This sense is intimated in "Last Walk of the Season," when the speaker asks, "Can it be that the world is but the great word / That speaks the meaning of our joy?" (21–22). The world and our joy converge in the speaking of language. There is no distinction between the language of the world and the world itself. In "Fear and Trembling" (*CP* 487), Warren is concerned to find a language that is not simply adequate but one that is meaningful so that he might "meditate on what the season has meant" (4). But, is that language comprised in human speech if a word is "but wind through the tube of the throat" (6)? Significantly, the poet asks not "what defines" but "Who defines the relation between the word *sun* and the sun?" (7). There is a necessary power or potency that does not originate in human language. The words that comprise human language cannot define such meditation, for "What word has glittered on whitecap? Or lured blossom out?" (8). Rather, nature itself provides the language and the text for such meditation. But he asks,

> Can one, in fact, meditate in the heart, rapt and wordless?
> Or find his own voice in the towering gust now from northward?
> When boughs toss—is it in joy or pain and madness?
> The gold leaf—is it whirled in anguish or ecstasy skyward? (13–16)

While the human heart yearns for language to be able to meditate, its words fall short, for if the boughs toss in joy or in pain, the meaning is much more than this. Human language is bound over to difference within the tension of the world. But the world provides a very real narrative for meditation:

> Can the heart's meditation wake us from life's long sleep,
> And instruct us how foolish and fond was our labor spent—
> Us who now know that only at death of ambition does the deep
> Energy crack crust, spurt forth, and leap
>
> From grottoes, dark—and from the caverned enchainment? (17–21)

Only a meditation by means of the meaningful language that the world speaks may wake us from "life's long sleep" and only then may meaning be found; only at the death of the ambition of human language to circumscribe the meaning of the world will meaning "spurt forth, and leap // From grottoes dark. . . ." This final vision is apocalyptic in character: only at the breaking up of human language is meaning revealed through the speaking of the unsayable.

In "Aspen Leaf in Windless World" (*CP* 430), Warren continues to meditate upon the world which is an "unworded revelation":

Watch how the aspen leaf, pale and windless, waggles,
While one white cloud loiters, motionless, over Wyoming.
And think how delicately the heart may flutter
In the windless joy of unworded revelation. (1–4)

By paying attention to the language of the world, Warren reads a narrative that is not mimetic or referential but one that is poetic. The imperatives to "watch" and "think" are really a call to listen to the voice of the world in which the poet discerns a revelation, even though he does not always know what it reveals:

Look how sea-foam, thin and white, makes its Arabic scrawl
On the unruffled sand of the beach's faint-tilted plane.
Is there a message there for you to decipher?
Or only the joy of its sunlit, intricate rhythm?

Is there a sign Truth gives that we recognize?
Can we fix our eyes on the flight of birds for answer?
Can the bloody-armed augurs declare expediency?
What does dew on stretched wool-fleece, the grass dry, mean?

Have you stood on the night-lawn, oaks black, and heard,
From bough-crotch to bough-crotch, the moon-eyed tree-toad utter,
Again and again, that quavery croak, and asked
If it means there'll be rain? Toward dawn? Or early tomorrow? (5–16)

Though the revelation made by the world is "unworded," it is nonetheless revealed within the worded. The poet perceives it in the "Arabic scrawl" of the sea foam, in sign made by Truth, and in the utterance of the tree toad. The poet and the world are bounded by language within which the unsayable speaks. There is no doubt in the poet that the world is itself a revelation, but the question is, what does it mean? Warren's allusion to Gideon's fleece in Judges 6 confirms this question; Gideon used the fleece to test the meaning of the Lord's revelation to him. In the same way, the poet listens to the voice of the world and asks if the quavery croak of the tree toad means that there will be rain. This revelation of the world speaks joy, just as in "Language Barrier" the snow peaks scream joy to the sun. It is this joy which is Coleridge's "beauty-making power" in "Dejection: An Ode" (433). But, does the world speak of more than simply the joy of its own rhythm? For the poet, the world does utter a message, a sign, a meaning, but these are not always completely discernible. The world is, as he says in the sixth stanza, a "shadowy world / Of miracles, whispers, high jinks, and metaphor" (21–22). It is significant that Warren does not focus on any single metaphor in this poem but lists in catalog fashion the myriad ways that the world speaks this unworded revelation. There is no longer any room in Warren's poem for metaphors or symbols because the whole poem is a metaphor—or rather, the poet's understanding of the whole world is symbolic. The world declares itself and provides the language by which we might begin to understand it and might begin to speak. But at the end of the poem, Warren asks if the world tells us of anything more than itself:

> What image—behind blind eyes when the nurse steps back—
> Will loom at the end of your own life's long sorites?
> Would a sun then rise red on an eastern horizon of waters?
> Would you see a face? What face? Would it smile? Can you say?
>
> Or would it be some great, sky-thrusting gray menhir?
> Or what, in your long-lost childhood, one morning you saw—
> Tinfoil wrappers of chocolate, popcorn, nut shells, and poorly
> Cleared up, the last elephant turd on the lot where the circus had been?
>   (25–32)

What will the world reveal at death? The power of this unworded revelation is limited to itself; that is, it reveals nothing that is supernatural. When Warren comes to the very edge of the worded utterance of the poem, he does not leap into what Coleridge calls in his *Notebooks* a "transcendental Idea of infinity" (3.4047). He does not propose that, having heard the unworded revelation of the voice of the world, he might now say the unsayable. Even the language used to probe the possibility of the death-image is bounded by the natural within that the unsayable speaks. And, though the language of the world gives of itself, there is no means of grasping any final image by means of human language. In Warren's vision, human language before the absolute nature of death is only "the last elephant turd on the lot where the circus had been."

Warren's confrontation with the unsayable within the voice of the world finally involves a vision that is decidedly paradoxical. Although the poet may not say the unsayable, the unsayable nonetheless speaks within the voice of language which is given utterance in the moment of the poem. That which may not be spoken is grasped within paradox. In the first section of a poem entitled "Synonyms" (*CP* 433–36) Warren questions the power of paradox:

Where eons back, earth slipped and cracked
To leave a great stratum, snag-edged, thrust

As margin to that blind inwardness, water
Now plunges in cosmic racket, sempiternal roar,

White-splintered on masses of stone, deep-domed or spired,
Chaos of white in dark paradox. What is the roar

But a paradox in that
Tumultuous silence—

Which paradox must be a voice of ultimate utterance? (1–9)

In tones and images that recall Coleridge's "Kubla Khan," Warren comes to a place and moment of paradox at the margin of "blind inwardness" that marks off the darkness of earth from the "white-splintered" waterfall. At this margin, the water plunges with an unending roar over rocks and forms the paradox of "white in dark."[13] But this paradox is not simply visual; it also encompasses the juxtaposition of the roar of the water's chaos with the silence of earth. In this moment and space, Warren declares that there is a voice making an "ultimate utterance." What is it that speaks, though? It is neither the roar nor the silence that speaks in isolation, but the paradox that speaks. The voice is heard within the radical and sustained tension of the world.

Warren's notion of the voice of language that speaks within this tension approaches a point close to Coleridge's understanding of the language of nature. In Lecture XII of his *Philosophical Lectures*, Coleridge suggests that the Book of Nature will "become transparent to us, when we regard the forms of matter as words, as symbols, valuable only as being the expression, an unrolled but yet glorious fragment, of the wisdom of the Supreme Being" (367). Nature functioned for Coleridge as a book alongside the Bible, which is a revelation of God's power and being. Warren, however, never suggests that the world is divine nor does he claim that the world is God. Instead, he consistently makes recourse to the fallenness of the world as it bears the inescapable contrariness that is the result of the Fall. While nature is not a transparent medium through which we see God's wisdom, Warren shares Coleridge's emphasis upon the world as a symbolic language—it partakes of the reality of which it speaks—and bears the full contrariness of being—it is an unrolled and a glorious fragment. Warren's poetry claims that that which is more than concrete manifests in the concrete elements of the world. So, the poet does not encounter the unsayable in some undefinable "out there" but in the "here" of the moment and the poem.

CHAPTER FIVE

The Act of Naming

What is it that the poet reaches? Not mere knowledge. He obtains entrance into the relation of word to thing. This relation is not, however, a connection between the thing that is on one side and the word that is on the other. The word itself is the relation which in each instance retains the thing within itself in such a manner that it "is" a thing.—Martin Heidegger[1]

As Warren pursues this story of deep delight through his exploration of participation in the world, he also engages in a very particular interrogation of what he calls "the name of the world." In the midst of the long and grotesque second section of *Audubon: A Vision*, the narrator demands at the very moment he anticipates the murder of Audubon in the cabin in the woods, "Tell me the name of the world" [II[G].13].[2] This is both an appeal for understanding and a plea for a place of articulation. In order to speak the name of the world, the poet must know the name, which is comprehensive of participation in the world. The name of the world expresses what he repeatedly longs for at various points throughout his poetry—the name of truth, of time, of wisdom itself. All of these together make it clear that the poet longs for some sort of ultimate utterance. For Warren, the world is a place of "tangled and hieroglyphic beauty," as he says in "The Mission" (*CP* 359). The world is itself linguistic, made up of pen-strokes and calligraphy, of whispers and screams. This is how the world declares itself, as he asserts in *Audubon*. As with language itself, the name of the world is never the given from which the poet works but is the given toward which he moves. The name of the self is equally elusive—not easier or more present. Just as he longs for the name of the world, he longs for his own name. In seeking the identity of the world and of the self, he looks for that place where the two might be co-terminus. This is why, for Warren, to speak the name is to say the unsayable.

Audubon pursues the name of the world by continuing to walk in it, knowing that the name speaks of that "season past all seasons" in which the "wild-grape cluster, / . . . Unripening, ripens" (V[C].3–6) as well as of that "story of deep delight" for which the poet longs. To speak the name of the world involves the knowledge that is marked by love and joy. But, the question of naming heightens the poet's sense not so much of linguistic arbitrariness as of linguistic instability. Who is it that gives the name and what makes the name "stick"? And what about entities that share a name? These, too, are crucial linguistic issues for the poet. To be able to name the world is to be able to grasp the world in its fullness, in its complexity and completeness. So, the quest for the name is the quest after the unified utterance in which word and thing finally share identity. And yet, in the poet's experience, there is no such stable word or name. Even an individual's name does not lead to stability; the identity of the individual is never fully fixed but is always being made and remade, according to Warren. So, Audubon thinks at toward the end of section III, "I do not know my name" ([E].11). Does the name equal identity? If not, where is identity found and what relation does the name bear to it? Warren's quest to name the self opens up his thinking about the construction of identity and reveals the way the poem and the self are analogous in his aesthetic. His desire to know the name is another way in which he pursued the unsayable and sought to hear the voice of language speak. But, even as Warren confronts the voice of the world throughout his later poetry, he faces his own inability to speak the name of the world.

One of Warren's early unpublished poems foreshadows the way he would confront the unsayable in the search for the name.[3] "Love's Voice" (*CP* 27–29), originally included in a volume entitled *Problem of Knowledge* and compiled sometime after the publication of *Thirty-Six Poems* in 1935, is among the lengthiest of his early works and bears a similar narrative and structural density to many poems of this period.[4] It is, however, one of the more openly philosophical in its approach and bears a striking self-consciousness in its meditations on the unavoidable tension of the poet's articulation and search for meaning. In this way, it foreshadows the confrontation with the unsayable in the act of poetic creation throughout the later poetry. Warren's persistent desire as a poet was to find that place of articulation from which he might gain access to the unsayable and might be able to humbly speak a unified utterance that would destroy what Coleridge called "the old antithesis of words and things" (*CL* 1.625–26). The poem is an early attempt to work out that problem by means of an extended syllogism, working from the "If" of the first stanza to the "Then" of the final stanza. He begins with the desire to hear the unadulterated voice of love which has the power to unite word and action:

> If once we dreamed love had a tongue
> Tuned not to flatter but command
> Gross ear and grosser thought, and strong
> Enough to stay the ravening hand..." (1–4).

But, he goes on to acknowledge that if there had ever been a code word of love—or what he calls "that master-sound" (14)—the soul cannot hear it, no matter how hard she may listen. The potential danger is that the soul falls into a certain naturalism when there is no answer from love's voice:

> ... then hope deferred,
> Faith fainter, and the absolute
> Of joy forgot, reviled, a word
> For fools, and nothing but the brute
> Disorder for the anarch ear ... (33–37)

And, yet, the soul continues to listen, knowing that such aversion still speaks of the necessity of love. But neither ancient nor modern science can answer the question. In the seventh stanza, he recalls the Pythagorean theory of the cosmos in which the spheres are held in place by "music of accord so pure" (52) that all things worked together in harmony and an "excess / of joy ..." (53–54). But just as this fable fails to account for the experience of love, so our modern ones cannot solve this problem.

In the final stanzas, the narrator suggests that the problem must be turned around to be understood. Rather than looking for the grand meta-narrative to provide an answer, it is the individual words and deeds of our lives that give meaning.

> For, no: not faith by fable lives,
> But from the faith the fable springs
> —It never is the song that gives

Tongue life, it is the tongue that sings;
And sings the song. Then, let the act
Speak, it is the unbetrayable
Command, if music, let the fact
Make music's motion; us the fable . . . (81–88)

And the final stanza makes clear that the act is love itself, and it is enacted between two people in speaking, even if the words spoken are not a "master-sound" or final word.

. . . then speak and know
That speech, half lost, can yet amaze
Joy at the root; then suddenly grow
Silent, and on each other gaze. (93–96)

This is why in the middle of the poem the narrator does not give in to linguistic nihilism. He gets a glimpse of a place where he can approach the unsayable in the ongoing act of speaking in the limited, fragmented, and unstable language available to him within the tension of the world. His only recourse to the unsayable lay in saying itself within the inevitable limits of language. So much of our language may be just "wild sounds" that are silent "to purer sense" and "brutish tumult that confounds / In vanity the unpregnant ear" (41–44). And yet, even these may be as "rank oil [that] feeds the steady flame" (46) and serve as "syllables for a clear name" (48). In the context of the poem, that name is more than likely the name of love itself, in its purest expression, but a name that may not be spoken. In the ninth stanza, the narrator questions the way we think our fables give us meaning. He asks, "What glass unwinking gives our trust / Its image back, what echo names / The names we hurl at namelessness?" (68–70). We try to speak the name, but all our words fall short and leave us within the tension between "joy or distress" (72).

Although the mention of the name may be brief, it links "Love's Voice" to that place from which Warren speaks in so many of his later poems—the place from which he seeks to engage the world for what it is. His desire to speak the name of the world is not an attempt to define the extra-linguistic referent of his poetic enterprise. "Time as Hypnosis," from *Or Else: Poem/Poems 1968–1974,* makes this clear (*CP* 272–73). In the first stanza, the poet asks, "What / Is the name of the world" (2–3), and returns to that question late in the poem, acknowledging, "All day, I had wandered in the glittering metaphor / For which I could find no referent" (46–47). As a poet, he is not concerned about *mimesis* by which he might capture something about the world; rather, he is committed to the creative act of *poiesis* through an imaginative engagement in the world in which he dwells which reshapes and modifies his understanding. Speaking the name of the world or of the self is a particular way of participation, one that enacts. In linguistic terms, naming is a commonly understood as a performative act rather than a denotative or prescriptive one.[5] To name someone or something is an instance of language seemingly doing what it says. A name is language, a specific way that language reveals itself. In Warren's aesthetic, however, naming is never an absolute and pure act. To name something involves embracing the tension of the world. In *The Possibilities of Order* published in 1976, Warren muses with his long-time friend and collaborator Cleanth Brooks about experience and what he calls "enactment" in an extended conversation about literature in both its critical and social contexts. At various points, Warren urges that literature embodies a certain kind of experience because of the nature of language itself. Early on, he says, "So even in the most minimal dimension, part of the medium of language is not *mere* medium but an experience in itself" (22). At a later point, he queries Brooks, "Would you say that literature is knowledge by enactment, imaginative enactment?" And Brooks agrees, "That's good phrasing and perhaps superior to 'dramatic,' . . . Yes, knowledge by imaginative enactment" (48). In the same year that he and Brooks had this conversation, Warren published *Democracy and Poetry* in which he argues that poetry as a "made thing" that "embodies the experience of a self vis-à-vis the world, not merely as a subject matter, but as translated into the experience of form" (72). Because of this, there is a surplus to a made thing that marks its uniqueness as that which may not be exhausted, "any more than love is exhausted by the sexual act" (72). In its inexhaustible character, a poem "stands as a perennial possibility of experience, available whenever we turn to it . . . " (72). Later, he sums up his appeal to the necessity of poetry in a society that is prone to "de-create" by stating, "For the basic fact about poetry is that it demands participation, from the secret physical echo in muscle and nerve that identifies us with the medium, to the imaginative enactment that stirs the deepest recesses where life-will and values reside" (89). Warren does not shrink from speaking of language as *medium*, but it is never a "*mere* medium" that is neutral and pliable. There is a necessary vitality to it as it enacts experience. In his 1970 acceptance speech for the National Medal for Literature, he argued that there is a kind of poetry necessary in an age marked by "the sense of being cut off from reality" ("Hawthorne *was* Relevant" 87). He urges that what makes poetry real has to do with the way language is conceived.

> In our communication-numbed society, we are buffeted and drowned in a flood of language, but it is a language that is debased, with the makedo word taking the place of the right word. Worse, even, language is used as merely a convenient way of pointing. It becomes bleached out, not a thing expressive in itself. It is no longer a part of experience and an index of the speaker's own reality; and of the reader's or the listener's, too, as he senses the ripple of language in the throat, the deep and complex bodily response. (88)

There is a power to language that is "expressive in itself," not reliant upon the use of the speaker, one that is able to enact reality, or being. So, he argues, when "primitive man" spoke whatever word he used to name "tiger," that word was not an abstract pointer but and enactment of his own "awe, fear, admiration" (88).

Naming defines a relation of difference, a way of distinguishing one person or entity from another. The person or entity is never isolated, and neither is the name ungoverned by relations to other names or words. Naming is a specific moment of utterance. It is not simply a matter of designation, as if a name were simply a sign that designates a thing.[6] Rather it is a word that enacts even as the creative act is a moment of experience and instancy. Warren consistently attempted to avoid what he considered the abyss of abstraction by dealing with vital experience in the moment rather than speaking in platitudes. Speaking of Truth or Happiness or Despair is pointless apart from the concrete act of the moment in which Truth is not spoken but enacted. In "Preternaturally Early Snowfall in Mating Season" (*CP* 398–99), he puts it in this way: "This is one name for happiness: the act" (32). The act gives definition not simply to an idea but to life itself in Warren's vision. During his first dialogue with Laetitia Lewis, wife of Lilburn Lewis, in *Brother to Dragons* (1979), R.P.W. states that

> . . . every act is but a door
> Between two rooms, on equal hinges hung
> To open either way, on either room,

And every act to become an act must resolve
The essential polarity of possibility,
Yet in the act polarity will lurk,
Like the apple blossom ghostly in the full-grown fruit.
Yet all we yearn for is the dear redemption of
Simplicity. (38–39)[7]

Though the act and the possibility are distinct from one another, they can never be separated. The act always dwells within the contrariness of possibility. However, though action is inescapable if one is to live at all, the act itself is not a given; it is not simply necessitated by a chain of cause-and-effect relations. The act is generated by the exercise of the conscious will within which the polarity of possibility lurks. The act does not destroy that tug of possibility. The polarity of possibility is not resolved so that it is dispelled but is resolved by incorporating that polarity within the one moment of the act. The act incorporates the possibility just as the "full-grown fruit" incorporates the apple blossom. The polarity of possibility is found not only in binary oppositions, but also in a plethora of possibilities available to the individual. In order for the act to become an act, it must enter into one of the rooms available to it. But the act cannot evade an inherent doubleness similar to the doubleness the poet experiences in language. The act is never stable.

In the 1953 edition of *Brother to Dragons*, R.P.W. goes on in this same exchange to meditate on the relationship between act and possibility.

No, that's not the thought I have meant to follow.
I had meant to say that if the act resolves
The essential polarity of possibility,
It yet will carry that polarity,
As deep in the inner flesh of autumn fruit
We trace the frail configuration of spring's flower.
But that image, with its sense of beauty and delight,
Is scarcely appropriate for my notion, and my own line
Has a sort of conventional euphony and sweetness. (55–56)

Like the concrete utterance of the poet, the act is always marked by the tension of the world and inevitably carries the doubleness of the "essential polarity of possibility." Even as R.P.W. seeks an appropriate image that can capture the way the act carries that polarity within itself, he is alert to the incapacity of his language and hints that any image will be limited in itself. He is suspicious about his own ability to articulate the unified experience that he appears to be describing. Though he speaks of the polarity of possibility, his impulse is to move toward resolution and yet he must struggle against that. R.P.W. complains, "No, that's not the thought I had meant to follow." Tension is not superseded but inevitably remains. But even when he seeks to translate this into metaphor, both his own impulse and his own language fail him: the image is inadequate to convey the fullness of the experience of which he speaks and his "own line / Has a sort of conventional euphony and sweetness" that tames and destroys the tension. R.P.W. continues in the 1953 edition:

> All wrong: For the origin of no human action,
> No matter how sweet the action and dear, is ever
> Pure like the flower. For if sweetness is there, then bitterness too,
> In that hell-broth of paradox and internecine
> Complex of motive and murderous intensity
> We call the soul, and from that
> Anguish of complication any act,
> Any act at all, the bad, the good, affords,
> Or seems to afford, the dear redemption of simplicity:
> The dear redemption in the mere fact of achieved definition,
> Be what that may. (56)

There is no pure act, just as there is no pure language, and no pure poem. Though an act may want to be pure, it partakes of the tension of the world: it is a mixture of sweetness and bitterness, a "hell-broth of paradox and internecine/ Complex of motive. . . ." The poet's understanding of this tension, though, is achieved through the exercise of the pure imagination in the poem.[8] The act bears this tension because such is the ontological condition of the human soul. The soul—if the poet can speak of such an abstract idea—is itself a paradox and a complex of motive, brimming with murderous intensity. Warren's mention of motive calls to mind "A Poem of Pure Imagination," in which he deals with the role of motive in the Mariner's act of killing the albatross. There, the severity of the crime that made it a reenactment of the mystery of the Fall was due to its apparent lack of motive. This concern for motive and act reappears in *Audubon,* where Warren redefines, in the light of *The Ancient Mariner,* the act of poetic creation as a willful act that involved blessing and cursing and was in its own way a necessary reenactment of the mystery of the Fall. Warren's lines here in *Brother to Dragons* seem to coincide with these other instances of his concern for the act and motive. They even seem to be illuminated by Coleridge's comment from the *Table Talk*, which Warren used as a sort of guiding statement for his analysis of the Mariner's act. For Coleridge, the Fall created the nonabsolute out of the absolute by which "every phenomenon is explicable" ("APPI" 359). As a result of the Fall, no human action is ever absolute, but involves a mixture of nonabsolute motives and values. No single human action can ever stand apart from other actions without any effect upon them. Though a given action may be without apparent motive, it is never an absolute and pure action. The human soul bears an "anguish of complication" in any act; but, because each act achieves a moment of definition out of the haze of possibility, each affords a sort of redemption, a buying back of each moment, though there is no clear promise attached to this redemption.

Warren's quest to know the name of the world is a quest after something primordial, a search for the "right word." To know the name of the world is to know the name that brings it into being and in which it exists as it does, full of tension and paradox. This quest, though, is ever a paradoxical one—the object of his search constantly runs ahead; and when he has reached the point where it was, it has moved on.[9] And yet this is the poet's passion, to name the world in which he lives and moves and has his being. In the dramatic dialogue of *Brother to Dragons* (1979), R.P.W. narrates how he first came to the ruined place of the Lewis home on a hill overlooking the Ohio River Valley. After climbing the hill, R.P.W. encounters a snake that slithers out from under one of the rocks. The "manifestation" of the snake "was only natural," he claims. It was not a supernatural revelation but a natural phenomenon. R.P.W. then muses:

No, none of these, no spirit, symbol, god,
Or Freudian principle, but just a snake,
Black Snake, Black Pilot Snake, the Mountain Blacksnake,
Hog-snout or Chicken Snake, but in the books
Elaphe obsoleta obsoleta,
And not to be confused with the Black Racer,
Coluber constrictor—oh, I remember

> That much from the old times when, like a boy,
> I thought to name the world and hug it tight,
> And snake and hawk and fox and ant and day and night
> All moved in a stately pavane of great joy
> And naked danced before the untouchable Ark of Covenant,
> Like Israel's king, and never one fell down.
> But when you're not a boy you learn one thing:
> You settle for what you get. You find that out.
> But if that's all you settle for, you're good as dead. (25)

Warren establishes a tension between the innocence of the boyish urge to "name the world" and the somewhat bitter voice of experience that resigns, "You settle for what you can get." To name the world supposedly means that you are able to "hug it tight," to grasp the world for what it is. The proliferation of names here is significant: as a boy, the speaker thought that to have the command of these names and distinctions was to be able to name the world. But the names, either in English or in Latin, all seem to refer to the one snake, the one that is not to be confused with the Black Racer.[10] The names do not bring him any closer to experiencing the snake confronted in this narrative. What is innocent about the desire to name the world is the expectation that he might actually be able to speak the word. In that vision of innocence, speaking the name enacts all the elements of nature "in a stately pavane of great joy" as they dance "before the untouchable Ark of Covenant . . . " without falling down. However, like the presence of Michal in the biblical narrative (2 Samuel 6), the voice of experience impinges, and R.P.W. realizes that he may not speak the final name of the world that will set nature to dancing. Rather, he claims that you learn to accept what little bit you can apprehend about the world, and apparently the world teaches you that fairly quickly. But, the speaker's final note unveils the relentless tension of the world and the passion of the poet: "But if that's all you settle for, you're good as dead." This is not simply irony; rather this is the paradoxical situation of the poet who yearns to name the unnameable. Within this paradox, the poet finds that hope that sustains him in his quest after the name of the world.[11]

Elsewhere in *Brother to Dragons*, Warren returns to the necessity of this yearning to name the things in the world, or to name the condition of life in the world. During her account of her relationship with Lilburn, Laetitia Lewis describes how at one point something changed in her relationship with her husband but she could not name what that thing was. "Just how it started I don't know. It wasn't / A thing to lay a name to, and I reckon / There's just no name to lay to the worst thing" (45).[12] As R.P.W. interviews her, she recounts different things in her relationship that could be considered the worst—to include the trauma of being raped by her husband—as she seems to try to name what it was that really changed her. She had experienced severe violence at the hands of her husband, but the "worst" thing she experienced was her husband's demand on the following day that she describe the act to him. When he commands her, "Laetitia—now tell me exactly what happened," she says, "But my words wouldn't come and my poor chest was a bigness / That hurt like something swelled there . . ." (50). The presence of her absent voice was the pain that she endured. It was her inability to speak that she felt so viscerally. This is made clear when she concedes to speak what she could not name. As she is confronted by her husband, she says:

And the bigness that in my chest had hurt me so
And was not words, was words now, and they came,
And some were words I never named before,
They were so awful, nor heard tell. . . . (51)

Even though she speaks by recounting the act, she cannot name the act itself. In her state of emotional and linguistic debility, she lacks the name for this worst thing and so lacks the fullness of knowledge of the experience. The act or the experience is only brought to fullness of being when the name is spoken. Only then may it be fully known. Laetitia acknowledges not simply her inability to name the thing that changed and led to the dissolving of her marriage but more so her encounter with the unsayable in the midst of her trauma. By doing so, she draws together here the necessary relationship between naming and knowledge, implying that one may only name that which may ultimately be known. When language withdraws and conceals the name searched for, there is no real knowledge of the thing. The worst thing, like the best thing, is that which cannot be fully known and for which there is no name. And yet we are bound to experience them, though we do not know the name.

Warren's pursuit of the name of the world is particularly evident in several poems in *Being Here*, a volume deeply attuned to the unsayable in the voice of the world.[13] Hidden within the poet's experience of radical tension is a persistent hope for that place from which he may raise his own voice and name the world. This hope, however, is wed to an extreme sense of his own inability. Warren consistently turns to the instancy and necessity of the poet's experience in the world in light of his own inability to speak the name of the world. Yet, that experience in the world encourages him nonetheless that he might hear the unsayable speak even as it cautions him that, in himself, he may never make that ultimate utterance. In the "Afterthought" to this volume, Warren describes the way he conceived of the structure of the book as an expression of this tension.

> Rather early, as the book began to take shape in my mind and in some poems, I began to feel that I needed a preliminary poem and another as a sort of coda, both very simple in method and feeling, to serve as a base for the book, or better, as a bracket to enclose the dimly envisaged tangles and complications of the main body. (441)

In the preliminary poem, "October Picnic Long Ago" (CP 381) Warren introduces both the narrative voice that is heard in so many poems throughout the collection and the trope of memory that provides the means by which that voice speaks. This poem is the memory of a Sunday afternoon family picnic, long ago, when the narrator was a young child. It is set in a time of innocence, both "before the auto had come, or many" (18) and before the narrator could "know what a Future was" (35). But, the narrator speaks from the standpoint of experience, recognizing the tension between the voice of the mother, who affirms her love for the moment and place and exclaims, "Could a place so beautiful be!" (27), and the voice of the father who longs for more of the world beyond the moment: "My ship will come in yet, / And you'll see all the beautiful world there is to see" (28–29). In the final stanza, the mother sings as the family "*clop-clopped* homeward while the shadows, sly, / Leashed the Future up, like a hound with a slavering fang" (33–34). But the narrator confesses that, in his youthful lack of experience, he did not know the name of the future. The voices of the mother and the father express the tension between the moment and the possibility, and each names the world in its own way. The irony, though, is that "bird-note" song of his mother's voice is telling the name of the world more so than anything he could know in the future.

From this originating poem, Warren pursues the name in two early poems within the volume, "Boyhood in Tobacco Country" (*CP* 384–85) followed by "Filling Night with The Name: Funeral As Local Color" (*CP* 385). In the first of these two, the poet dreams of "an autumn sunset" in which the tree-lined horizon is "blackened / To timelessness" (1, 4–5). "Far off" in the dream the blue smoke "from the curing barns of tobacco / . . . clings" (5–6) to the world's horizon. In the second stanza, the poet hears a voice:

> Far past slashed stubs, homeward or homeless, a black
> Voice, deeper and bluer than sea-heart, sweeter
> Than sadness or sorghum, utters the namelessness
> Of life to the birth of a first star,
> And again, I am walking a dust-silent, dusky lane, and try
> To forget my own name and be part of the world. (8–13)

In the midst of his dream, the voice "utters the namelessness / Of life" at the moment that a first star appears in the evening sky. The namelessness of life is not defined by the specific experience of the one who utters, who is either moving homeward or is homeless. Regardless of situation, the speaker cannot utter the name of life even as he watches "the birth of a first star." In fact, his utterance is not only nameless but also wordless, perhaps sung like the melodious "bird-note" of the mother's song in "October Picnic Long Ago." The suggestion is that voice utters something that cannot be named, and this is what reveals the tension of the world. The speaker may give utterance to— but he may not make any final predication about—life except that it avoids such predication. The name that might be spoken is a name that he cannot speak. And yet, the final two lines of the stanza intimate that this is what it means to be a part of the world. The poet, once again walking along a country lane in his dream, suggests that he must forget his own name before he can be a part of the world. Rather than asserting his own name, he embraces the namelessness of the world.

In the first lines of the third stanza, though, the poet encounters another voice as he moves in the timelessness of the dream world:

> . . . From the deep and premature midnight
> Of woodland, I hear the first whip-o-will's
> Precious grief, and my young heart,

As darkling I stand, yearns for a grief
To be worthy of that sound. Ah, fool! Meanwhile,
Arrogant, eastward, lifts the slow dawn of the harvest moon. (14–19)

In the previous stanza, the black voice was "deeper and bluer than sea-heart, sweeter / Than sadness or sorghum . . ." and seemed to possess a certain joy-fulness in its ignorance of the world's name. The whip-o-will, however, utters its "Precious grief," and the sound of his voice defines the grief he bears; it is a grief that the poet in his youth "yearns . . . / To be worthy of. . . ." There is a sense of need for both the grief and the joy that will inevitably be encountered in his pursuit of the name of the world. In the final stanza, as the poet awakens from his dream and memory to stand once again under an autumn moon, he wonders why his perception that the moon presides over "what the year has wrought" does not give to him the knowledge that he desires.

Enormous, smoky, smoldering, it stirs.
First visibly, then paling in retardation, it begins
The long climb zenithward to preside
There whitely on what the year has wrought.
What have the years wrought? I walk the house.
Oh, grief! Oh, joy! Tonight
The same season's moon holds sky-height.

The dark roof hides the sky. (20–27)

In the poet's persisting tension between grief and joy, he encounters the limit of his knowledge in the recognition that the "dark roof hides the sky." Within the dark confines of that limit, though, he must continue to pursue the name of the world while the voice of the world speaks all around him.

What can neither be spoken nor understood in "Boyhood in Tobacco Country" is given utterance in the following poem, "Filling Night with The Name: Funeral as Local Color," in which the whip-o-will speaks the word that is unavailable to the widower. In this poem, the name of the world is closely linked to the conviction that the language of the world speaks the word that the poet cannot articulate. Nature itself constitutes that word. When Warren questions the name of the world, he surmises that the name must be spoken by the world itself before he will be able to know it. The question of the name enacts the poet's longing for a unified word that the world alone can give.

The same narrative voice introduced in "October Picnic Long Ago," which recounts the boyhood memory of joy and sorrow, appears now to tell the tale of an elderly husband's learning to cope with his wife's death during the night after her funeral. But there is a clear tension in the poem not simply between the silence and the saying but between the spoken word and the unutterable word. The tension is sustained between the words that seem so thoughtful and are yet spoken so easily, and the word that is necessary but may not be spoken.

> It was all predictable, and just as well.
> For old Mrs. Clinch at last lay gut-rigid there
> In the coffin, withered cheeks subtly rouged, hair
> Frizzled and tinted, with other marks of skill
> Of the undertaker to ready his client to meet
> Her God and her grave-worm—well, Mrs. Clinch had heard
> The same virtues extolled for the likes of her, word for word,
> With no word, true or false, that she couldn't exactly repeat. (1–8)

Before the face of death, the speaker confronts the emptiness of the "predictable" and the virtuous. The words of the minister in his overused eulogy reveal that the predictable words could not suffice to speak the necessary word. By their endless repetition, the words had become trite and fell flat before the exigency of death, whether true or false.

Even the husband's words in the second stanza, spoken in response to "a friendly old couple," cannot stave off the reality of death: "'When a thing's gonna be,' he replied, 'git used to it fast'" (11). When he sits "down to write to his boy, / Far away," there is no word to speak what must be spoken: "But no word would come, and sorrow and joy / All seemed one . . ." (22–24). Caught between the joy of the living son and the sorrow of his dead wife, what can he write? But Warren suggests that the word he cannot find in himself is given by the name that the world speaks: " . . . just the single, simple word *whip-o-will*. // For the bird was filling the night with the name: *whip-o-will*. // *Whip-o-will*" (24–26). The name and the call converge in the one word that simultaneously speaks the husband's sorrow and joy. What cannot be spoken as a single word in human speech without privileging one word over another is given utterance in the voice of the whip-o-will. In the previous poem, the whip-o-will utters his precious grief, and here that grief is brought into the realm of being by one unified, competent word that is both the call and the name. It is significant that the poem ends with this call which utters the name; the poet has receded and given way to the voice of being itself. That spoken name now opens up being instead of closing off from being, and so this final word/name is not an ending but an invocation similar to that at the end of *Audubon*: "Tell me a story of deep delight."

"Youthful Truth-Seeker, Half Naked, at Night, Running down Beach South of San Francisco" (*CP* 392–93) marks the beginning of the second section of *Being Here* and advances the theme of memory. But if the poems in the first section give voice to the desire to name the world, this poem now frames a more urgent expression of the heart's yearning to embrace the world "in its fulness and threat." The connection that this bears to the description of the truth-seeker as being youthful is confirmed by the boyish desire that R.P.W. remembers in *Brother to Dragons*, when he "thought to name the world and hug it tight" (*BD 79* 25).[14] The desire to embrace the world incorporates the hope to engage the tension as the place or moment within which the poet may speak. By speaking its name, the poet embraces the world and enacts that moment in which being is shaped and changed. In the thirteen stanzas of the poem, the speaker narrates his own experience many years before of running alone down the beach in the darkness. In his youthfulness, he runs away from "the glow of the city of men" into the darkness, the encroaching fog, and the sound of the surf. In the midst of his memory, he muses:

> What was the world I had lived in? Poetry, orgasm, joke:
> And the joke the biggest on me, the laughing despair
> Of a truth the heart might speak, but never spoke—
> Like the twilit whisper of wings with no shadow on air.
>
> You dream that somewhere, somehow, you may embrace
> The world in its fulness and threat, and feel, like Jacob, at last
> The merciless grasp of unwordable grace
> Which has no truth to tell of future or past—
>
> But only life's instancy.... (17–25)

The dream expresses the desire to embrace the world so that the poet might be grasped by the "unwordable grace," which speaks "life's instancy." Warren's allusion to the biblical Jacob in his experience of wrestling with God (who perhaps presented the patriarch with his own fulness and threat) heightens the tension of this paradoxical desire to grasp in order to be grasped. Jacob survives his encounter but walks away with a limp that reminds him of the instancy of that moment. This unwordable grace contrasts with the truth "the heart might speak" but never is spoken precisely because it comes from within the speaker who must admit his own inability. The truth cannot be spoken any more than "the twilit whisper of wings with no shadow on air." The name of the world after which the poet yearns is itself unwordable and gracious.

The poet continues this emphasis in the eighth stanza:

So lungs aflame now, sand raw between toes,
And the city grows dim, dimmer still,
And the grind of breath and of sand is all one knows
Of the Truth a man flees to, or from, in his angry need to fulfill

What? ... (29–33)

The moment of instancy in which the youth feels "the grind of breath and of sand" is the only truth that he can name, though he cannot define it. It is at once something that "a man flees to, or from"; it draws him on but it can also repel by its power. But there is still the question of fulfillment that goes unanswered; there is the lack of stability for the self. As Warren asserts in *Audubon*, the answer can be found only in the asking the question. The youth is a truth-seeker walking in the world and asking the world to speak its truth. He stares at the stars and listens with ear to the wet sand for this word or name. So, in the eleventh and twelfth stanzas, he listens:

Below all silken soil-slip, all crinkled earth-crust,
Far deeper than ocean, past rock that against rock grieves,
There at the globe's deepest dark and visceral lust,
Can I hear the *groan-swish* of magma that churns and heaves?

No word? No sign? Or is there a time and place—
Ice-peak or heat-simmered distance—where heart, like eye,
May open? But sleep at last—it has sealed up my face,
And last foam, retreating, creeps from my hand. ... (41–48)

He can imagine the layers of the earth down to the very core of the planet, but he cannot hear the word or sign that would speak the truth after which he seeks. In a way parallel to the dream of the sixth stanza, he longs for a moment of articulation, a moment within time and space, where the heart may finally gain vision not shrouded by the dark. For the poet, listening and articulation are part of the same act. The heart opens both to listen and to speak. This is ultimately a moment of knowledge, as part of being itself, and is therefore necessarily related to "being here." Knowledge is tied to the concreteness of the world—whether the ice-peak or the heat-simmered distance.

In "Sila" (*CP* 400–02), Warren confronts the need to name the world within its concreteness by creating a concrete narrative which drives this poem forward.[15] The poem sketches out the relationship between "the tawny great husky" (6) named Sila and the boy or young man whose perspective defines the vision of the narrative. The poem highlights the sense of connection between the dog and the boy through their repeated eye contact, much like in other poems where Warren displays contact between eyes and hands and bodies. But this connection is still bounded by a degree of helplessness that each bears before the inescapability of death. "Sila" parallels both *The Rime of the Ancient Mariner* as well as *Audubon: A Vision* in the way its narrative hinges on death and the doubleness of blessing and cursing. Early in the narrative, the boy and dog come upon the ruins of a cabin, and the boy ponders the exigency of death. He thinks, "*Two hundred years back—and it might/ Have been me*" (10–11). He wonders "what name the man / Might have had" (12–13) who built and inhabited the cabin, then he imagines coming back in the summer to find gravestones and even imagines a skull rotting deep in the ground beneath those stones. When the husky is released from his harness, a doe leaps from its thicket-cover and bounds over the snow in beauty before the moment of death when Sila pounces on it. In an intense section in the middle of the poem, the boy's eyes are in contact with the dog's and then alternately with the deer's, suggesting a distinctly sacramental quality within the tension of the world. There is no escaping the connection between the self and the world, a connection bound up in violence, blood and death. After the dog has wounded the deer, the boy decides that he cannot leave it to die slowly in the winter sunset:

> . . . So the boy's knees bend,
> Break the snow-crust like prayer,
> And he cuddles the doe's head, and widening brown eyes
> Seem ready, almost, to forgive.

Throat fur is cream color, eyes flecked with gold glintings.
He longs for connection, to give explanation. Sudden,
The head, now helpless, drops back on his shoulder. Twin eyes
Hold his own entrapped in their depth,
But his free hand, as though unaware,
Slides slow back
To grope for the knife-sheath. (60–70)

There is a clear redemptive element at work here, comparable to the sacramental theme Warren explored in *Rime of the Ancient Mariner*, and it encompasses both the boy and the deer in a moment of transformation. Though "helpless" and "unaware," they both participate in the act of redemption. After the boy has cut the deer's throat and watched the blood flow "Red petal by petal" (85) onto the white snow, the poem makes the sacramental notion of participation all the more explicit:

He lifted his head, knife yet in hand, and westward
Fixed eyes beyond beech-bench to the snow-hatched
Stone thrust of the mountain, above which sky, too,
More majestically bloomed, but petals paler as higher—
The rose of the blood of the day. Still as stone,
So he stood. Then slowly—so slowly—
He raised the blade of the knife he loved honing, and wiped
The sweet warmness and wetness across his own mouth,
And set tongue to the edge of the silk-whetted steel.

He knew he knew something at last
That he'd never before known.
No name for it—no! (90–101)

Just as the boy had set his eyes on the dog's and the deer's eyes for a sense of connection, here he fixes his eyes on the "Stone thrust of mountain," and when he stands he seems to have been transformed by this connection, for he stands "Still as stone. . . ."

This notion of sacramental participation is sharpened, though, into explicit eucharistic imagery. The blood that flowed out onto the snow like the fallen petals of a rose has now flowed into the day itself as the sun sets; above the mountain "The rose of the blood of the day" (94) blooms. When the boy sets the blade to his mouth and partakes of the "sweet warmness and wetness" (97), it is not simply the blood of the deer that he drinks but the blood of the day, and even mingles it with his own as he sets "tongue to the edge of the silk-whetted steel" (98). The eucharistic union is comprehensive with life in the world, and it becomes a sort of revelation, an entry into a new knowledge. However, even though he has such new knowledge, he cannot name what it is he knows. Though the violent act is unavoidable, it holds within itself the possibility of the blessing of that knowledge that opens up being and changes the self and the understanding of the world. But the change in being that the boy experiences might be said to be paradoxical: he knows that a change has occurred but he does not have a name for it. It is unclear why he cannot name this, though; it may be because of an implicit sense of holiness of this knowledge received through this act, or it may be simply because of the inability not only to grasp the moment but also to articulate this experience. And yet, it appears that the boy finally does speak the word to name the knowledge that he has received.

> He snow-cleaned the knife. Sheathed it. Called: "Come!"
> The dog, now docile, obeyed. With bare hands full of snow,
> The boy washed him of the blood and, comblike,
> With fingers ennobled the ruff.
>
> Then suddenly clasping the creature, he,
> Over raw fur, past beeches, the mountain's snow-snag,
> And the sky's slow paling of petals,
> Cried out into vastness
> Of silence: "Oh, world!"
>
> He felt like a fool when tears came. (102–11)

Even here Warren emphasizes that this new knowledge, limited as it is, is a sort of redemption through a washing of blood. In the former stanza, the boy washes the dog "of blood," a prepositional phrase whose antecedent is ambiguous. The dog is being cleaned from the stain of the blood on his fur, but there is also the hint that the boy and the dog and the day have all been washed in blood. In the second of the two stanzas, the sky still bears the stain of this blood in its "slow paling petals." But such a redemption in the world is momentary and its power is found in the instancy of the experience. In this moment, the boy utters his cry in which we hear him name the only name he can utter before the silence and the vastness of the world, and that is, "world." The name of the world is, in the end, "world." For the poet, even with such a sacramental vision, this is the only name that may be named for the world and for life in the world. The knowledge that the boy received was of the character of life in the world as he confronts death. So the poem ends with his confrontation with his own death:

> Some sixty years later, propped on death's pillow,
> Again will he see that same scene, and try,
> Heart straining, to utter that cry?—But
> Cannot, breath short. (112–15)

At the horizon of his own being, will he still "utter that cry" that is the name of the world? In the tension of the world, he will find that the name he learned is what he will not be able to pronounce, because he, like the pioneer and the deer, has succumbed to life itself. His last cry of the name of the world will be the sound of his final expiration. This will be the speaking of life's name, as R.P.W. suggests in *Brother to Dragons*: "For all life lifts and longs toward its own name, / And toward fulfillment in the singleness of definition" (*BD 79* 77).

The final two poems of *Being Here* recapitulate the relentless yearning to name the world as a means toward the redemption of life within the world. In his "Afterthought" to the volume, Warren notes that the poems of this final section are "concerned with the reviewing of life from the standpoint of age" (*CP* 441). The first-person narrative of "Night Walking" (*CP* 438) makes this explicit both by the parallels with other poems early in the volume which recall more youthful forays into the world of the night as well as by introducing the figure of the speaker's son. It also ties together the various thematic elements of this collection by a kind of transference of the quest to name the world from the aging speaker to the youthful son, rooting it concretely in "here" in which being is to be achieved—if it is going to be achieved at all. From its perspective of age, the poem heightens the endless character of the quest to name the unnameable, which he terms here as a sort of wisdom. In contrast to many of the poems in this volume, that narrative line of "Night Walking" is not rendered in the past tense, as if it were recounting a memory. Rather, the poem is the event; the narrative constitutes the episode in such a way that it brings the unsayable into the open of the sayable. So, the poem begins by opening up the poet's own thought:

> *Bear*, my first thought at waking. I hear
> What I think is the first bear this year
> Come down off the mountain to rip
> Apples from trees near my window—but no,
> Its the creak of the door of the shop my son stays in. (1–5)

Upon seeing his son, "Now booted and breeched but bare / From waist" (6–7) standing in the late light of a full moon, the father dresses and waits, although he does not know what he is waiting for. He creeps slowly at a safe distance away from the son as he makes his way "up the track" into the blackness of the forest. While the son is captivated with the vastness of the moonlit night, the father is fixed on his son and desires what knowledge he can derive "in love" about what his son is experiencing. But, when he is overcome with a "mixture of shame, guilt, and joy" (43), he turns away to leave his son to his own experience, as if a mantle had been passed on.

The world into which the father and son walk is a world full of tension, "Where from blackness of spruces great birches / Stand monitory, stand white" (21–22). The contrast between light and dark is also seen in the interplay of moonlight and shadow as the full moon shines "now late and zenithward high / Over forests as black as old blood / And the crags bone-white" (9–11). The son gazes over the "light-laved land" (32) as if to accept it for what it is, knowing that the "clambering forest" would claim even him if given the chance. When he moves on to "the next range to westward" (36), he pauses and "lifts up his light-bleached arms" (38). In the light he stands frozen, and the poem itself pauses in that moment before "Arms down, [he] goes on" (40).[16] The son lifts his arms to the moonlight without shame, embracing the world in its tension. After watching this act of participation, the father knows from his own experience that the son can only go on alone. In his own shadowed solitude, the father too must move on by turning back to "the proper darkness of night," that interior darkness into which the light of the moon cannot reach.

> I start, but alone then in moonlight, I stop
> As one paralyzed at a sudden black brink opening up,

For a recollection, as sudden, has come from long back—
Moon-walking on sea-cliffs, once I
Had dreamed to a wisdom I almost could name.
But could not. I waited.
But heard no voice in the heart.
Just the hum of the wires.

But that is my luck. Not yours. (47–55)

When confronted with his own loneliness in the night, his imagination is engaged to open up the memory of his experience as a young man. In his own moonlight walk, he perceived a wisdom that he desired to name but he could not speak the name itself. He was able to apprehend the presence of such wisdom as the world opened itself to him, but he was bound by his own inability to give utterance to the name in that moment. Like truth, this wisdom cannot be named but may only be enacted in a way that invokes its presence, even when its name is withheld. The father waits in order to listen for the name now in this night shared with his son, but he hears "no voice in the heart. / Just the hum of the wires" (53–54). The poet then admits that this absence of voice is his own "luck" (55) and not his son's. This is a burden that he must bear as he listens for the voice of the world.[17]

The final stanza avoids resolving the tension created by this confrontation with the world and issues an exhortation spoken to both the son and the reader alike.

At any rate, you must swear never,
Not even in secret, the utmost, to be ashamed
To have lifted bare arms to that icy
Blaze and redeeming white light of the world. (56–59)

The father affirms the goodness of participating in the world and not being silenced by what is the unsayable. While so much of the poem is set in darkness, he ends by pointing to the "redeeming white light of the world." This is the only name that he can give to the wisdom of the world, because this is the name that is brought into the open by the world itself. It reveals itself in the blaze and light the father confronted in the darkness of night. But this is not something that the father alone has experienced. There is a shift in this final section to the second person personal pronoun and to a past perfect verb tense, a shift intended to draw in the reader and place the name of the world on the reader's own lips. Here, it is not the father that has lifted his arms but the reader who stands before the blaze and light of the world as he reads the poem.

Even as Warren tracks the name of the world through his ongoing and imaginative engagement with "being here," he engages in a relentless hunt for the name of the self. These two paths of pursuit are not really separate in his thought but really make up the one quest to speak the name. Throughout his later poetry, they cast light and shadow on one another. In the same section in *Audubon* in which the poet says, "The world declares itself," Audubon thinks, "I do not know my own name" (IV[E].1, 11). Yet, he continues to walk in the world because it is here that he learns the nature of the self in its relation to the world. There is, however, a certain irony in the pursuit of the name of the self because it would appear to be the one word that is clearly defined and can be grasped with relative linguistic ease. The self, itself, is not the given from which the poet works but, like the name of the world, it must be worked toward. Just as his concern for the name of the world functions according to the desire to come into the being of the world and to participate in its unfolding through language, so his desire to find the name of the self involves the task of creating the self, of bringing it into being.[18] Warren maintains that the self must be created and worked toward, not as a teleological goal but as an ever-present possibility. While he never contends that reality is a linguistic construct or that language is all we may know, his poetry does demonstrate that reality is linguistically perceived and that the self is not free from such a poetic condition. There must be such linguistic perception if the poet ever hopes to find the place from which he can speak.

Warren clearly is exploring this urgent need in "Sunset" (*CP* 583), part of his final collection of poetry, *Altitudes and Extensions 1980–1984*. The poem begins with that moment in which the self confronts the world in its tense power, and the world becomes not a thing but another self. In the terminology of Martin Buber, for whose thought Warren had a great affinity, the world is transformed from It to Thou.[19] He envisions an apocalypse of nature that happens each day but is never the same from one day to the next.

> Clouds clamber, turgid, the mountain, peakward
> And pine-pierced, toward the
> Vulgar and flaming apocalypse of day,

In which our errors are consumed
Like fire in a lint-house—
Not repetitious
But different each day, for day to day nothing
Is identical to eye or soul.
At night, at a late hour, I
Have asked stars the name of my soul. (1–10)

Each "apocalypse of day" is unique, as individual as each day is, but every one consumes our errors. Every apocalypse is a moment full in itself and never identical to another moment. But each and all point toward the inability of the poet to speak the name of his own soul. Even as in other poems Warren listens to nature to speak the name of the world, so here he interrogates the stars to hear them speak his own name.[20] The timing of his interrogation is significant: he petitions the stars *after* the apocalypse has burned up his sins like fire on the altar, after he has been cleansed so that he might hear what is spoken. In the second stanza, he states his question explicitly: "Oh, what shall I call my soul in a dire hour?" (11) The poet's question is filled with a sense of urgency because of the "dire hour," that moment in which he must speak but cannot. If the day is able to consume his errors, then the night should be able to tell him what he might call his soul. But, when the poet asks the stars the name of his soul, he learns that they are unable to give him the answer that he desires:

But there is no answer from
Heavenly algebra, and you are left with
The implacable gaggles and military squadrons
Of ignorance . . . " (12–15).

The source of this inability appears to be that the stars, unlike the daily apocalypse, are locked in a repetition from day to day.[21] Each night is identical to them because they do not have a soul that cries out in the dire hour. The poet is able, though, to name this "Heavenly algebra" even when he does not know the name of his own soul. He is able to discern the constellations, and, though they know no originality, they continue to speak without any hope of appeasement. When the poet questions the stars regarding his own name, all he hears is their "implacable gaggles," their own unrelenting questioning that announces themselves.[22] The self, though, is confronted with its own originality and each day's lack of repetition. The poet wonders in the final stanza what then is available to him in light of life's necessity:

> Who knows his own name at the last?
> How shall he speak to a soul that has none?
> "Tell me that name," I cried, "that I may speak
> In a dire hour." . . . (19–22).

The self is caught in the necessity of having to speak, but in order to speak, the self must know its own name. There is an important shift from the apocalypse of the day in the first stanza to the apocalypse of the self in the final stanza. The apocalyptic moment of the self—that simultaneous time of uncovering and hiding, of scattering and coming together—is the dire hour, the moment when of necessity "you must speak / To your naked self. . . " (23–24). In that moment, the name is hidden from sight, but the self is revealed; what has never before been seen or known is brought to the light and made known, though the poet remains unable to give the final name for the soul.

In that tension between the urgency to speak and the inability to name, the name of the self, like the name of the world, appears to be a significant part of that "given" toward which Warren contended the poet must work. It is not a given, just as identity is not a static and isolated entity or quality. Rather, to speak the name is to say the unsayable. But how can one do this, poet or otherwise? In Warren's vision, the self that we wish to name must be created via the imagination. But this creation is not abstracted from life in the world; the world shapes and influences, even as it is shaped and influenced. In the creation of the self, there is a sort of reciprocal relationship. Like the poem, the self is a "made thing," as he put it in *Democracy and Poetry*. Even in "The Ballad of Billie Potts," in which Little Billie is made and remade, this is revealed through the narrator's emphasis upon the "new name."[23] However, Warren states more explicitly his understanding of the creation of the self in his discussion of Coleridge's distinction between the primary and secondary imagination in "A Poem of Pure Imagination." The connection Warren makes in this essay between the imagination and the self is not only crucial for understanding his later comments in *Democracy and Poetry* but also an important addition to the on-going reading and interpretation of Coleridge's aesthetic. Warren's interpretation, if not quite unique, does pursue a valid line of thinking often overlooked in Coleridge criticism. After quoting in full Coleridge's distinction and definition of the primary and secondary imagination, Warren goes on to comment:

> It is the primary imagination which creates our world, for nothing of which we are aware is given to the passive mind. By it we know the world, but for Coleridge knowing is making, for, "To know is in its very essence a verb active." We know by creating, and one of the things we create is the Self, for a subject is that which "becomes a subject by the act of constructing itself objectively to itself; but which never is an object except for itself, and only so far as by the very same act it becomes a subject." ("APPI" 342)

Only by the primary imagination can we know the world or the self because the primary imagination creates both. In this creation, there is a fusion of the two horizons of subject and object. When Warren turns to the secondary imagination, the necessity of creating the self becomes all the more obvious. Here he is dealing not with "creation at the unconscious and instinctive level" (343) but with creation as an act of the conscious will. There is clearly an analogous relationship between the poem and self, in that they are both made things. In both cases, the act of creation is never pure in itself, free from the tension of the world. Warren asks, "Does Coleridge imply, however, that the poet in composing his poem acts according to a fully developed and objectively statable plan, that he has a blueprint of intention in such an absolute sense? To this question the answer is *no*" (343). Neither the poem nor the self are created according to an objectified plan or "blueprint of intention." While the act of creation functions according to an unconscious activity, it does not deny the role of the conscious will. Warren reconciles this "both/and" argument of Coleridge in the following way:

> It seems clear that the secondary imagination does operate as a function of that permanent will, and in terms of the basic concerns by which that will fulfills itself, but the particular plan or intention for a particular poem may be actually developed in the course of composition in terms of that "unconscious activity," which is the "genius in the man of genius," and may result from a long process of trial and error.... In other words, the plan and meaning of the work may be discovered in the process of creation. (343–44)

Warren adopted this aesthetic in his own thinking about poetic creation, stating in an interview with Ruth Fisher in 1970 that "[the writer] is not working deductively from a highly articulated image, a careful scheme of values; he is trying to find the values, find the ideas, by a process of trial and error, as it were" (Watkins, Hiers, and Weaks 171). This process, he goes on to say, is a matter of "the test of experience" (171). In fact, "Life is a process of trial and error about our own values" (171). It is not only the poem but also the self that is created through a process of trial and error. This process is always carried out by the imagination; in the same interview, and in language drawn directly from his earlier reading of Coleridge, Warren explores the role the imagination plays in this process. He says that "the writing is the process in which the imagination takes the place of literal living; by moving toward values and modifying, testing, and exfoliating older values" (171–72).

In "Poetry and Selfhood," the second essay that makes up *Democracy and Poetry*, Warren confirms this relation between the poem and the self in his aesthetic. "I am trying to indicate how, in the end, in the face of the increasingly disintegrative forces in our society, poetry may affirm and reinforce the notion of the self" (42). In the first half of the essay, he traces out these disintegrative forces and the way they militate against the proper understanding of the self. He argues that a relentless "contempt of the past inevitably means that the self we have is more and more a fictive self, . . . for any true self is not only the result of a vital relation with a community but is also a development in time, and if there is no past there can be no self" (56). He considers those forces within a democratic society that encourage "the abolition of the self" (68) rather than the establishing of the self. These work both from without and from within, but especially through the manipulation of images in a media culture that produces an endless string of fictive selves. Against this, he suggests that poetry is one of the things which serves to make democracy possible. "For poetry—the work of the 'makers'—is a dynamic affirmation of, as well as the image of, the concept of the self" (68). As a "made thing," he argues, the poem "stands as a 'model' of the organized self" (69). "The "made thing" becomes, then, a vital emblem of the struggle toward the achieving of the self, and that mark of struggle, the human signature, is what gives the aesthetic organization its numinousness. "It is what makes us feel that the 'made thing' nods mysteriously at us, at the deepest personal inward self"(69). The poem is not a model for the self simply because both are static and discrete entities that reflect each other. Rather, the poem acts as a model for the self because each involves an ongoing struggle toward some sort of presence. The poem bears the mark of this struggle and becomes "the human signature" for the work. The relationship between the poem and the self is not, then, simply a formal one, but is a mysterious relationship in which the two echo one another. This continues to clarify Warren's shift from formalist concerns to more openly ontological questions in his quest for the unsayable. Warren does acknowledge a difference between the way poetry functions with regard to the self and the way other literary genres do; what distinguishes the poem is a unique form.

> But the "made thing" that the poet produces represents a different kind of form from all the others we know. Its characteristic quality springs from the special fullness of the relation of a self to the world. The form of a work represents, not only a manipulation of the world, but an adventure in selfhood. It embodies the experience of a self vis-à-vis the world, not merely as a subject matter, but as translated into the experience of form. . . . The "made thing," the "formed thing," stands as a perennial possibility of experience, available whenever we turn to it; and insofar as we again, in any deep sense, open the imagination to it, it provides the freshness and immediacy of experience that returns us to ourselves and, as Nietzsche puts it, provides us with that "vision," that "enchantment," which is, for man, the "completion of his state" and an affirmation of his sense of life. (72)

The poem is a moment of the self's "being in the world," a moment of vital experience and enactment within the world. That experience is not simply objectified "subject matter" able to be studied; rather the relation of the self to the world provides the basis for the form of the poem. As we have already seen in Warren's attention to the language of the world, it is the tension of the world experienced by the self that provides the basis for the poem itself. In turn, then, the poem becomes a possibility of experience that not only "returns us to ourselves" but returns us to the world as well. And the vision this provides is necessary for the fullness of selfhood.

Warren says later in the same essay that the self is not "a preexisting entity" or "a Platonic idea existing in a mystic realm beyond time and change" (88).

Neither is the self "an object like the nugget of gold in the placer pan, the Easter egg, under the bush at an Easter-egg hunt, a four-leaf clover to promise miraculous luck" (88). This is, he says,

> the essence of passivity, to think to find, by luck, one's quintessential luck. And the essence of absurdity, too, for the self is never to be found, but must be created, not the happy accident of passivity, but the product of a thousand actions, large and small, conscious or unconscious, performed not "away from it all," but in the face of "it all," for better or for worse, in work and leisure rather than in free time. (88–89)

Warren's language here echoes his analysis of Coleridge's imagination in his earlier essay. By virtue of exercise of the conscious will, the self must be worked toward. It cannot be found by the passive mind, "for nothing of which we are aware is given to the passive mind" ("APPI" 342), least of all the self. The actions that create the self do not form an "objectively statable plan" or "a blueprint of intention in such an absolute sense" ("APPI" 343). Rather, these "thousand actions" form the process of trial and error that *is* life, in Warren's vision. And these actions are enacted (to use another of Warren's terms) in the face of—in the presence of—the being of the world.

One of the necessary actions by which the self is created is the act of naming the self. In this act, the self is returned into its own presence through the poem. Toward the end of "Poetry and Selfhood," Warren states, "Poetry even, in the same act and the same moment, helps one to grasp reality and to grasp one's own life. Not that it will give definitions and certainties. But it can help us to ponder on what Saint Augustine meant when he said that he was a question to himself" (92). The question of the self, and of the self's name, is really the only answer that the poet can come to, as Warren suggests in his "Afterthought" to *Being Here*: "Here, as in life, meaning is, I should say, often more fruitfully found in the question asked than in any answer given" (*CP* 441). It is this question that accounts for so much of the fruit of Warren's late poetry. In a number of poems, Warren confronts this question of the self in a very raw and exposed way, relentlessly searching for what, in the end, may not be fully spoken. For example, "Immanence" (*CP* 472) is a series of fifteen unrhymed couplets written in varying meters in which Warren pursues the name of the self as it relates to identity. The beginning of the poem suggests that one's name, if it can be known, cannot deflect the urgency of self-knowledge, nor can one's position within the world.

Stop! Wait! Wherever you are.
Whatever your name. It may well be

At the corner of one of the Fifties and Fifth Avenue,
Where the City of Things gleams brightest, and

Your name does not matter .... (1–5).

Even where "the City of Things gleams brightest," a person can feel the immanence of the self without knowing the self. The crux of the matter is that the
referent for your name—the signified of the signifier that is your name—"is
obscure to you . . ." (6). Speaking the name cannot simply designate the self
and then seal it off. There is still this matter of the obscurity of the self, which
in the middle of the poem parallels the darkness that swells like an orchid. The
obscurity of the darkness, though, is that it appears as benign and inimical; its
intention is hidden in its own darkness so that you cannot know if it means
good or ill. The poet contends that all you can know is the immanence of this
darkness and obscurity. In the immanence of the darkness, "something / Plays
cat-and-mouse with you, veiled, unrevealed . . ." (13–14).[24]

The "something" that plays the cat-and-mouse game is the knowledge
after which the self yearns, though it is constantly veiled and unrevealed. If
it could be unveiled and revealed so that "Its face is seen, name known" (19),
that knowledge would become powerless and would elude the grasp. Its fleeing
scream would bring pity to even a "horn-scabbed" (23). But the possibility of
trapping such knowledge remains just that: a possibility. This is the "teasing
enigma" (24) of the self. As in other poems where Warren uses the notion of
Zeno's paradox to portray this relentless quest, here he uses the notion of the
enigma; it is the riddle of the self that the poet is trying to solve. And yet the
question is the only answer he will receive. If he were to be able to name the
self, it would disappear in a consummation like the apocalypse of the "dire
hour" that Warren confronts in "Sunset" (*CP* 583). But the poet remains convinced that there is a *telos*, that there will be a day of unveiling and revealing.
If not, the only option is the naturalistic vision that he considers at the end of
the poem. If the "swollen Immanence turns out to be all" (26), the self—"Yet
yearning, . . . / yet ignorant . . ." (27–28)—will only be sucked into the abyss
and into a blind chemical reaction. "But that possibility is simply too distress-
ing // To—even—be considered" (30–31). Rather, the poet clings to his yearning after the possibility that one day he will know and be able to speak the

168 | The Act of Naming

name of the self. Within the nearness of the immanence, the poet carries on the quest and in the midst of that quest the unpresentable is presented in the act of creation.

Warren pursues this same quest in a similar poem in *Rumor Verified*, "Nameless Thing" (*CP* 456). As in "Immanence" and "What Was The Thought?", Warren here attempts to track down the relationship of the name to the self or to identity, questioning the givenness of the referent. He begins, "I have no name for the nameless thing / That after midnight walks the house" (1–2). Though usually moving about without a sound, the nameless thing betrays its presence through the creak of a stair, the sound of a soft breath, or simply "the effluvium / Of its being" (5–6). Caught between the silence and the sound, it reveals itself through "the odor of / A real existence lost in the unreality . . ." (9–10). This odor is itself paradoxical, a "sickening sweetness" like funeral flowers or sweat (7–8). The image of the funeral flowers is powerful: even though the flowers might suggest life in the face of death, they will nonetheless themselves die, and their death is made known through the scent of the not-yet-dead flowers. The effluvium of their death points to the time when what is nameless will be finally named in death. More strikingly, though, it is a "real existence" perceived in the "unreality / Of dead objects of day . . . " (10–11). That which is nameless though real is made known through that which is unreal; being is announced in the midst of nonbeing. It is a "real existence" rather than simply an idea or a thought. The irony of the final line of the third stanza is sharp: we know that every stone has its life, and yet we cannot name that which is of the fullness of being. But the speaker tries to hunt down the nameless thing, only to be confronted with being in the midst of unreality: "Barefoot, in darkness, I walk the house, a heavy / Poker seized from the hearth . . . " (13–14). Just when he thinks he might catch the nameless thing, it recedes and hides itself again. Warren suggests here a conviction similar to what he states in "Sunset": that nature is unable to give us the name that we seek so diligently. As the speaker stalks the nameless thing, he opens a door to find "Only a square / Of moonlight lies on the floor inside" (18–19), but the moonlight seems to dissipate the name he seeks. Nonetheless, it subtly intimates itself as he goes back to bed and hears "the blessèd heart beat there" (20). He proceeds to recount another experience on another night when he was certain he had trapped the nameless thing in a bathroom. But when he opened the door, ready to strike, he was confronted by his own reflection in a mirror and "Recognition // Came almost too late" (24–25). In this apophatic moment, the nameless thing both presents itself and makes it absence known. It lives in the fissure between recognition and nonrecognition, between life and death, between existence and unreality. And, in that moment, the speaker almost smashes the bathroom mirror, thinking to kill the nameless thing. His question—"But how could I / Have been expected to recognize what I am?" (25–26)—reveals this tension of the moment, a tension between "I have been" and "I am." This is where the self lies. To know this, however, does not mean that name may be finally known; rather it remains nameless, continuing in its restless existence. The sight of his own reflection in the mirror did not capture the nameless thing, as if the poet had finally pinned the name to its referent. In its namelessness, though, the self is propelled into that space and moment in which it might continue to pursue the name. So, the poem ends in the same way it began, with the poet lying in bed hearing "namelessness stalk the dark house," wondering "why it cannot rest" (28–29).

In his pursuit of the name, Warren's engagement with the enigmatic nature of language brought him face to face with the very nature of being itself. On the surface, his inability as a poet to perform what appears to be a very simple task—that is, to speak a name—makes obvious his sense of finitude within the tension of the world. However, this radical tension declares that the poet's desire to speak not just *a* name but *the* name is never simple, though it is necessary. Warren's vision of language and articulation looks toward some sort of an ultimate blessing in which language unfolds itself in the midst of the present tension. And yet this vision of blessing is endlessly deferred. He can imagine the time and the place from which he will be able to know the name of the world and to name even the fullness of his own self. But that place is only found in the consummation of the self, that moment in which the self *is*, in its truest and fullest sense, and in which it radically altered. He may not know how it is altered, though, until he dies. Death is the very real horizon of life and being in Warren's vision; it is the moment when the self may know even as it is known. It is also for the poet the moment of linguistic fullness in which the sayable and the unsayable converge and are said in that one word. While there is a sort of eschatological hope in his vision, the name of that hope can never be spoken, or it will disappear into the mist. Rather than being given over to a linguistic determinism, though, Warren persists in his conviction that language is the only means of articulating that hope.[25]

Limited, arbitrary, and unstable as it is, language nonetheless provides a means of experiencing that hope of a possibility in the present moment. And it is in the poem that language speaks and provides the ground for such a hope. This is the hope given by poetry itself. Though it bears the tension of the world, that tension points to a hope beyond it. For Warren, it is the real, though undefinable, presence of the unsayable that makes speaking at all possible. At the end of *Democracy and Poetry*, Warren makes his vision explicit. If what he calls "the oscillation, [and] the vibrance" of the tension of the world ceases, then "life, as we know it and esteem it, will cease" (93). He then quotes the end of Alexander Pope's *Dunciad* (1728) as evidence of this nihilistic vision: "Thy Hand, Great Anarch! let the curtain fall; / And Universal Darkness buries All." He goes on to comment:

> We are not, however, for all our dunce-ness, necessarily condemned to that—even if process may be thought to be all, even if there is to be no millennium of any kind. As a last word, I'll quote again from the *Confessions* of Saint Augustine:
>
>> "There is a dim glimmering of light unput-out in men; let them walk, let them walk that the darkness overtake them not." (93–94)

The presence of the unsayable does not condemn us to a darkness that buries us under the limits of the sayable. Rather, the unsayable reveals itself in the sayable as a dim-glimmering light that gives us a hope to speak at all. Bolstered by that hope, Robert Penn Warren continued to walk in the world and to love it.

CHAPTER SIX

Warren as Witness to the Unpresentable

Poetry is largely a matter of being able to open yourself to possibilities, rather than to fulfill ideas.—Robert Penn Warren[1]

Warren pursued the work of a poet to the end, which is to say, he continued working toward the given, yearning to say the unsayable. His unrelenting pursuit carries on through the final stages of his work because he never achieved the given that would be the final word, the ground truth that would unify understanding and relieve the tension of "being here" in the world as creatures full of our own power and limitation. "Poetry is a way of thinking" (Watkins, Hiers, and Weaks 293), he told David Farrell in 1977, and so much of Warren's thought is worked out in poetry caught between the two horizons of the past and the future—neither of which are a given for him. The burden of history really is an inescapable presence for Warren, but the reality of death is also the ineluctable boundary that must be faced and even crossed by the poet. Together with his engagement with the voice of the world and his search for the name of the world, these two horizons open up the unsayable as that which is present but whose content cannot be finally spoken.

The way in which Warren approached these horizons places his poetry and thought firmly within the broader theoretical context of the 1970s and 1980s, usually referred to under the broad banner of postmodern thought. During these years of Warren's final phase of poetic labor, literary theorists and philosophers alike were mapping the new critical landscape in the wake of the seismic shifts of the 1960s. Whether described as "deconstruction" or "post-structuralism," postmodern thought moved decidedly from epistemology to ontology, from assertion to questioning, and from "language as form" to "language as problem." The work of Saussure laid bare the linguistic foundations of thought. David Jasper summarizes the impact of Saussure's project: "The structure of thought is also the structure of language, without which there can be no thinking, and at the heart of language there is no *reference* . . . but only relationships" ("From Modernism to Postmodernism" 302). The thought of Martin Heidegger brought into the open the relation of being and language, and by doing so he became the unavoidable intellectual father to whom so many postmodern thinkers were both indebted and at odds— chief among whom was Jacques Derrida.[2] The ways in which these thinkers called attention to the structure of being in the world and exposed language as the mode of that being are the very directions in which Warren's thought went during this period. Warren himself, however, saw a certain distance between his own work and the work of those heralded as postmodern critics. Though he taught his last class at Yale University in 1973, he was still there at the same time as noted American critics and theorists J. Hillis Miller, Paul de Man, Geoffrey Hartman, and Harold Bloom, who later published the volume *Deconstruction and Criticism* (1979).[3] Bloom, however, is apparently the only one of these with whom Warren had a relationship.[4] In a November 1982 letter to Louis D. Rubin, Jr., Warren wrote, "I don't really know that gang at Yale. I know [Harold] Bloom very well . . . , but he doesn't belong to the gang. He and I disagree on various things and get heated . . . but he does have a real taste for poetry and an open mind about approaching it . . . " (*SL* 6.153–54). And, it was poetry that made the difference for Warren. Criticism or theory were only valid and appropriate if they return the reader to the poem. Any consideration of his work within the context of postmodernity must keep that in view.

Certain critics have provided their own assessments of the relationship between Warren's work and postmodernism. Charlotte Beck identifies *Brother to Dragons* and *Promises: Poems 1954–1956* as Warren's "bridge into Postmodernism" because of his radically new style that fit what she characterizes as "postmodern poetics" ("The Postmodernism of Robert Penn Warren" 211). Following the work of Jerome Mezzaro, whose *Postmodernism and American Poetry* describes certain common patterns and techniques in the poetry of Auden, Jarrell, Berryman and others, Beck sees a similar "evolution into postmodernism" (212) in Warren's open subjectivism and looser form. Victor Strandberg argues that both Warren and his precursor T. S. Eliot were "quintessential Modernists" in whose thought and work "the Postmodern lay dormant and waiting" ("R.P.W. and T.S.E" 35). He then justifies this claim by developing "three important Postmodern postulates" (35): literature as an agent of social change, the self as a social construct, and the equivalency of high art and pop culture. Anthony Szczesiul draws a connection between Warren and "the single feature most commonly associated with postmodernism: an antifoundational perspective" ("'Language Barrier'" 2). He points out "a general sense of uncertainty and instability" in Warren's later work— especially in regard to the conception of truth—concluding, "It is this expression of uncertainty which provides perhaps the strongest link between Warren and postmodernism" (2). Of these critics, Szczesiul is the most helpful in the way he compares Warren's thought in *Democracy and Poetry* with Lyotard's *The Postmodern Condition*. But, while there are affinities between Warren's thought and that of the larger theoretical context, these do not justify labeling him a "postmodernist" who espoused some sort of "postmodernism." Rather, his thought dwelled within the atmosphere of postmodernity that marked the history of ideas during this period.

There is another way of assessing the relation of Warren's work to postmodernity. Richard Palmer describes the "postmodernity" of Martin Heidegger by arguing that his thought is "of a special kind, . . . a thought and a path that resists categories, so that he himself wishes to leave it in the nameless" (87). He observes, though, some of Heidegger's "suggestive articulations of that path of thought: the step back from metaphysical thinking, the search for the unthought within the thought, the between-character of man's existence, the importance of co-responding to the Saying of language . . . " (87–88). These articulations are significant reasons, in Palmer's estimation, to consider Heidegger neither an idiosyncratic "mystic" and "crank" (71) nor one whose irrelevant thought has been superseded by contemporary philosophy. Rather, his work "points to a new 'site' for thinking . . . " (88), situating a path in a new geography of language and being. Warren's later poetry does much the same thing in the way it confronts the unsayable within the tension of the world. Through this poetry, he has given some suggestive articulations of his own path of thought: in its step back from the formalistic to the ontological, in its sense of being as "in the midst of" the world, and in its pursuit of the unsayable within the sayable. Warren's poetry moves toward a postmodern poetics, shifting its sights from representation "as the reproduction, for subjectivity, of an objectivity that lies outside it" (Jameson, Forward viii) to presentation in which language becomes the matter itself and the agent of poetic creation.

Jean François Lyotard frames a description of "postmodernism" specifically in relation to the question of the unpresentable.[5] In his estimation, the distinction between the presentable and the unpresentable is rooted in the ontologically prior question regarding the means of legitimating knowledge. In his "Introduction" to *The Postmodern Condition* (1979), Lyotard defines the postmodern with confessed extreme simplicity as "incredulity toward metanarratives" (xxiv). He goes on to sharpen what he means by such incredulity: "Postmodern knowledge is not simply a tool of the authorities; it refines our sensitivity to differences and reinforces our ability to tolerate the incommensurable. Its principle is not the expert's homology, but the inventor's paralogy" (xxv). In "What is Postmodernism?" he states that the postmodern "is undoubtedly a part of the modern" (79). In a reversal of a strict chronological approach to the development of ideas, he argues that "postmodernism thus understood is not modernism at its end but in the nascent state, and this state is constant" (79). The postmodern is not simply a sequential consequence of the modern but an approach that rivals and questions the modern. Like other thinkers working outside the Analytical tradition, Lyotard poses "totality" as one of the key problems of modernity as the heir of the Enlightenment. Knowledge is not legitimized by appeal to a common foundational authority, rooted in agreement, correspondence, and identity. Rather, knowledge properly resides in something other than a reasoned explanation of reality. Paralogy, like paradox, brings together the incommensurable in order to open up something beyond reason. Lyotard applies this distinction specifically to the question of how the unpresentable may be presented. The unified word of the expert presents a discourse of calculation in which the unpresentable may finally be presented through both progressive rational thought and the nostalgic sublime.[6] Homology "allows the unpresentable to be put forward only as the missing contents," and in the poetry of the homologous word, "the form, because of its recognizable consistency, continues to offer to the reader . . . matter for solace and pleasure" (81). However, postmodern knowledge is instead characterized by the paralogy of the poet. The poetic word is the unexpected and uncertain word which dwells within the tension of the incommensurable. In that poetic word there is the play of creativity by which the unpresentable is not simply presented as the "missing contents" of our speech that are reinscribed within the sayable, but it is approached in the midst of the world. According to the paralogy of the poet, then, the unpresentable is put forward in the act of presentation itself, a move that "denies itself the solace of good forms" and "searches for new presentations . . . in order to impart a stronger sense of the unpresentable" (81). If, according to Lyotard, the modern form of legitimation leads to narcissism and nihilism as the ends of a naturalistic and deterministic perspective, then postmodern legitimation, which is indeterminate, on-going, and ex-centric, could lead to a hopefulness *in the midst of* the limitations of our knowledge and understanding.

Warren's later work demonstrates a similar concern for the effect of the unpresentable upon human understanding under the guise of the unsayable as it is encountered both within the world and within the self. As the poet confronts the unsayable, he is bound to the paralogous word with its persistent questioning and refusal of nostalgia; at the same time, he eschews the homologous word of closure, meaning, and formula that can speak the final word of Truth. For him, the question of legitimate knowledge—a question he wrestled with throughout his career—is not answered by affirmation but by the courage to continue asking the question. The poetic word does not work from a stable given but toward language speaking through the world and through the poem itself. In "The Use of the Past," Warren rejects any means of legitimizing historical knowledge rooted in the expert's homology that would seal off the past as a self-contained and absolute entity.[7] His concern precisely for the *use* of the past bears similarities both to Lyotard's emphasis upon the necessity to tell our "little narrative [*petit récit*]" (60) and to Charles Jenck's notion of the "paradoxical dualism, or double coding" of postmodernism, in which the traditions of the past are used and simultaneously transcended (10, 14). Warren holds in contempt the idea of tradition "in the sense of formula" (47); rather, his recurring question is, "what is the legitimate use of the past?" That question sums up his concern for the character of our knowledge not only of ourselves but also of the world in which we dwell. His contempt for tradition as formula also reflects a clear incredulity toward that metanarrative of American history that would destroy the necessary sense of temporality for living in the world. Ironically, this contempt for the past is bred by a discourse that has envisioned America as a new Eden in which "the dimension of space redeemed man from the dimension of time" (32).[8] This discourse denies the relation of the self to time through an ongoing sort of nostalgia for the "Edenic moment" (36) of America's founding. "We began our great project with the notion that with the past wiped out, perfection and universal prosperity were just around the corner" (33). But Warren rejects this sort of American idealism, which "runs true from Emerson's drip-dry Christianity, with no Blood of the Lamb required, to B.F. Skinner's *Walden II*" (33). Warren's aversion to this line of thinking stems from what he perceives to be the danger of "moral narcissism": "If perfection is just around the corner, and we have the blueprint, the magic word, and a Hot Line to the Most High, who can prevail against us?" (33). For Warren, however, the importance of the study of the past is not found in any nostalgia by which the past forms the given from which the poet or individual may work. Warren rejects such nostalgia and argues instead that the past must be worked toward. Only then can the past give us a sense of time within which the self may be created.

> The past must be studied, worked at—in short, created. . . . There is no absolute, positive past available to us, no matter how rigorously we strive to determine it—as strive we must. Inevitably, the past, so far as we know it, is an inference, a creation, and this, without being paradoxical, can be said to be its chief value for us. In creating the image of the past, we create ourselves, and without that task of creating the past we might be said scarcely to exist. (51)

Warren's remarks about the creation of the self expand his earlier notions developed in "A Poem of Pure Imagination," but his emphasis here, though, stresses that "the self, of course, is never finally created" (51). The act of creation never ceases so that knowledge is never completed or totalized. There is, for Warren, no finally self-transparent identity of the self that may be found. Rather, the self is formed within the play of difference. "Without differences, any recognition of identity would be meaningless" (46). We need knowledge both of identity and difference, a knowledge that operates according to a symbolic understanding within the imagination.

> For we need difference *and* identity, fused in the thing created by the imagination, to make us comprehend imaginatively our own nature and our own plight. . . . The shifting arcades and perspectives of being and fate, the wilderness of mirrors, the ever unfolding and fluctuating ratio of identity and difference— we need these things in all their increasing complexity if we are to pursue the never-ending task of knowing the self. (46)

The kind of fusion he describes betrays the ongoing influence of Coleridge on his thought. Rather than providing the final resolution in which difference and identity melt into one, this fusion holds them together without mixture or confusion. Precisely because we cannot apprehend the fullness of identity as an infinite concept, the imagination falls back into difference, into "the wilderness of mirrors," in which there is no clear distinction between discrete object and reflection.

In 1983, Warren published *Chief Joseph of the Nez Perce* (*CP* 489–526), his last long-form poem, which, like *Audubon: A Vision* and *Brother to Dragons* before, provides an example of the poet working toward the past.[9] Warren became fascinated with the story of Chief Joseph and his band of the Nez Perce tribe in the 1930s when he visited Montana for the first time, and the dramatic character of the events captivated him just as did the life and art of Audubon.[10] It was not until the 1970s, however, that he began to work on the poem. It is significant that Warren himself drew a comparison between this poem and his work on Audubon. In an August 1980 letter to T. G. Rosenthal, publisher at Secker and Warburg in England, he describes how "for years I've been trying to do a poem about [Chief Joseph], in late years 'projecting' with something sort of like my *Audubon*—a little book. Well, I think I've hit it" (*SL* 6.52). Later that same year, he writes to Floyd C. Watkins about his work on the poem: "I knew I didn't want a straight narrative poem. I keep trying to find something like my solution for *Audubon*. Well, of late years I've hit on the solution, I hope . . ." (*SL* 6.66). In both of these works, Warren's "solution" is not so much an authoritative account of accurate detail as it is the way creative reflection on the experience of these historical figures opens up possibilities for understanding both the self and the world within "the ever unfolding and fluctuating ratio of identity and difference" ("The Use of the Past" 46). *Chief Joseph*, however, is perhaps Warren's most self-consciously constructed work; that is, this poem—more than *Audubon* or *Brother to Dragons*—foregrounds the confrontations and complications of language in an effort to create a work that qualifies as a legitimate use of the past. But it is also a work that gives itself to the reader and requires more from the reader in a way unlike most of his poetry. In this way, *Chief Joseph* approaches what Roland Barthes, in *S/Z*, calls a writerly text in which the reader is "no longer a consumer, but a producer of the text" (4). Barthes explains:

The writerly text is a perpetual present, upon which no *consequent* language (which would inevitably make it past) can be super-imposed; the writerly text is *ourselves writing*, before the infinite play of the world (the world as function) is traversed, intersected, stopped, plasticized by some singular system (Ideology, Genus, Criticism) which reduces the plurality of entrances, the opening of networks, the infinity of languages. (5)

Chief Joseph is not simply "about" a past event in its dramatic play. Rather, Warren writes in such a way that brings the experience to the present in the act of reading, providing both a plurality of entrances to the text and a sensitivity to the "infinity of languages." Terence Hawkes summarizes Barthes in this way: "*writerly* texts require us to look at the nature of language itself, not *through* it at a preordained 'real world.' They thus involve us in the dangerous, exhilarating activity of creating our world *now*, together with the author, as we go along" (*Structuralism and Semiotics* 114). Rather than constructing the poem in a way that places the writer out of view, *Chief Joseph* draws attention to the various demands that language itself makes on readers.

Warren accomplishes this by making the poem a strikingly intertextual work.[11] On one level, he does so by interspersing the narration with a variety of other texts, drawn from memoirs, journals, government reports, presidential executive orders, interviews, communiques, and an art catalog from the Metropolitan Museum of Art—none of which is a particularly "poetic" text. These introduce a variety of voices into the work as well—from civil servants to army generals, from Charles Dickens to Chief Joseph himself. Warren especially highlights the voice of Chief Joseph by casting almost half of the work in the first-person voice enclosed in quotation marks. That device creates a subtle distance between the reader and the supposed speaker, which undercuts the presumption of identity and points to the unavoidable difference between the two. Rather than being a pure speaking subject, the quotations point to the work of the poet himself. In the parts outside of those quotations, Joseph is spoken of in the third person by the other voices recorded in the text as well as by the poet himself, who appears as "I" in the final section of the poem. By placing himself as a speaking subject within the narrative, Warren acknowledges both a consciousness of the tensions of language and a self-consciousness as a writer. Reflecting on *Audubon, Brother to Dragons,* and *Chief Joseph,* Steven Ealy observes, "It is significant that Warren himself is a character in each of these poems, engaging in a process of historical recovery and creation simultaneously with poetic and self-creation" (202). Warren writes himself into the narrative as he recounts his visit to Snake Creek to see the site of the final battle, knowing the consequences that resulted from that day a century before.[12] While he describes the landscape that he saw—"Vastness of plains lifting in twilight for / Winter's cold kiss, its absoluteness" (IX.139–40)— he gives more attention to the power of the imagination to fuse identity and difference in the act of poetic creation.[13] Speaking of Chief Joseph, he writes:

> ... I,
> In fanatic imagination, saw—
> No, see—the old weapon
> Outthrust, firm in a hand that does not
> Tremble. I see lips move, but
> No sound hear. (IX.107–12)

Warren is not so much speaking about the historical figure as he is about the character who lives in his imagination as a poet. He speaks not of the past but of the present, and in this perpetual present the poet is able to articulate his own approach to the unsayable.

> ... And he—
> He strove to think of things outside
> Of Time, in some
> Great whirling sphere, like truth unnamable.... (IX.128–31)

On another level, Warren calls attention to the play of language by creating a tension within the poem between speech and writing. Specifically, there is a contrast between the speech of Joseph and his people and the written documents of the government. After the Nez Perce Cession of 1855 had been broken, Joseph describes the original agreement as "mist in dawn wind" (I.103) that burns away to nothing. Even when President Grant, whom Joseph describes as "the Great White Father," ordered in 1873 the original boundaries established in that cession to be honored, Joseph says that this word "faded like mist in the day's heat" (I.106, 109). The second section begins with a piercing question about the validity of such writing.

> But what is a piece of white paper, ink on it?
> What if the Father, though great, be fed
> On lies only, and seeks not to know what
> Truth is, or cannot tell Truth from Lie?

So tears up the paper of Truth, and the liars,
Behind their hands, grin, while he writes a big Lie? (II.1–6)

Later, when Chief Joseph agrees to sign the treaty that will remove them from their home in Wallowa, he says, "'For now you know what a treaty is— / Black marks on white paper, black smoke in the air'" (II.82–83). At the council with General Howard and his army representatives, Joseph stands to speak, struggling to find words of wisdom, but then hears the voice of his deceased father.

'Oh, who will speak!' Cried the heart in my bosom.
'Speak for the Nimipu, and speak Truth!'

"But then, my heart, it heard
My father's voice, like a great sky-cry
From snow-peaks in sunlight, and my voice
Was saying the Truth that no
White man can know. . . . " (II.100–06)

In Joseph's understanding, writing cannot communicate Truth but can only deceive. Rather, Truth may only be spoken and that by virtue of what is beyond language itself—his father who is not present. By setting up this opposition, Warren is tapping into a long-standing discourse on speech and writing central to the Western metaphysical tradition. Derrida identifies this as one of the central binary oppositions that has driven Western thought, in which speech is given priority over writing because of its sense of the presence of the speaker.[14] This is in part the point made by Socrates in his discourse with Phaedrus, when he argues that the written word is but an "image," like a painting, of the "living and breathing word" in the speaker (*Phaedrus* 567). Socrates likens writing to a "garden of letters," planted for the amusement of the writer "to treasure up reminders for himself, when he comes to the forgetfulness of old age, and for others who follow the same path" (569). He goes on to argue that "serious discourse . . . is far nobler" (569).

But the man . . . who thinks that only in words about justice and beauty and goodness spoken by teachers for the sake of instruction and really written in a soul is clearness and perfection and serious value, that such words should be considered the speaker's own legitimate offspring, first the word within himself, if it be found there, and secondly its descendants or brothers which may have sprung up in worthy manner in the souls of others, and who pays no attention to the other words,—that man, Phaedrus, is likely to be such as you and I might pray that we ourselves become. (573–75)

Of course the irony within this text is that these "spoken" words are communicated to the reader because Plato wrote them, undercutting the very opposition that Socrates posits. Warren's text appears to be aware of this very irony as it relates to language and the creation of the self. His use of extended quotation to communicate the voice of Joseph alerts the reader to this very tension. *Chief Joseph* is not so much about privileging speech over writing as it is about the inescapable problems of language and the struggle for articulation, which for Warren is distinct from direct speech. Whether dealing with Chief Joseph or with General Howard, Warren is grappling with the same tension he encountered throughout his poetry: the limits as well as the power of language.

Chief Joseph is also one of Warren's texts that has a particular apophatic quality about it, both in its encounter with the unsayable and in its encounters with the boundary of death. In Denys Turner's estimation, "The apophatic is the linguistic strategy of somehow showing by means of language that which lies beyond language" (qtd. in Franke, *A Philosophy of the Unsayable* 152). This is Warren's strategy in a poem that does not simply narrate history but creates an entrance to what is beyond the narrative itself. It is much like the way he describes the struggle of the writer against "the great creators of the past" ("The Use of the Past" 47). "He is like Jacob, who wrestled the angel all night in the place to be called Peniel and, though at the break of day he received the mystic wound in the thigh, would not let go of the mysterious stranger until he had exacted the blessing he craved and could say that he had 'seen God face to face'" (47). The poem becomes both a place and a moment in which writer and reader alike must wrestle with what the language itself points to. And when reading becomes wrestling, there is a blessing to be found. In *Chief Joseph*, that blessing is found in the encounter with death. One of the formative moments for Joseph is the death of his father, Old Joseph, and his dying words to his son. From beyond death, Old Joseph is able to see what cannot be seen: " . . . sees / The shadow of thought in my heart—the lie / The heel must crush" (II.31–33). There is something fundamental in his language, alluding to both the temptation in the Garden of Eden and the promise that the serpent's head would be crushed by the seed of the woman (Genesis 3:15). This is what Joseph understands to be the "Wisdom" that his father has entered into through death (II.34). Later, as Joseph approaches his own death, he remembers his father and looks to him for some justification for what he has done and been as a man (VII.29–34, 40–42). Warren carries that same desire into the final lines of the last section in which he imagines his return "into the squirming throng, faceless to facelessness" (IX.153), where some stranger pauses on a crowded street corner when the light turns green and the mob rushes past him. He wonders if the stranger looks,

> ... standing paralyzed in his momentary eternity, into
> His own heart ... while he asks
> From what undefinable distance, years, and direction,
> Eyes of fathers are suddenly fixed on him. To know. (IX.161–64)

This stranger, like Joseph, looks for some justification from beyond himself of his life as a men among men. With a certain degree of irony, Warren ends the poem with his own sort of ontological pause.

> I turned to my friend Quammen, the nearer. Called:
> "It's getting night, and a hell of a way
> To go." We went,
> And did not talk much on the way. (165–168)

The poem brings the reader to the edge of darkness and silence as the entrance to what lies beyond it. Warren says in "The Use of the Past" that the past "is the tonic for self-pity," because "it tells us that we, too, shall soon be part of the past" (52–53). Poetry and history alike bring us to that boundary of death where what lies beyond language speaks.

Like the rest of Warren's later poetry, *Chief Joseph* presents the increasing complexity and the ever-unfolding quality of difference that is necessary for understanding. Just as poetry provides a means of pursuing this "never-ending task of knowing the self" ("The Use of the Past" 46), so it furnishes the moment in which the poet may approach the unsayable through persistent questioning and openness. Such poetry does not use form as a means to achieve closure but strives for a dis-closure through continual and new presentations of the unpresentable. Throughout Warren's later poetry, there is this ongoing repetition of the moment—not the recollection of some absolute and origi-nating moment, but the repetition of moments at the boundaries of experi-ence. The word of the poet is that paralogous word beyond calculation and that functions through questioning to move us as readers to the boundaries of being. The poet, then, is that man described in Heidegger's "A Dialogue on Language":

> *I:* Man is the message-bearer of the message which the two-fold's uncon-cealment speaks to him.
>
> . . . .
>
> *I:* Then, man, as the message-bearer of the message of the two-fold's un-concealment, would also be he who walks the boundary of the boundless.
>
> *J:* And on this path he seeks the boundary's mystery . . .
>
> *I:* . . . which cannot be hidden in anything other than the voice that determines and tunes his nature. (41)[15]

In Heidegger's vocabulary, the "two-fold" hearkens to what he considered the originating issue of philosophy—that is, the difference between being and be-ings, a difference never overcome nor resolved in identity.[16] Heidegger insists that language defines the hermeneutic relation between man and the two-fold as it shows itself in what he calls "the presence of present-beings" (30). In the apocalyptic moment of the unconcealment of this relation, then, it is language that speaks. The poet is the message-bearer who walks along this boundary of the boundless hidden in language itself. And it is language that is the voice that determines and tunes the nature of the poet. For Heidegger and Warren alike, the poem is this moment of unconcealment—this apocalyptic moment—that brings us up against that mysterious boundary time and again and reveals to us the boundary of our own death. This is what Warren consid-ers to be an important use of the past: it reminds us of our own mortality by telling "us that we, too, shall soon be part of the past" (53).

When William Spanos wrote his introductory essay for the volume *Martin Heidegger and the Question of Literature* (1979), he perceived that he was writ-ing in a literary critical context still governed by "the continuing authority of the formalist interpretive orientation of the New Criticism in literary stud-ies and broader semiotic contexts" (xv). He perceived that even then in 1979

New Critical formalism was "an authority in the process of being" and that it was not superseded by but was being "theoretically shored up by Structuralist poetics" (xv). In this context, he describes a postmodern poetics—schooled in Heidegger's concern for time and language—which is marked by "experiments in open, or, as I prefer to call them, 'dis-closive' or 'de-structive,' forms of much of the most dynamic and powerful contemporary writing; forms whose mastered irony assigns us as readers to ourselves and activates rather than nullifies consciousness of being-in-the-world as our *case*" (xv). Although Warren is typically associated by contemporary criticism with "the formalist interpretive orientation of the New Criticism," his later poetry is undoubtedly marked by these very "postmodern" characteristics described by Spanos. In his final volume, *Altitudes and Extensions 1980–1984*, Warren repeatedly presses the boundary of the boundless and self-consciously brings the matter of the unsayable to the forefront.[17] This is a poetry that dwells in a radically temporalized space and resists closure by persisting in an openness to and an expectancy for the speaking of language in its approach to the unsayable. No longer does form provide sufficient solace in the presence of the unsayable, nor can structure wrestle time into its boundaries. Instead, Warren works out a poetics that often subverts structure and form through what Spanos calls the "generous measure" (xii). It is a poetry of "mastered irony" that reveals its own limitations and possibilities, and in so doing, it assigns us as readers to ourselves. This is something that Warren emphasizes in *Democracy and Poetry* and reiterates in "The Use of the Past"; the acts of poetic creation and of reading poetry enact a plunge into the abyss of the self for poet and reader alike. But Warren follows Henri Bergson in suggesting that the power of the work is that, in the abyss, it returns us to ourselves, "into our own presence."[18] Within the abyss—the fissure or *Riß*, to use Heidegger's term—poet and reader alike encounter the moment of possibility.[19] Returned and assigned, the reader is then engaged in an on-going participation of being-in-the-world.

Such poetics of exploration must be understood as a mode of calling into question and dis-covering (as an uncovering). Heidegger described this sort of searching out activity in "A Dialogue on Language": what we need is "to give heed to the trails that direct thinking back into the region of its source" (37). He emphasizes that these trails may not be found in our own attempt. Rather, "I *find* them only because they are *not* of my own making, and are discernible only quite rarely, like the wind-borne echo of a distant call" (37).

Warren's later poetics searches out these trails, which lead back into the region of poetry's source, language itself. These trails are not of the poet's own making but are announced to him by the voice of the world. However, neither do these trails lead back to what Warren calls an "absolute, positive past" ("The Use of the Past" 51) or what Spanos describes as "an absolute or privileged origin" ("Heidegger, Kierkegaard, and the Hermeneutic Circle" 122). Instead, these trails are the *Holzwege* described by Heidegger, which lead into that forest that is the "region of its source" and soon disseminate among the trees.[20] According to Miller, "a *Holzweg* is a woodcutter's path that goes into the forest and stops, peters out. It is not a way to get from here to some definite 'there'" (*Illustration* 84). The trails are working toward what might be revealed as language reveals itself in the poem.

Altitudes and Extensions includes several poems that lead the reader repeatedly to that uneasy edge between the sayable and the unsayable, that continually shifting nonsite where the process of generation never ceases or is overcome. They provide an entrance to the boundary of the boundless, or to the *eschatia*, which is the furthest part of being and the verge of understanding. This boundary, though, is not found in some indefinite "out there" beyond the concreteness dwelling in the world; rather it is found within the concrete actualities of being in the world. The boundless is encountered within the bounds of the bounded. The volume begins with "Three Darknesses" (*CP* 529–30), a tripartite poem perched at this eschatological edge that welcomes the reader to plunge in and confront the darkness of the abyss from three possible perspectives.[21] The first poem of this sequence is ironic, though, in that it begins at the end, only to fall back upon the supposed innocence of childhood and memory. The poem begins at the limit of the poet's thought:

> There is some logic here to trace, and I
> Will try hard to find it. But even as I begin, I
> Remember one Sunday morning, festal with springtime, in
> The zoo of Rome. (1–4)

The poem begins at both a moment and a place simply called "here," which is not located in the zoo of Rome nor in the poet's mind but is announced in the poem itself. Here is both everywhere and nowhere. This place, however, is not spatially isolated from time, locked in timelessness; it is defined temporally as the poetic moment of being in the world. Within the space of the poetic moment, we are brought to the edge of the unpresentable, the end at which the poet hopes to find the logic he might trace out in order to provide a sort of wisdom for being in the world. Behind this willful statement—"There *is* some logic here to trace . . ."—there is a yearning for identity and resolution, for that final place in which the poet may find the absolute origin. But as the poet approaches this edge of understanding and experience, there is the engagement of the self through the imaginative enactment, " . . . and I / Will try hard to find it. But. . . ." But human effort cannot find the essential place beyond space and time; the human imagination fails to find the final logic. Such an inevitable failure, however, does not result in passivity for the poet but actively engages him in grasping after whatever traces of meaning and truth might be found through experience in the world.

As soon as the poet attempts to approach final meaning in identity, he is thrown back upon difference, and there is an unending deferral of meaning even as he attempts to name the unnameable. The poet can name neither the logic of his own existence nor the place in which such a logic might be found. But the weight of the unnameable bears so heavily upon the poet and the presence of the unsayable compels him to speak. As in "Passers-By On Snowy Night" (*CP* 439), the poet may not name the logic after which he seeks but may only name the journey he must pursue as he walks in the world. In this way, the poet gives heed to the trails that direct thinking back into the region of its source. He pursues these trails, though, not at the outer limit of his logic but in the moment of concrete experience. As he tries hard to find this logic, he is thrown back into the world on a springtime Sunday morning in the zoo of Rome. Through the poet's relation to the world in language, he is able to begin searching out the vestige or trace of this logic. Within the world, the unsayable announces itself through the rhythmic beating of the bear against the iron door.

> . . . Minute by minute, near, far,
> Wheresoever we wandered, all Sunday morning,
> With the air full of colored balloons trying to escape
> From children, the ineluctable
> Rhythm continues. You think of the
> Great paws like iron on iron. Can iron bleed?
> Since my idiot childhood the world has been

Trying to tell me something. There is something
Hidden in the dark. The bear
Was trying to enter into the darkness of wisdom. (11–20)

As in *Audubon*, the poet finds that "the world declares itself," speaking of its own mystery. The poet must listen for what may be brought to light in the act of poetic creation as the voice of language is heard in the midst of the world. It is the sound of the bear's slugging against this iron door that follows the poet throughout the poem; its sound and rhythm are "ineluctable." He cannot escape the repetition of the beating, just as the poet cannot escape the repetition of moments in which he presses the boundary. This repetition does not look back, though, but is the forward-looking movement generated by a yearning for the other.[22] Even so, the confrontation with the borders of our knowledge and understanding are inescapable, and in this poem the imagination provides the notion of its own failure.

The exploration of the poetic moment in "Three Darknesses: I" follows the movement of Kant called the "imaginative regress." In "Sublimity and Theatricality: Romantic 'Pre-Postmodernism' in Schiller and Coleridge," Linda Marie Brooks examines that aspect of Kant's notion of the sublime in which the "reconciling or connecting function of the imagination . . . fails," so that what remains "is the component of the imagination that makes no attempt to draw relations, that does not connect or reconcile randomness but simply engages it, unordered, in all its chaos" (945). While Coleridge's notion of the imagination is distinct from Kant's formulation, it does bear some important similarities to Kant's description of the "imaginative regress." In the moment of regress, the imagination confronts its own inability to fully apprehend the "manifold" character of being or reality and, after halting this effort to apprehend infinity, the imagination within a single moment comprehends multiplicity in such a way that it "is able to contain or circumscribe a type of whole, an entirety in which all the discrete entities of phenomena can be 'intuited,' in Kant's words, to 'coexist'" (946). Coleridge's description of the imagination and the symbol makes it clear that, because the imagination, unlike the fancy, recognizes this limit, the symbol becomes this means of engaging the unordered chaos. The symbol is a means by which the poet engages difference, and if there is to be understanding, then this engagement with difference is not only necessary but "ineluctable." This is the possibility presented by Warren's poetry. But this is not a possibility that resides in specific symbols; thus, our concern has not been Warren's use of specific symbols throughout his poetry. Rather, the possibility that his poetry offers rests painfully in the symbolic understanding, which is characterized by recurring moments of engaging difference through imaginative regress.

Within the symbolic moment, the imagination grasps the multiplicity of experience. Warren describes the imagination in a similar way in "A Poem of Pure Imagination": "The symbol affirms the unity of mind in the welter of experience; it is a device for making that welter of experience manageable for the mind—graspable. It represents a focus of being and is not a mere sign ..." (352). It is important that Warren does not speak of the "unity of experience" but instead of the "unity of mind" in the midst of the seemingly random or chaotic nature of experience. The symbolic moment is, for Warren, a particular "focus of being." Coleridge's formulation of the symbol, then, does not present a unified whole of apprehended infinity but presents what in postmodern discourse is called an aporetic moment: it does not unite but brings into light the gaps and breakdowns of language and understanding. Even here, though, the formulation of the aporetic moment must be seen as a radically metaphorical construction that grasps at the unsayable. As Linda Marie Brooks points out, following Rudolphe Gasché, "What is seen in this moment of imaginative regress is the 'unseeable'" (946). And Warren repeatedly stands in his later poetry as a witness to the unseeable and unpresentable.

In "Mortal Limit" (*CP* 530–31), the second poem of *Altitudes and Extensions*, Warren continues to explore the way that poetry takes the reader to the edge of the abyss in the symbolic moment of grappling with difference. This poem returns to familiar territory for Warren as he envisions the hawk set against the sunset sky. The limit that the poet confronts in this poem is that *eschatia* of language itself.

> I saw the hawk ride updraft in the sunset over Wyoming.
> It rose from coniferous darkness, past gray jags
> Of mercilessness, past whiteness, into the gloaming
> Of dream-spectral light about the last purity of snow-snags.
>
> There—west—were the Tetons. Snow-peaks would soon be
> In dark profile to break constellations. Beyond what height

Hangs now the black speck? Beyond what range will gold eyes see
New ranges rise to mark a last scrawl of light? (1–8)

The poem follows the hawk's motion of rising in the first stanza and reaching the mortal limit in the second. Within this motion, the poem confronts the tension of the world, as this moment stands poised between day and night and between darkness and light. This is not a moment of recollection but one of repetition. The hawk rises from the "coniferous darkness" of the landscape, floats past the "gray jags" of the mountains, and even passes "whiteness" and "purity" before reaching "the gloaming / Of dream-spectral light" of the twilit sky. At the peak of its upward motion, though, the hawk does not experience the pure identity of vision but has a view of difference: its vision is bounded by the horizon of snow-peaks that are discernible because of the their dark profile against the star-light. Even the farthest point within this vision is marked by the scrawl of light. As it reaches the moment of mortal limit, the hawk finds itself in that place where it might have a wider vision, but to remain in this place would mean its death.

Or, having tasted that atmosphere's thinness, does it
Hang motionless in dying vision before
It knows it will accept the mortal limit,
And swing into the great circular downwardness that will restore

The breath of earth? Of rock? Of rot? Of other such
Items, and the darkness of whatever dream we clutch? (9–14)

The moment of turning is the very moment of the "dying vision." In that place, the atmosphere is thin and tastes not of immortality but of mortality—death. The eschatological moment, then, is a moment that both reaches to the uppermost limits and falls into the lowest depths. It can take the reader to the uttermost point where, after all saying has ceased, all that can be presented is the unpresentable. And in this confrontation there is a returning to a possible new understanding. This motion toward the *eschatia* and then falling away back from it is similar to what John Burt calls "a simultaneous evasion and experience of primary truth" (112) in Warren's poetry. But that truth is what may not be named or spoken; it may be known only in death. This is the same limit that Warren confronts in the unnameable. Death is the horizon of being but it is also the ultimate moment of ripeness or of turning. It is a fullness that is also a consummation.

The mortal limit confronted by the hawk is the same limit that the poet confronts when presented with the unsayable and the unpresentable; and, like the hawk, the poet too is turned back to "swing in that great circular downwardness. . . ." The hawk does not take what Coleridge calls the *salto mortale* into some existence beyond "the gloaming / Of dream-spectral light above the last purity of snow-snags," but somersaults back into the material world. Coleridge wrote in his *Notebook* of the tendency for the imagination to continue adding description upon description "and as if to hide from itself its perpetual failure . . . it takes the *salto mortale*, and vaults at once into the transcendental Idea of Infinity" (3.4047).[23] Linda Marie Brooks argues that Coleridge's notion here is ironic and that, similar to Kant's notion of the sublime, his notion has in view a sort of regressive move. She describes Kant's notion in this way:

> Instead of soaring *up*ward in some transcendental flight toward the "supersensible," toward some *im*material "truth" decreed by Reason as the "ground" of thought—Wholeness, Unity, Coexistence and the like, as Kant had expected—the subject vaults, in a kind of regressive somersault or *salto mortale*, into the non-rational "substrate" or incomprehensible materiality of the negative sublime. (949)

The poet's vision is not some soaring flight into the transcendental or into identity; it is a dying vision that confronts his own finite existence with the insurmountability and intractability of the world in which he walks. In such a vision, then, what is the substance of poetry itself? It is the radical materiality of life found in the concreteness of language. And it is this experience of his own limit at his own death and in the death of language that provides the grounds for his speaking in the world. It is a vision not of the blessedness of immateriality but of the possibility of understanding rooted in materiality. In Warren's vision, this *salto mortale* can be restorative within the fallen and finite experience of reader and poet, but there are limits to what can be restored. What is restored to the hawk is the breath of earth, rock, rot, and other elements of this darkness in which we live. Among these concrete elements of a fallen world, the poet must find traces of the unpresentable and vestiges of the unsayable. In this way, the eschatological moment in Warren's poetry is also an apocalyptic moment; at the borders, there is a pulling back of the veil so that we see our experience for what it is, even if that is "the darkness of whatever dream we clutch."

"Mortal Limit" also illustrates another critical shift in Warren's understanding of poetry and language. While modernist poetry would not deny or reject these claims about the unpresentable or the mortal limit, it functions according to a formalism in which poetic structure might erase the boundary of the unsayable so that there might be the communication of truth. However, in this poem, the poet rejects any effort to traverse this mortal limit by attempting to cancel it through word-play or poetic structure. He refuses the nostalgia of good forms that would contain truth through statements about language and the unsayable. But this would only be a transgression of the limit. Warren manifests the poet's confrontation with the "mortal limit" of language even in the formal structure of the poem by allowing content to subvert form. In effect, Warren defamiliarizes the familiar form of the sonnet. The poem follows the pattern of an Elizabethan sonnet in its rhyme scheme and in its division into quatrains, and yet this use of the sonnet form displays the poet's mastered irony: this "constructive" structure designed for the communication of meaning is not able to sustain the poem as it becomes de-structive and collapses in on itself. The language here is what it says it is: the mortal limit. Rather than ending with a final solution to the problem raised, the poem closes with a dark question that returns us to ourselves. The form is deceptive; though there is the positive element in the rhyming of the lines, this is subverted by the question that the poet asks. Here Warren uses form as a negative means of communication, turning upside down the concern among early Formalists and Symbolists with what Hawkes describes as "form as a viable communicative instrument" (60). If Warren's use of the sonnet form is an instance of the sublime, then it is a presentation of the negative sublime. The presentation of the unpresentable is not attempted by supplying what Lyotard calls "the missing contents." Rather, it is only present in its absence, named only as the unnameable. The mortal limit remains.

In light of the claims Warren makes about the act of poetic creation, we may make certain concomitant claims about the act of reading. Reading takes us to that place of the dying vision where the atmosphere is thin and we stand motionless before the mortal limit. We are taken to the verge of our understanding and ability. In this act of reading we are confronted with a paradox: in death do we find life, in the emptying of ourselves do we find fullness. The poem returns us to ourselves by bringing us as readers to the edge of this abyss and reading becomes a plunge into this abyss. But Warren does not see this plunge as nihilistic; rather it offers the possibility of the celebration of life itself. As in the act of poetic creation, the symbolic moment in our reading is one that simultaneously shapes and dissolves, or, to borrow another phrase from Coleridge, one that "fixing unfixes" (*CN* 3.4066). This eschatological moment is also an apocalyptic one in which what is buried may be uncovered, and in this uncovering there is a celebration of life. The dying vision has the power to give new life to our understanding. Upon this view of reading, though, it is not the reader who operates upon the text, but the text that "reads" the reader. Warren states this more explicitly in "A Poem of Pure Imagination": "...We may say that the reader does not interpret the poem but the poem interprets the reader. We may say that the poem is the light and not the thing seen by the light. The poem is the light by which the reader may view and review all the areas of experience with which he is acquainted" (347). The reading of poetry, then, becomes this simultaneous and paradoxical moment of blessing and cursing that Warren observes in the poet's act of creation in *The Ancient Mariner*. To have your experience interpreted by the poem necessarily involves both a blessing and a cursing, that is, a consecration of life in the world and an affliction of the knowledge of the reader's own fallen and finite ability. In the apocalypse of reading, there is an unveiling of the incommensurate relationship of our yearning to our ability; our yearning far outweighs our ability. But it is an activity that calls for response as well; in the apocalyptic quality there is an implied ethic, a call to live willfully and not passively. As Warren says in *Democracy and Poetry*, poetry "demands participation" through "imaginative enactment" (89), calling on the reader to participate through a sort of sacramental engagement.

The significance of Warren's contribution toward contemporary thought about language and poetics does not lie in his having formed a new linguistic philosophy or in the claim to have developed a new principle of poetic creation. Rather the significance is found in the poetry itself and in the way that it calls into question our notions of language and our understanding of "being here" in the world. Warren does this in "The Whole Question" (*CP* 566), a poem that moves from birth to age as it longs for a language that can enact the unsayable. The speaker begins by challenging the reader with the question of being:

> You'll have to rethink the whole question. This
> Getting born business is not as simple as it seemed,

Or midwife thought, or doctor deemed. It is,
Time shows, more complicated than either—or you—ever dreamed.
    (1–4)

As in "Three Darknesses," the poet begins at the edge of the boundless, which
is being itself. But after voicing his sense of urgent need "to rethink the whole
question," there is a similar motion of imaginative regress: from the ultimate
question, he does not make the death leap into the infinite but is thrown back
upon the concrete materiality of existence within space and time. The poet
finds, however, that the question of being leads to the question of language. To
rethink what is real leads one to the source of understanding the real, which is
language in all of its concreteness. So Warren explores here the inadequacies
and possibilities of language. On the one hand, it is the limitations of language that make it necessary to rethink the whole question. Throughout the
poem, the speaker highlights the ways that we use language to try to nail down
concepts of being, but he recognizes that language cannot be nailed down in
order to fulfill his yearning for a final answer. In the second stanza, he alludes
to "what Paul called the body of this death" (8). In the third, he speaks of "the
terrible thing called love" (9) and describes how the infant's twisted face is
"called" a smile (12). In these early stanzas, the poet is calling into question
the ability of language to provide an adequate understanding of experience
in the world by raising the problematic of referentiality. The poet's emphasis
upon naming and calling has to do with the referential quality of language,
but reference does not answer the question that he is asking. There is the sense
in each of these statements that the reference always goes wide of the mark.
The poet has a deep sense of the *hamartia* of language in its fallen and finite
condition.[24] In light of the instability of reference, one cannot, then, attempt
to understand his being in the world by virtue of vocabulary or diction. The
accumulation of words still leaves you with nothing:

You noticed how faces from outer vastness might twist, too.
But sometimes different twists, with names unknown,
And there were noises with no names you knew,
And times of dark silence when you seemed nothing—or gone. (13–16)

Though the speaker may know more words, he cannot avoid the "times of dark
silence" in which the presence of nothing announces to him the weightlessness
of such accumulation of words. "You knew more words, but they were words

only, only— / Metaphysical midges that plunged at the single flame / That centered the infinite dark of your skull . . . " (18–20). This negative presence persists through the years under the realization that words are only words. In this instance language collapses in its own apocalypse as it plunges "at the single flame" of the mind. This sense of nothing, though, is countered by the seeping in of the dawn light and the humming of the tires. Clearly, the poem refuses to become nostalgic about language and experience.

One way the poet could rethink "the whole question" would be to invoke the expert's homology—to return to Lyotard's terms—by which he could then make the move to absolutizing thought, especially thought about language. This would be a return to the logocentrism of metaphysics. But such a return would have the effect of destroying experience. To absolutize would end in death. Coleridge makes a similar point in his reading of Schelling, rejecting the way in which Schelling makes nature absolute by reducing multëity to that which may be thought rather than remaining at the level of the imagination. Coleridge writes, "It cannot be thought—the thought would destroy, annihilate. Annihilation of all reality would be the consequence" (*CN* 3.4449). It is the imagination, though, that can grasp in the symbolic moment the plenitude of multëity without annihilating it in an absolutizing thought. But this moment is not the timeless and ego-centric measure of an earlier modernist poetics; rather, it is the moment in which the self is decentered in what Spanos calls "the ec-centric measure of mortality" (xiv). Even so, Warren here brings the reader to the edge of the absolute without jumping into an absolutizing language and can only fall back on the limitations of language. Rather than acquiescing to a metaphysics as presence that secures and defines reference between word and experience, Warren moves toward a sort of Heideggerian overcoming of metaphysics that "leaves behind the aesthetics that is grounded in metaphysics" ("A Dialogue on Language" 42).

Joan Stambaugh notes, however, in her translation of Heidegger's essay, "Overcoming Metaphysics," that "overcoming" has the sense of incorporating instead of defeating or leaving behind. "Thus, to overcome metaphysics would mean to incorporate metaphysics, perhaps with the hope, but not with the certainty, of elevating it to a new reality."[25] Warren's poetic vision overcomes his earlier formalistic concerns and suggests a certain amount of hope for the possibilities of language and articulation. By openly grasping the limitations of language, he avoids the inevitable annihilation brought about by a nostalgia for a sort of innocent language untouched by experience. His hope, though, is precisely a poetic hope—that poetry can provide the moment of a possible means of recovery through language. Such a recovery would not be a recapturing of a lost linguistic innocence, nor would it be a mere rehabilitation of our own fallen language. The recovery would come from the power of fallen language to bring us to the edge of the unpresentable and to provide a sort of momentary but real redemption. The hope that pervades his final stanza is not simply ironic—although it certainly involves paradox—but it is a hope vested in poetry itself.

> Yes, you must try to rethink what is real. Perhaps
> It is only a matter of language that traps you. You
> May yet find a new one in which experience overlaps
> Words. Or find some words that make the Truth come true. (25–28)

As the previous stanzas reveal, it is precisely the limitations of language that trap us and bar us from any absolute and pure origin of identity. It is language that obstructs any *final* rethinking of the real. But such a situation does not negate the necessity to *try* to rethink what is real, for language offers the possibility and the hope of being brought back again and again to the unsayable that makes speaking or articulation possible. Warren's hope here seems to point again to the consummating and apocalyptic moment of death in which we will find that language in which experience overlaps words. In that moment, we will find that death is the word which makes "the Truth come true."

The poet must continue to speak, undeterred by the confines of a fallen language. Like the Mariner of Coleridge's poem, he seeks that place of articulation that is rooted in a "woful agony" but compels him to speak. The agony of language is inescapable if one is to be able to speak; just as the agony provided for the Mariner the "strange power of speech," so for the poet it provides his moment of rejoicing that is the moment of articulation. The burden of this agony is its insatiable quality; language will ever strive outward. But, the agony affords a moment of hope and possibility as well. The poet is also like the Wedding Guest in that same poem, who

> went like one that hath been stunned,
> And is of sense forlorn:
> A sadder and wiser man,
> He rose the morrow morn." (*The Rime of the Ancient Mariner* 58)

Stunned by the inevitable limits of language, he is nonetheless a "wiser man" who has learned that he may no longer speak *about* language. Heidegger makes this point in "A Dialogue on Language":

> *I:* Speaking *about* language turns language almost inevitably into an object.
>
> *J:* And then its reality vanishes.
>
> *I:* We then have taken up a position about language, instead of hearing from it.
>
> *J:* Then there would only be a speaking *from* language . . .
>
> *I:* . . . in this manner, that it would be called *from out of language's* reality, and be led *to* its reality. (50–51)

The danger of letting language become an object of thought and speech is that our understanding of reality—not simply the reality of language—vanishes, for both Warren and Heidegger presuppose that language defines the relation of our being in the world. But the position of the poet must be one of humility in which he listens to language and he speaks from its reality so that he might be led back to the region of the source of thinking. In this way, Heidegger calls for the very thing that Warren yearns for: saying, in the sense of letting language show itself, letting it appear and shine, letting it insinuate itself in the articulation of the poet.[26]

In the final poem of *Altitudes and Extensions*, "Myth of Mountain Sunrise" (*CP* 584), Warren seems to have heard that wind-borne call of the voice of the world and to have followed the trail announced by that call back to the region of poetry's source. He comes in these lines to a moment of articulation, that moment toward which the poet has striven. But in this moment, it is not so much the poet who speaks as it is language itself. This poem opens up the time of language's own saying in which it brings to light truth in the event of its own speaking. Frances Bixler helpfully points out Warren's careful placement of this poem as the final selection in *Altitudes and Extensions*. By placing it after "Sunset" (*CP* 583), these two poems appear to be "companion poems" that elucidate Warren's characteristic dark/light contrast (95). In each of these, the reader is brought to the borders of experience as Warren continues to subvert any notions of beginning and ending. Whereas the first two poems of this collection brought us, as a beginning, to the end of logic

("Three Darknesses: I") and to the edge of the day at sunset ("Mortal Limit"), so here the poet approaches an ending in "Sunset," which is overturned by an apocalyptic beginning in "Myth of Mountain Sunrise." The more striking contrast between the two poems is found, however, in the distinction between the poet's striving to speak his own name in "Sunset" ("Who knows his own name at the last? / How shall he speak to a soul that has none?" [19–20]) and the outward bulging and announcing character of language itself in "Myth of Mountain Sunrise." In the former poem, we overhear the yearning of the poet for a way to speak, for a place in which he can articulate his own being. He longs to know his name so that he might speak "in a dire hour," and yet this name appears as the unpresentable. But this contrast is made clear in the absence of the poet's "I" in the latter poem. The cry voiced in "Myth of Mountain Sunrise" comes from language through the world.

> Prodigious, prodigal, crags steel-ringing
> To dream-hoofs nightlong, proverbial
> Words stone-incised in language unknowable, but somehow singing
> Their wisdom-song against disaster of granite and all
> Moonless non-redemption on the left hand of dawn:
> The mountain dimly wakes, stretches itself on windlessness. Feels its
>   deepest chasm, waking, yawn. (1–7)[27]

In the sunrise, the unsayable approaches the poet as he discerns the saying of language in the voice of the world, sensing that this concrete utterance gives what he is unable to articulate. This is not a language posited upon reference or representation but upon the power of language itself in the function of the pure imagination—what Coleridge called the verbal imagination. This poem does not refer to any single mountain or to some extra-verbal notion of mountain-ness; rather, it creates and transfigures a world as a possibility. This is a poem of concrete images in which the language is what it says.

This prodigious and prodigal poem is an instance of a sacramental moment in which the language, the reader, and experience participate together in striving toward the unnameable. Warren suggests something similar in some of the opening lines of *Audubon*, in which the artist sees

> Eastward and over the cypress swamp, the dawn,
> Redder than meat, break;
> And the large bird,

> Long neck outthrust, wings crooked to scull air, moved
> In a slow calligraphy, crank, flat, and black against
> The color of God's blood spilt, as though
> Pulled by a string. (I[A].6–12)

The calligraphy of the heron inscribed upon God's spilt blood is transformed here in "Myth of Mountain Sunrise" into the wisdom-song of joy sung by the mountain. Just as the heron in *Audubon* appears to be writing what has already been written, so Warren presents here the vision of a language already written and already spoken in the concrete existence of the mountain. The mountain is brought into being by "proverbial / Words stone-incised in language unknowable. . . ." In this mountain, we see what Coleridge called the coïnherence of act and being (*CN* 4.4644). But this coïnherence sustains a tension between the sayable and the unsayable: these crags of the mountain are etched out in a "language unknowable," but they are "somehow singing / Their wisdom-song. . . ." The poet is a witness to that audible song, which eludes his comprehension, which cannot be reduced to thought. Even the song of the mountain participates in a sort of imaginative regress that cannot transcend the agony of the fallen creation; it cannot lift its voice beyond but is uttered against and amidst the disaster and nonredemption. The song is a negative utterance "against disaster of granite and all / Moonless nonredemption on the left hand of dawn." In this tension, the act of speaking and the condition of being inhere in the same moment; if the poet questions the one, then he must question the other.

The second stanza presents a sort of yearning similar to what it encountered in "Sunset," but here it is the agony of the mountain's inwardness that "strives dayward," as darkness moving toward light.

> The curdling agony of interred dark strives dayward, in stone strives
>   though
> No light here enters, has ever entered but
> In ageless age of primal flame. But look! All mountains want slow-
> ly to bulge outward extremely. The leaf, whetted on light, will cut
> Air like butter. Leaf cries: "I feel my deepest filament in dark rejoice.
> I know that the density of basalt has a voice." (7–12)

Inasmuch as the language is what it says—if the mountain cannot be divided from the language in the poem—then it is language that participates in this agony of outwardness. Language strives in its own "curdling agony of interred dark," wanting to slowly bulge outward. Even the poet's line cannot contain this outward bulging, as the word "slowly" breaks into pieces within the text's terrain. The mountain's yearning is given voice in the cry of the leaf, which, being one with the mountain and earth, feels its "deepest filament" rejoice in the dark agony of the mountain, paralleling the mountain feeling its "deepest chasm … yawn" at the end of the first stanza. The leaf "whetted on light," however, does not rejoice in that light but in the consummation of the mountain's striving in its own entrance into the brightness of dawn. The agony and the voice of the mountain find their destiny in the cry of the leaf: "I know that the density of basalt has a voice." But, if what is envisioned here is the yearning of language itself, then the agony of language find its voice and destiny in the agony of the poet, who feels his "deepest filament in dark rejoice" and who knows the density of the darkness within language. The poet perceives how language resists being contained within thought but wants to give outness to thought; he knows the slow but extreme outward bulging of language. And, like the leaf, the poet cries out in the midst of the world. The poet carries with him the agony of words and of language, which is displayed in a simultaneous burden and hope.

In the final section of "Myth of Mountain Sunrise," the poet turns to the powerful effect of this outward movement from dark to light.

> How soon will the spiderweb, dew-dappled, gleam
> In Pompeian glory! Think of a girl-shape, birch-white sapling,
>   rising now
> From ankle-deep brook-stones, head back-flung, eyes closed in first
>   beam,
> While hair—long, water-roped, part curve, coign, sway that no
>   geometries know—
> Spreads end-thin, to define fruit-swell of haunches, tingle of
>   hand-hold.
> The sun blazes over the peak. That will be the old tale told. (13–18)

It is not simply the leaf that rejoices in the midst of the light, but now it is the spiderweb that is also whetted on light as it gleams "In Pompeian glory." Bixler points out the irony of this phrase: "Dashing the reader against the stern memory of what happened to mortals at Pompeii, the poet acknowledges his mortality. . . . Human existence is, indeed, most fragile and most ephemeral" (96). But the poet seems to be considering more than his own mortality here, as the images of the spiderweb and the "birch-white sapling" imply. What is in view is the paradoxical moment of consummation that is both violent and lovely. The consummation of the "glory" of Pompeii consists in the extreme outward bulging of the lava through the basalt and the crust of earth and in its eruption, that is, its striving into daylight. This eruption is an outgrowth of the "ageless age of primal flame" of the second stanza. The eruption participates in the outward bulging of language. The image of the Pompeian glory also coalesces with the image of sexual consummation and climax: the "girl-shape, birch-white sapling" flings its head back with eyes closed while hair falls in such a way as "to define fruit-swell of haunches, tingle of hand-hold." This consummation, however, eludes the coign of fundamental perspective and the knowledge of geometry. It is a consummation found only in the blazing light over the peak. It may not be reduced or translated. And it is this irreducible moment that "will be the old tale told."

The tale that is told *is* the myth of the mountain's sunrise. In "John Crowe Ransom: A Study in Irony," Warren summarizes Ransom's use of the term "myth" into a working definition for his essay: "Myth represents a primary exercise of sensibility in which thought and feeling are one: it is a total communication" (95). In this poem, though, Warren's notion of myth would appear to have retained the concern for the "primary exercise of sensibility" while rejecting the possibility that he as a poet can articulate a "total communication." Rather, the world itself declares "the old tale told" that may be considered a trace of the foundational notion of Logos. Coleridge proposed in his *Notebooks* that the Logos consists in a coïnherence of act and being and forms the grammatical correspondent of the absolute I AM of the Jewish and Christian scriptures (4.4644). Warren, however, seems to find in this poem not the equivalent of the I AM as a total communication but the trace of the unsayable after which he sought in "Three Darknesses." He has not found a final logic that will provide the Archimedean point from which he may rethink the whole question of being; rather he has found a trace of the power and energy of language through the act of poetic creation that enables thought to begin. He has not been able to finally define the appropriate relation between mind and nature, but he has caught a glimpse of the energy that might speak to the condition of man's being in the world. His notion of the Logos here follows Heidegger's use of the term: an overcoming return to the Logos not as absolute presence but as *legein*, saying. And in this movement there is a return not to Truth but to truth that uncovers what has been forgotten. In "The Postmodernity of Heidegger," Palmer states that for Heidegger, "The concept of truth, then, is not a matter of correspondence to an already perceived nature of a thing; it is a matter of placing that thing in the light of understanding for the first time" (82). Truth is an event of being, and the moment of that event is, for Warren, the saying of language in the poem, in which language shows itself to be that "shaping, projecting, light-shedding structure in which every extant thing is 'announced' in a certain way as it is 'seen'" (Palmer 82). Warren makes a similar point in "A Poem of Pure Imagination," when he says that "the poem is the light and not the thing seen by the light. The poem is the light by which the reader may view and review all the areas of experience with which he is acquainted" (347). Warren's vision seems to have found the moment—the *eschatia*—from which he may speak, a site that avoids definition and is continually shifting, but one in which the Logos of "the old tale told" provides the space and time for the symbolic understanding. The Logos as an understanding of the power and nature of language provides a means of interpreting that circumvents logocentricity. No longer founded upon the notion of absolute presence in language or upon the idea of final identity, this vision of the Logos opens itself to new possibilities in which presence and absence mingle and in which meaning recedes just over the horizon of your sight.

In the end, Warren's search for and yearning after the given of language brought him back to the source of poetry itself. However, his Logos cannot be reduced to the name or the concept, as such, of this given. Rather, it names the ongoing reading of and responding to the tale. In his seminal essay, "Différance," Jacques Derrida writes of this notion which "is neither a *word* nor a *concept*" (441). Rather, the term both "indicates difference as distinction, inequality, or discernibility" and "expresses the interposition of delay, the interval of a *spacing* and *temporalizing* that puts off until 'later' what is presently denied, the possible that is presently impossible" (441). In Warren's notion of Logos, we find this deferral of the possible that is presently impossible. Derrida expands this tension later in this essay as he expounds his reading of Heidegger's 1946 text, "Der Spruch des Anaximander." In the context of that discussion, Derrida writes:

"Older" than Being itself, our language has no name for such a difference. But we "already know" that if it is unnameable, this is not simply provisional; it is not because our language has still not found or received this *name*, or because we would have to look for it in another language, outside the finite system of our language. It is because there is no name for this, not even essence or Being—not even the name "differance," which is not a name, which is not a pure nominal unity, and continually breaks up in a chain of different substitutions. (463)

Though language may be the given toward which the poet works, it remains unnameable. The poet never becomes the master of language. What is called for, though, is a new conception of language that is affirmed in the play of *différance*. What is not available to the poet is a nostalgia for an Adamic language, or as Derrida puts it, "the myth of the purely maternal or paternal language belonging to the lost fatherland of thought" (463). However, Derrida affirms that, on the other side of nostalgia, there may be what he calls "Heideggerian *hope*" in "the quest for the proper word and the unique name" (463). This quest, following Heidegger's trails back to the region of thought, is carried on through persistent questioning. Derrida translates the following passage from Heidegger's *Holzwege* as capturing the question of the unique word:

> Thus, in order to name what is deployed in Being..., language will have to find a single word, the unique word.... There we see how hazardous is every word of thought ... that addresses itself to Being.... What is hazarded here, however, is not something impossible, because Being speaks through every language; everywhere and always. (464)

Warren's later poetry takes up this hazardous quest after the unique word with all the joy of the poet's persistent, active engagement with language. It is a joyful labor, for in the moment of poetic creation the poet hears the voice of being speak in language. Joy sustains him in the quest that returns him to the region of the source of thought—language itself. For language is the poet's own country. When the poet has the vision of his country, he experiences joy as language speaks in the midst of silence and the silence sinks like music on his heart.[28] But the silence does not negate the poet's role as a witness to the unpresentable. At the end of his essay, "What is Postmodernism," Lyotard declares, "Finally, it must be clear that it is our business not to supply reality but to invent allusions to the conceivable which cannot be presented.... Let us wage a war on totality; let us be witnesses to the unpresentable; let us activate differences and save the honor of the name" (81–82). Silence characterizes and distinguishes the poet's testimony: no longer is he speaking about language but letting language speak in order to return the reader in its light to the world in which he dwells. For Warren, the effect of the pure imagination is to return the reader in such a way. By the illuminating quality of language, the reader becomes a creative being brought within the poetic moment to the place where language speaks. The poem moves the reader in a yearning "toward truth as experience" ("The Use of the Past" 48) so that he might continue the constant work of understanding the self in the world.

AFTERWORD

The Poet's Portrait

... I started as a poet and I will probably end as a poet.—Robert Penn Warren[1]

The eyes stare straight into the unseen camera, the left eye slightly darker than the right, surrounded by a ruddy face atop a shirtless torso that confirms the realities of time and gravity. The hands grip the edge of the bed on which the body is seated, as if they need to be ready to hold fast for the unknown of the next moment. On each side lay the undershirt, the shirt, and the jacket, removed like layers of a costume that can no longer hide the vulnerability of flesh. The mouth forms a perfectly straight line centered in the top half of the shot, and, though there may be much to say, the lips do not say a word. It is the eyes that speak within the square of the photograph in the same way the words of a poem stand on the blank paper. Set off in a relationship of difference from all the other elements that give the photograph its unity, they are trying to tell you something.

The eyes belong, of course, to Robert Penn Warren, and the photograph is the portrait shot by the American photographer Annie Leibovitz in 1980. In what is arguably the most iconoclastic image of this eminent man of letters, Leibovitz set out to show what Warren's poetry looks like, what he was writing about. In order to prepare for the shoot, she said that she read "his last book of poetry ..., and it was all about time and coming toward the end of life. And I really felt that he had totally accepted life" (Felton).[2] "It was part of the portrait," she told Jordan Reife in an interview for *The Guardian*. According to Riefe, "At the last moment, she asked Warren to take off his shirt, transforming the shot into a moment of vulnerability. The septuagenarian poet seems to be baring more than just his chest." By her own admission, she was "trying to penetrate his eyes and soul; trying to peel his skin back to expose his heart" (Christenson). What she saw was a man who "had a peace about himself in the world.... Robert Penn Warren is so assured of himself that it does not matter how he's photographed" (Felton). If, however, the portrait is meant to show what Warren's poems look like or what he was writing about, then perhaps self-assurance is not the best description. Rather, there is an honesty about life in the moment and a confidence that one articulation—even a photograph— can express more than what it says. The portrait does not declare Truth, but it does present a truth. It is not a metanarrative that explains everything about the poet and his work or that betrays its technical expertise; instead, it is a *petit récit* that presents a moment of "imaginative invention" (Lyotard 60). It is not the homologous word of the expert, but the paralogous expression of the artist that embraces the tension of power and limit in one image. It cannot be "summarized" by what it presents, but it must be seen as an invitation to the unpresentable.

Leibovitz's portrait does what Warren set out to do in his poetry—to say the unsayable. To do that, the poet must be willing to undress himself of all the costumes of convention and expectation and sit bare-chested in the presence of being and time. He exposes what may be considered a wounded body—even a left eye injured in his youth—but within that weakness is an unmistakable vitality and life. Perhaps this is why Warren returned time and again to the image of Jacob wrestling the angel. In two late poems, Warren probes the notion of the poet in active engagement with language through the image of Jacob. In "Dream" from *Now and Then* (*CP* 353), he affirms the necessity of this struggle.

> Yes, grapple—or else the Morning Star
> Westward will pale, and leave
> Your ghost without history even, to wander
> A desert trackless in sun-glare.
>
> For the dream is only a self of yourself—and Jacob
> Once wrestled, nightlong, his angel and, though
> With wrenched thigh, had blackmailed a blessing, by dawn. (15–21)

What is true of the self is true of the poet; the blessing of language to make known what might otherwise pale like a ghost must be won through wrestling and wrenching. The poet cannot be lost in a trackless desert of articulation. Warren comes back to this image in "Youthful Truth-Seeker, Half-Naked, at Night, Running down Beach South of San Francisco" (*CP* 392).

> What was the world I had lived in? Poetry, orgasm, joke:
> And the joke the biggest on me, the laughing despair
> Of a truth the heart might speak, but never spoke—
> Like the twilit whisper of wings with no shadow on air.
>
> You dream that somewhere, somehow, you may embrace
> The world in its fullness and threat, and feel, like Jacob, at last
> The merciless grasp of unwordable grace
> Which has no truth to tell of future or past—
>
> But only life's instancy.... (17–25)

The experience of the young poet is one of tension, caught between the "might" and the "never" of truth and the shadowless whisper of wings. The world in which he dwells is one of fullness and threat where the unsayable speaks in life's instancy. In order to hear the word, though, the poet submits himself to the merciless grasp of language. In "The Use of the Past," Warren compares the poet's struggle to find his own voice to the experience of Jacob. "He is like Jacob, who wrestled the angel all night in the place to be called Peniel and, though at the break of day he received the mystic wound in the thigh, would not let go of the mysterious stranger until he had exacted the blessing he craved and could say that he had 'seen God face to face'" (47). The reality of this in Warren's own experience is unmistakable. Though his wound was received not in his thigh, he wrestled with the stranger of language in order to have poetic vision. For him, perhaps, this was his experience of coming face to face with God.

Warren held that language is the living power and agent by which the imagination functions not only in the act of poetic creation but also in any enactment of being in the world, that is, the exercise of the conscious will in creative engagement with the world. His poetic vision is rooted in the act of *poiesis* itself. But *poiesis* is not merely the making of an object, constructed out of the material of language so that the poem becomes a lifeless thing. Rather, *poiesis* is as much a matter of doing as a matter of making, and language is the life-giving energy that generates the act. The act of creation does not cease when the poem is "finished," but it continues on through the event of reading and the reader's activity—itself enacted by language—participates in the *poiesis*. This is even what distinguishes genuine criticism. Warren told Peter Stitt,

> Criticism when it really functions in the full sense of the word leads to a creative act in the sense of appreciating the work of art, whatever it is. You have to redo the work. You repaint the picture, rewrite the book, recompose the music, by going inside, if you are really experiencing it properly . . . . This is clearly a creative act, and it's a very difficult creative act. (Watkins, Hiers, and Weaks 177)

For the poet and the reader alike, language brings us into the moment of enactment, and in this moment, the work of art illuminates being by uncovering the unsayable within the sayable itself. The poem, however, does not become a statement of the contents of the unsayable. The unsayable cannot be equated with any one thing or any single statement; it cannot be reduced even to the concept of Truth. But the unsayable is ineluctably present in every articulation. Far from being "unreal," the magnitude of its being presses on the poet and makes articulation possible. This is what accounts for the irreducibility of a poem and why it is not the poet who finally says the unsayable. Rather, the poet—the artist—acts as a steward in the house who welcomes the reader as a guest into the hospitality of the language.

In *Brother to Dragons: A Tale in Verse and Voices, A New Version*, R.P.W. (who is identified in the *dramatis personae* as "the writer of this poem") describes the memory of his father teaching his granddaughter "some small last Latin" on a Sunday afternoon "after the chicken dinner and ice cream. . . ." He then says:

> There's worse, I guess, than in the end to offer
> Your last bright keepsake, some fragment of the vase
> That held your hopes, to offer it to a child.
> And the child took the crazy toy, and laughed. (22)

It is significant that the father's "last bright keepsake" is language—the crazy-sounding words of Latin vocabulary in the ears of a five-year-old girl. Even more striking is that these words should be compared to "some fragment of the vase / That held your hopes. . . . " But, as the writer of the poem, R.P.W.

knows that what he offers to his readers is his own last bright keepsake, even if it is a fragment of what he once thought was a beautiful vase. As with his father, the poet's hopes seem to have changed, shifting from what the mastery of language could have once done for him to what it now does for the child. What was once considered his possession now becomes an offering, freely given. The hopes move outward from the ambitions of the self to the satisfaction in the joy of others. For him, perhaps, this is the nature of love. Warren's last bright keepsake is this story of the poet's own confrontation with language and the unsayable that provides not only the moment within which he is able to speak but also the moment of our joy as readers. Although the keepsake may only be a fragment of the vase that once held our hopes, it nonetheless engenders a hopefulness as we embark on the hazardous course of encountering language. In this way, Warren's poetry becomes an offering that not only mirrors certain arcs of critical thought within postmodernity but also contributes in an ongoing way to a vital critical discourse. The voice speaks of the power of paradox and of the necessity of meaning without allowing either to become rarified into an abstracted foundational concept. The voice counters any bent toward linguistic nihilism by calling the reader to continue to walk in the world. And the voice reminds us that there is always something more to be thought.

The purpose of this work has been to return the reader to the poems themselves and to encounter there the voice of the unsayable, confident that there remains a rich future of meaning in the poetry of Robert Penn Warren.[3] As readers, we are the child whose joy it is to take this crazy toy into our hands and laugh.

NOTES

Introduction

1. Quoted in Graziano, "Matter Itself" 17.
2. See Rogers 40, 44.
3. Cronin and Seigel acknowledge, "Several interviews collected here were reprinted earlier in two companion books, *Robert Penn Warren Talking: Interviews 1950–1978* (Random House, 1980) and *Talking with Robert Penn Warren* (University of Georgia Press, 1990)" (xviii). Indeed, sixteen of the nineteen interviews or conversations included were previously published in these earlier volumes.
4. See, for example, Sarnowski; and Corrigan, *Poems of Pure Imagination*.
5. One exception is Richard Jackson's 1980 interview with Warren in which he asked the poet, "Is there, for you, a 'suspicion' about language, as some modern philosophers call it?" Warren's response, however, diverts from any philosophical discussion of language. "You have raised many deep questions here. I'll simply stick to the simplest of answers." See Jackson "On the Horizon of Time" 59.
6. I do not mean to suggest here that what is required is some sort of Schleiermachian hermeneutic in which we reach back into the author's mind, and I do not think Warren was suggesting this either. The goal is to get back to the texts themselves, cleared from the encrustment of the writer's reputation.
7. Grimshaw states this view most succinctly: "Warren's poetry may be conveniently categorized in three phases: the early poems, 1921–1943; the middle poems, 1953–1975; and the late poems, 1976–1989" ("Warren as Moral Philosopher" 103). See also Strandberg, *Poetic Vision* 1–20; Runyon, *Braided Dream* 2–8; and McClatchy 82–85.
8. See Blotner 337–38.
9. See Van Dyke, "A Critical Sense Worthy of Respect."
10. See chapter four for a lengthier consideration of this poem.
11. For instance, compare "The Ballad of Billie Potts," ll. 353–54 (*CP* 88).
12. Warren explores the same function of wind in "The Return: An Elegy" (*CP* 33–35), "Calendar" (*CP* 56), and "The Ballad of Billie Potts" (*CP* 92).

Chapter One

1. *The Essence of Truth* 71.
2. See also Franke's essay, "Apophasis and the Turn of Philosophy."

3. See McKusick, *Coleridge's Philosophy of Language* 9–10, 152, 157.

4. English devotional writer and mystic William Law (1686–1761) translated Boehme's work into English during the latter years of his life. His work was published posthumously in four volumes in 1765. Warren returns to Boehme in a later poem "When the Tooth Cracks—Zing!" (*CP* 360).

5. See Hagberg's discussion of Langer's distinction between discursive and nondiscursive symbols in *Art as Language* 12–17.

6. Compare Franke's analysis of Rosenzweig at this point. See his "Franz Rosenzweig" 168.

7. See Szczesiul, *Racial Politics* 141–52.

8. "The Briar Patch" was published in the Agrarian manifesto, *I'll Take My Stand* (1930). See also Warren's comments in *Robert Penn Warren Talking* 34–36 and 183–86.

9. Compare Warren's earlier remark in "Why do We Read Fiction?": "Fiction brings up from their dark oubliettes our shadowy, deprived selves and gives them an airing in, as it were, the prison yard. They get a chance to participate, each according to his nature, in the life which fiction presents" (60).

10. Compare Warren's statement in "Why Do We Read Fiction?":

> We have all observed how a person who has had a profound shock needs to tell the story of the event over and over again, every detail. By telling it he objectifies it, disentangling himself, as it were, from the more intolerable effects . . . If a child—or a man—who is in a state of blind outrage at his fate can come to understand that the fate which had seemed random and gratuitous is really the result of his own previous behavior or is part of the general pattern of life, his emotional response is modified by that intellectual comprehension. (61)

11. "In recent, postmodern apophasis (seen already, for example, in the 17th century Kabbalah) the tendency has been to emphasize the breaking and shattering of all meanings as what opens language to intimations beyond its possibilities of saying. Where discourse ruptures, meaning spills out and spreads without bounds, and in this sense becomes infinite" (Franke, "A Philosophy of the Unsayable" 71).

12. See Van Dyke, "Language at the End of Modernism." For other discussions of this lecture, see Strandberg, *Poetic Vision of Robert Penn Warren* 272; Westendorp 80–82; and Beck 97–99. *NB* Beck dates the original composition of the lecture in 1962, though it was never published or delivered prior to his 1966 lecture.

13. Compare Bowie's characterization of the holistic approach to thought in German philosophy over the past two centuries: "The focus of philosophy consequently shifts from a concentration on how language 'represents' things, to a focus on all the ways in which language 'expresses' or 'articulates' how we relate to the world" (3).

14. For a succinct description of the relationship between the Analytical and the Continental traditions and the "linguistic turn" that significantly defines this divide, see Bowie 84–96. Compare Bowie's remark: "The division [between 'Continental' and 'analytical' philosophy] is in fact probably best considered as a series of contrasting approaches to modern philosophical questions, rather than just one issue" (84).

15. Compare Preston 1–13.

16. For a discussion of the distinction between the natural sciences and the human sciences (*Geiteswissenschaften*) in the thought of Wilhelm Dilthey, see Palmer, *Hermeneutics* 98–106.

17. Compare Warren's remarks about the impact of technology in *Democracy and Poetry* 53–54.

18. *Heidegger* 72, 74.

19. At other points in his career, Warren also suggested that this crisis opened up new possibilities. He remarked in a 1986 interview that the First World War was a time both for fermentation and awakening among writers in the American South. During this period of crisis at the "end" of history, he says, "There was a questioning of all sorts of attitudes, new and old, in the South, and there certainly wasn't agreement or answers. But the world of the South was changing in that generation. It woke up in many ways and discovered its past in many, sometimes fallacious, ways, but ways that generally involved real issues" (Sanoff 73). It was in the midst of this crisis and questioning that Warren himself awakened as a writer.

20. See Longenbach's discussion of Jarrell's assessment of modernism and the shift toward postmodern poetry (3–21).

21. This volume was subsequently reissued in 1972 by The Johns Hopkins Press under the title *The Structuralist Controversy.*

22. Also, Grimshaw includes the full text of Kennedy's article in his *Dictionary of Literary Biography* volume on Warren (240–41).

23. See Franke, "Franz Rosenzweig" 166ff; Wolfson, *Language, Eros, Being* 17ff; and Buber 10.

24. Compare E. R. Wolfson's remark in "Heidegger's Apophaticism": "The unsayable, in other words, is not what is never said but precisely what is left unspoken in what is spoken" (189).

25. Hall's view of poetry is an example of what Warren describes as "poetry as art." Hall writes, "Poetry by its bodily, mental, and emotional complex educates the sensibility, thinking and feeling appropriately melded together" (7–8). Warren says that the view that regards poetry as art holds that poetry "should feed his love for the richness and variety of life, mollify his dogmatisms, and introduce him to imagination as the great 'as-if' of truth" (*APIM* 18).

Chapter Two

1. Watkins, Hiers, and Weaks 246

2. It is necessary to acknowledge that Warren also describes in this same interview his fascination with Melville, Whittier, and Dreiser. However, I am presently concerned with the obvious shaping influence of Coleridge's poetry and ideas on Warren's development. See Watkins, Hiers, and Weaks 245–46. See also Corrigan, *Poems of Pure Imagination* 121–22.

3. Compare Blotner 46–47.

4. This notion of ripeness is central to *Incarnations: Poems 1966–1968*. See especially "Where the Slow Fig's Purple Sloth" (*CP* 223), "Riddle in the Garden" (*CP* 225), "Where Purples Now the Fig" (*CP* 231), and "The Leaf" (*CP* 234–35).

5. Regarding the latter, see my analysis in chapter six of "Myth of Mountain Sunrise," in which Warren uses the same imagery of eruption.

6. For a survey of responses to Warren's essay up to 1985, see Schulz 386–88.

7. Near the beginning of *Brother to Dragons*, Jefferson interrupts himself and says "Yes, what was I saying? Language betrays. / There are no words to tell Truth." *Brother to Dragons: A New Version* 7.

8. This was the crux of Olson's objection to Warren's reading of *The Ancient Mariner*. "We may indeed worry about whether . . . it is not an absurdity to conceive of a poem—i.e., any imitative poem—as *having* a theme or meaning." See Olson 139n3.

9. It is worth noting that the first of Coleridge's *Notebooks* was not published until 1957. However, Warren would have had secondary access to some material from the notebooks and other works through Lowes's *Road to Xanadu* (1927), which includes extensive quotes from the *Notebooks*.

10. Warren quotes from both Griggs, ed., *The Best of Coleridge*, and Lowes's *The Road to Xanadu*.

11. Warren does not identify the source of this quote in the version of the essay included in both the 1958 *Selected Essays* and the 1989 *New and Selected Essays*. In the original version included in the 1946 Reynal and Hitchcock edition, he cites Shawcross from the preface to his 1907 edition of the *Biographia Literaria*. See *Rime of the Ancient Mariner* 120, n. 22.

12. Coleridge's concern for the imagination is evident in his earliest work and bears an important relationship to his subsequent thinking about language. Alluding probably to the year 1797, he begins Chapter 14 of the *Biographia* by recounting the growth of his thinking about the power of poetry: "During the first year that Mr. Wordsworth and I were neighbours, our conversations turned frequently on the two cardinal points of poetry, the power of exciting the sympathy of the reader by a faithful adherence to the truth of nature, and the power of giving the interest of novelty by the modifying colours of imagination" (II.5). At this early

stage, Coleridge links the emotive power of poetic language to a "faithful adherence to the truth of nature" and to a commitment to the modifying power of the imagination, by which poetry dissolves, diffuses, and dissipates what is given in order to re-create.

13. It is interesting to note that in the 1946 edition of the essay, Warren devotes more analysis to Priestley and Hartley's roles than in either the 1958 or 1989 editions of the essay. Also, Warren's notes in the earlier edition of the essay are far more extensive.

14. See *CN* 3.3605n.

15. Please note that references are to the book, chapter, and paragraph numbers in the text.

16. Abrams identifies this law as part of the overall mechanical theory of literary invention that was prevalent in eighteenth-century efforts "to import into the psychical realm the explanatory scheme of physical science, and so to extend the victories of mechanics from matter to mind"(159). According to Abrams, Hartley "set out to demonstrate rigorously that all the complex contents and processes of mind are derived from the elements of simple sensation, combined by the single link of contiguity in original experience" (162).

17. For Coleridge's unashamed admiration for Boehme, see *BL* I.146–49 and I.161–62

18. By specifying the corporeal nature of thought as motion, Coleridge is anticipating his later discussion of the symbol in *The Statesman's Manual*. Thought functions by symbols that "are the wheels Ezekiel beheld."

19. For a helpful summary of Berkeley's thought and its influence on Coleridge, see McKusick 26–32.

20. Coleridge is referring here to his son and not to David Hartley. See also his *Anima Poetae* 13.

21. See Coleridge, *Lectures 1795* 19; and McKusick 38–39.

22. Compare Warren's comment on the early work of Whittier from 1971: "In poetry, in fact, he could only pile up words as a mason piles up bricks; he could only repeat, compulsively, the dreary clichés; his meter-making machine ground on, and nothing that came out was, he knew, real: his poems were only 'fancies,' as he called them, only an echo of the past, not his own present." See "John Greenleaf Whittier" 278.

23. Compare Heidegger's discussion of the relation between word and thing in "The Nature of Language" 86–90.

24. McNiece observes a direct correlation between Coleridge's notion of logic and "the ancient and Christian idea of the Logos" as expressed by "several different attempts to define the appropriate relation between mind and nature." See *The Knowledge that Endures* 2.

25. See Perkins, *Coleridge's Philosophy* 16–21.
26. See also *Anima Poetae* 136.
27. See also *Aids to Reflection* 391n.
28. There is a curious parallel here to Lyotard's notion of *petit-récits* in *Postmodern Condition*. There is no grand metanarrative to explain and define "reality" but only little fables to creatively dramatize—a view which is symbolic in itself.

Chapter Three

1. Jackson, "Generous Time" 24.
2. See Watkins, Hiers, and Weaks 119, 163, 243–44, 333, 339; and Blotner 212, 381–82.
3. Butterworth notes, "Warren had become interested in Audubon during the forties while doing research for *World Enough and Time*, and while directing his critical attention to Eudora Welty's story 'A Still Moment,' but a method for using the Audubon materials in a poem eluded him for two decades" (93). For comparative analyses of Welty's and Warren's dealings with Audubon, see Cluck; and Corrigan, "Snapshots of Audubon."
4. For the textual history of this poem, see Szczesiul, "Robert Penn Warren's *Audubon.*"
5. See *Achievement of Robert Penn Warren* 87–96.
6. See Bedient 134–49 for his full discussion of the poem.
7. Compare Culler's formulation of the goal of structuralist criticism as an effort "to read the text as an exploration of writing, of the problems of articulating a world" (260).
8. See Sections III, IV[E], and V[A].
9. Compare Warren's discussion of "passion" in the thought of Kierkegaard in his 1974 Jefferson Lecture in the Humanities, published under the title *Democracy and Poetry*. In the second of his two essays in this volume, Warren explores the way that poetry might provide a place from which we may scrutinize "our own experience of our own world" (41). Warren goes on to describe the contemporary world, though, as one of scientific and technological predominance that denies the vital role of poetry in the formation of knowledge. He is skeptical, therefore, of the heritage of Cartesian thought that has led to abstract thinking and urges the essential place of poetry. In order to substantiate this claim, Warren points to Kierkegaard, who "affirmed that abstract thought cannot grasp the meaning of existence and that feeling—passion, as he termed it—provides the knowledge that is the key of existence and action" (48). Warren goes on to equate Kierkegaard's use of the term "passion" with the notion of the imagination held by the Romantic poets.
10. With regard to the former use of the term, Coleridge describes the way that demagogues seek to arouse the base passions of their hearers. These "political empirics"

use "arguments built on passing events and deriving an undue importance from the feelings of the moment. The mere appeal, however, to the auditors . . . is an effective substitute for any argument at all." In response, mobs fall into a state in which "passions, like a fused metal, fill up the wide interstices of thought, and supply the defective links: and thus incompatible assertions are harmonized by the *sensation*, without the *sense*, of connection." See "A Lay Sermon" 153. This statement affirms, however, the power of the passions: while it may be helpfully employed by the imagination of the poetic genius to approach the unsayable, it can also be exercised by ideology to unspeakable ends. There is both an inherent power and an inherent danger in passion, as in language.

11. This modifying and fusing effect of passion led Coleridge to link passion to meter and rhythm in verse. Coleridge distinguishes poetry from prose not simply by the arrangement of words or by the question of beauty but by the "essential difference" of meter. However, according to Marks, Coleridge disagreed with "Wordsworth's notion of verse as the mere superaddition of meter to an order of discourse essentially prosaic" (70). Meter for Coleridge would appear to relate not simply to order or arrangements of words but to a specific mode of expression (73). This mode of expression is generated by passion. Coleridge says that he "would trace [the origin of meter] to the balance in the mind effected by that spontaneous effort which strives to hold in check the workings of passion" (*BL* II.64). There must be in verse "an interpenetration of passion and of will, of spontaneous impulse and of voluntary purpose" (*BL* II.65).

12. There are striking similarities between Hopkins's poem and this image in *Audubon*. Hopkins is caught by the majestic motion of the falcon as it rides the morning air. His heart seems to be stirred by a similar passion as Warren's: "My heart in hiding / Stirred for a bird, - the achieve of, the master of the thing!" Each poem also has a distinct religious or theological aspect which shapes the living language of the verse. See Gardner and McKenzie 69.

13. See chapter five.

14. See "APPI" 360. Warren is quoting from *Statesman's Manual* 65–66.

15. Compare the final five lines of "Fear and Trembling" (*CP* 487):

Can the heart's meditation wake us from life's long sleep,
And instruct us how foolish and fond was our labor spent—
Us who now know that only at death of ambition does the deep
Energy crack crust, spurt forth, and leap

From grottoes, dark—and from the caverned enchainment? (17–21)

16. See *Statesman's Manual* 65.

17. In the image of the woman, Warren fuses his concern for nature and humanity, extending the implications of the sacramental vision to the artist's connection

with humanity. He develops in this passage what he calls in "A Poem of Pure Imagination" the "socializing function of the imagination," which was a fundamental concern of the Romantic poets. Warren refers to Shelley, who argues in the *Defense of Poetry* that the poet puts "'himself in the place of another and of many others' so that 'the pains and pleasures of his species must become his own'" (384).

18. Compare the image of the woman's body swaying "like a willow in spring wind" to the similar image in "Myth of Mountain Sunrise" (*CP* 584), in which the reader is asked to think "of a girl-shape, birch-white sapling, rising now / From ankle-deep brook-stones . . ." (14–15). There is a similar mixture of innocence and power in this image as in Audubon. This comparison is heightened by Warren's reference at the end of this poem to "the old tale told" that seems to answer the imperative at the end of *Audubon*, "Tell me a story." See the discussion of this poem in chapter five.

19. See Burt's textual note on this passage (*CP* 707).

20. Compare ll. 288–91 of *The Rime of the Ancient Mariner*:

The self-same moment I could pray;
And from my neck so free
The Albatross fell off, and sank
Like lead into the sea.

21. Third epigraph to *Being Here* (*CP* 379).

22. See Spanos, "Heidegger, Kierkegaard, and the Hermeneutic Circle" 139.

Chapter Four

1. Franke, *A Philosophy of the Unsayable* 5.

2. The "forthcoming novel" to which he refers is *A Place to Come To*, published in February 1977.

3. Warren's later poetry seems to reverse the order that Bedient observes in his 1984 study of Warren's major poetry, *In the Heart's Last Kingdom*. Rather than concentrating "on poetry as the extreme resource of . . . language being" (3), this later body of work continually confronts "language-being" as the extreme resource of poetry. Bedient's formulation is helpful, though, in the way that it brings to light the inseparable relationship between language and being in Warren's aesthetic and sacramental vision.

4. See *Selected Essays* 3–31.

5. Compare Burt's statement regarding *Audubon*: "Warren seeks in Audubon . . . a character who can look upon the truth and not be silenced by it" (92).

6. This poem, the second part of a two-poem sequence entitled "The True Nature

of Time," was originally published in *Incarnations: Poems 1966–1968*, but this sequence was republished in *Or Else—Poem/Poems 1968–1974*. Warren states in a prefatory note to *Or Else* that this sequence has a specific place within the thematic structure of that book that is conceived of as one long poem.

7. See the editors' remarks regarding the text-critical background of this quote. *The Statesman's Manual* 20 n. 1.
8. See, for example, "Better Than Counting Sheep" (*CP* 412).
9. See *Being and Time* 301–11; and Steiner, *Heidegger* 103–07.
10. See the discussion of "The Whole Question" in chapter six.
11. See Burt's Textual Note to line 18 (*CP* 730). In the first edition of *Now and Then: Poems 1976–1978*, line 18 reads "Identity of all?" (23). But in *New and Selected Poems 1923–1985*, the line was changed to "Nature of all?" (151)
12. Compare *Audubon: A Vision* II[J],17–21 and IV[B], 8. See *CP* 259, 262.
13. This juxtaposition is reminiscent of Warren's repeated contrast between light and dark in *Audubon*. See chapter three.

Chapter Five

1. "The Nature of Language" 66.
2. In his introduction to "The Dramatic Version of *Ballad of a Sweet Dream of Peace: A Charade for Easter*," Warren says:

The grotesque characteristically involved certain unexpected intensities and startling varieties of response to the "truth" thus isolated for assertion. Shock is of the essence of the grotesque. The grotesque is one of the most obvious forms art may take to pierce the veil of familiarity, to stab us up from the drowse of the accustomed, to make us aware of the perilous paradoxicality of life. (246)

3. See also "The Return: An Elegy" (*CP* 33–35) and "The Ballad of Billie Potts" (*CP* 81–92).
4. See *CP* 646–47. Burt notes that "Warren describes this poem as among the winners of the Caroline Sinkler Prize from the Poetry Society of South Carolina for 1936, 1937, and 1938" (646).
5. These linguistic terms derive from Speech Act theory and were first defined in the work of J. L. Austin and later developed by John R. Searle. Compare Lyotard's discussion of language games in *The Postmodern Condition* 9–11.
6. Heidegger suggests in "The Nature of Language" that a name is more than a mere designation. "What does 'to name' signify? We might answer: to name means to furnish something with a name. And what is a name? A designation that provides something with a vocal and written sign, a cipher. And what is a sign? Is it a signal? Or a token? A marker? Or a hint? Or all of these and something else besides?

We have become very slovenly and mechanical in our understanding and use of signs" (61).

7. Please note that references for both editions cite page numbers and not line numbers within the poem. For a discussion of the two editions of this poem (1953 and 1979), see Grimshaw, "Introduction." R.P.W., listed as one of the speakers in the *dramatis personae*, is identified as "The writer of this poem."

8. Compare Warren's remarks in "APPI" 394.

9. See "Paradox" (*CP* 328).

10. Warren makes this distinction between English and Latin in other places in *Brother to Dragons*. For example, see *BD 79* 22 and 115.

11. Compare Heidegger's statement, "Thus, in order to name what is deployed in Being, language will have to find a single word, the unique word." Quoted in Derrida, "Différance" 464. For a lengthier discussion of this passage, see chapter six.

12. This passage is pared down from a lengthier passage in the 1953 version, which makes "the worst thing" plural and then continues:

There's just no name to lay to the worst things,
And that's what makes them worse than anything,
For if they had a name, then you could name it.
At least to name it would be something then,
If you could bear to name it. And I think—
I mean I've come to think—that I could bear now
To name most anything if I could know,
Just only know, the name to name it with,
Even the worst. (67–68)

13. Runyan's thesis is relevant here: he contends that verbal threads tie Warren's poems together within specific collections, which fits with our own contention that Warren moved more toward the open-ended poem that can only be interpreted in light of other poems. See Runyan, *Braided Dream* 1–18.

14. Compare also "Youth Stares at Minoan Sunset" (*CP* 352).

15. *Sila* is an Eskimo word that Warren defines from *Larousse World Mythology*, which states that it "is the air, not the sky; movement, not wind; the very breath of life, but not physical life; he is clear-sighted energy, activating intelligence; the powerful fluid circulating 'all around' and also within each individual . . ." (*CP* 400).

16. Compare this moment to an earlier poem from *Now and Then*, "Youth Stares at Minoan Sunset" (*CP* 352), in which the boy in that poem "spreads his arms to the sky as though he loves it. . . . " (27).

17. In "The Ballad of Billie Potts" (*CP* 81–92), Warren links the identity and name of Little Billie to his birthmark, which is "Shaped lak a clover under his left tit, / With a shape fer luck . . ." (462–63). After the boy's father and mother have

brutally murdered him, thinking him to be some rich traveler unknown in their region, they open his shirt to find the birthmark "shaped for luck" and realize that they have sacrificed their own son. In the final section of the poem, the poet transfers this mark of identity to "you, wanderer," to the poet himself. Having heard "the wind's word," he kneels "in the sacramental silence of evening" with the little black mark—his name—under his heart, that mark "Which is shaped for luck, // Which is your luck" (512–13).

18. For a discussion of the different approaches to subjectivity in modern and post-modern discourse, see Davis.

19. "Before entering upon this topic we must, however, grant that in all times and places man has necessarily lived a large part of his life in what Martin Buber calls the realm of *It*—the realm of economics, politics, science, military activity, labor, and so on—as contrasted with the realm of the *Thou*, in which massive relations of recognition and reverence may prevail" (*DP* 57). See also *DP* 36, 90–91.

20. Compare "Interjection #5: Solipsism and Theology" (*CP* 299).

21. Notice how the "Not repetitious" of the first stanza falls into pieces in the "Nothing but repetition" in the second stanza.

22. Warren seems to play here upon the word "gaggle," which can be either the noise a goose makes or a flock of geese. The stars, then, hang in the heavens like a flock of geese.

23. For a variety of discussions on this poem, see for example Burt, *Robert Penn Warren* 84–91; Corrigan, *Poems of Pure Imagination* 61–70; Justus 57–60; Miller, "Knowledge and the Image of 'Billie Potts'"; Strandberg, *Colder Fire* 114–38 and *Poetic Vision* 148–63; and Walker 68–69.

24. Warren uses the same image of "cat-and-mouse" in an earlier poem in *Rumor Verified*, "What Was the Thought?" (*CP* 470–71). There, the cat has caught what the poet cannot catch—the elusive thought of the self that lurked the house through the night. When the speaker awakes, he is greeted by the cat, crouching at his knees and "There, blood streaking the counterpane, it lies— / Skull crushed, partly eviscerated" (58).

25. Compare Thiemann's description of Warren's avoidance of linguistic nihilism. See Thiemann 38–46.

Chapter Six

1. Wood 182.

2. "The French philosopher Jacques Derrida, it could be argued, is the true, though uneasy, heir of both Saussure and Heidegger" (Jasper, "From Modernism to Postmodernism" 306).

3. Although Jacques Derrida contributed a fifth essay to this volume, it is nonetheless attributed to the "Yale Critics." See Berman 223–24.

4. See *SL* 6.136, 212.

5. See *Postmodern Condition* 71–82.

6. See Lyotard 81.

7. See *New and Selected Essays* 29–53.

8. Compare Spanos's argument about the way modernism in Western literature "is grounded in a strategy that spatializes the temporal process of existence" (116). See "Heidegger, Kierkegaard, and the Hermeneutic Circle," 115–48.

9. The body of criticism on this poem is slight. See Callander; Shepherd; and Balla. See also Wood 186.

10. See *SL* 6.52, 92, 141.

11. Balla recognizes the layered quality of *Chief Joseph*: "*Chief Joseph of the Nez Perce* abounds with techniques that work. For one, it's a multifaceted story, with Warren relying on quotations from official documents, newspapers of the time, and historic memorabilia interspersed throughout . . . " (277). He misses, however, the writerly character when he goes on to state, "*Chief Joseph of the Nez Perce* is, in short, told so straightforwardly as a moving story that its devices seem unnoticeable. It doesn't rhyme. Lines don't measure against each other in evened feet and meter" (277).

12. Warren was compelled to visit the site in Montana again before being able to finish the ninth section, which would conclude the poem. See *SL* 6.105, 112, 113.

13. Please note that references cite the section number followed by the line number(s) from the text in *Collected Poems of Robert Penn Warren*.

14. For example, see "Plato's Pharmacy" and "The End of the Book and the Beginning of Writing" in *Of Grammatology*. See also Norris, "Derrida on Plato: Writing as Poison and Cure" in *Derrida* 28–62.

15. Heidegger's dialogue takes place between a Japanese (*J*) and an Inquirer (*I*). See "Dialogue" 1.

16. See Hoy 64.

17. Published as the first section of Warren's final selected volume, *New and Selected Poems 1923–1985* (1985).

18. See *Democracy and Poetry* 71; and "The Use of the Past" 46.

19. According to J. Hillis Miller, "The *Riß* is both the cleft of an abyss opening into 'noting' (in Heidegger's sense of that word: nothingness as manifestation of Being), and at the same time the sharp incised line, the 'trait' making a design that is a meaningful sign, whether letter or picture" (87).

20. *Holzwege* is the title of the volume in which Heidegger's "The Origin of the Work of Art" was originally published (1950), together with other essays, including "What Are Poets For?"

21. See *Democracy and Poetry* 71. Compare Spanos's statement regarding his own preface to *Martin Heidegger and the Question of Literature*: "It is intended, that is,

as a plunge in the midst: not to inform, but simply to provide a point of departure for an access *into* the 'open' hermeneutic circle" (xvii).

22. See Richard Jackson, "Deconstructed Moment" 319.

23. See also Brooks, "Sublimity and Theatricality" 950–51.

24. Compare Bloom's statement: "We are given a poetic art that dares constantly the root meaning of *hamartia*: to shoot wide of the mark" ("Sunset Hawk" 73).

25. Heidegger, "Overcoming Metaphysics" 84.

26. See "A Dialogue on Language" 47.

27. The text of *The Collected Poems* mistakenly has the word "deep" in the place of the correct language, "deepest." Compare Warren's *New and Selected Poem 1923–1985* 85. Burt includes the correction in the *errata* catalogued at www.robert pennwarren.com/collectedpoemserrata.html.

28. See Coleridge, *The Ancient Mariner* ll. 478, 80, 98–99. Compare one of Warren's earlier poems, "Joy" (*CP* 179):

If you've never had it, discussion is perfectly fruitless,
And if you have, you can tell nobody about it.
To explain silence, you scarcely try to shout it.
Let the flute and drum be still, the trumpet *toot*less.

Afterword

1. Watkins, Hiers, and Weaks 242.

2. It is difficult to know if Leibovitz read *Now and Then: Poems 1976–1978* or *Being Here: Poetry 1977–1980*, which was published in August of 1980. See Blotner 452.

3. See Kearney 110.

WORKS CITED

Primary Sources

Warren, Robert Penn. *All the King's Men*. New York: Harcourt, Brace and Company, Inc., 1946.

———. "The Briar Patch." *I'll Take My Stand: The South and the Agrarian Tradition*. Baton Rouge: Louisiana State UP, 1977. 246–64.

———. *Brother to Dragons: A Tale in Verse and Voices*. New York: Random House, 1953.

———. *Brother to Dragons: A Tale in Verse and Voices, A New Version*. New York: Random House, 1979.

———. *The Collected Poems of Robert Penn Warren*. Ed. John Burt. Baton Rouge: Louisiana State UP, 1998.

———. "A Conversation with Cleanth Brooks." *The Possibilities of Order: Cleanth Brooks and His Work*. Ed. Lewis P. Simpson. Baton Rouge: Louisiana State UP, 1976. 1–24.

———. *Democracy and Poetry*. Cambridge: Harvard UP, 1975.

———. "Dragon Country." *Yale Series of Recorded Poets: Robert Penn Warren Reads From His Own Works*. 14. Carillon Records. n.d.

———. "The Dramatic Version of *Ballad of a Sweet Dream of Peace: A Charade for Easter*, with the author's introduction." *The Grotesque in Art and Literature: Theological Reflections*. Ed. James Luther Adams and Wilson Yates. Grand Rapids: William B. Eerdmans Publishing Co., 1997. 243–74.

———. "Hawthorne *was* Relevant." *The Nathaniel Hawthorne Journal* (1972): 85–89.

———. *John Brown: The Making of a Martyr*. Southern Classic Series. Ed. M. E. Bradford. Nashville: J. S. Sanders & Company, 1993.

———. "John Crowe Ransom: A Study in Irony." *Virginia Quarterly Review* vol. XI (Winter 1935): 93–112.

———. "John Greenleaf Whittier: Poetry as Experience." *New and Selected Essays*. New York: Random House, 1989. 235–83.

———. "Knowledge and the Image of Man." *Sewanee Review* vol. 62 (Spring 1955): 182–92.

———. "Love and Separateness in Eudora Welty." *Selected Essays*. New York: Random House, 1958. 156–69.

———. *New and Selected Poems 1923–1985*. New York: Random House, 1985.

———. *Now and Then: Poems 1976–1978*. New York: Random House, 1978.

———. *A Place to Come To*. New York: Random House, 1977.

———. *A Plea in Mitigation: Modern Poetry at the End of an Era*. Macon: Wesleyan College, 1966.

———. "A Poem of Pure Imagination: An Experiment in Reading." *New and Selected Essays*. New York: Random House, 1989. 335–423.

———. "Pure and Impure Poetry." *New and Selected Essays*. New York: Random House, 1989. 3–28.

———. *Selected Letters of Robert Penn Warren, Volume Five: Backward Glances and New Visions, 1969–1979*. Ed. Randy Hendricks and James A. Perkins. Southern Literary Studies. Ed. Fred Hobson. Baton Rouge: Louisiana State University Press, 2011.

———. *Selected Letters of Robert Penn Warren, Volume One: The Apprentice Years, 1924–1934*. Ed. William Bedford Clark. Southern Literary Studies. Ed. Fred Hobson. Baton Rouge: Louisiana State University Press, 2000.

———. *Selected Letters of Robert Penn Warren, Volume Six: Toward Sunset, At a Great Height, 1980–1989*. Ed. Randy Hendricks and James A. Perkins. Southern Literary Studies. Ed. Fred Hobson. Baton Rouge: Louisiana State University Press, 2013.

———. *A Study of John Marston's Satires*. Thesis. Oxford University, 1930.

———. "The Use of the Past." *New and Selected Essays*. New York: Random House, 1989. 28–53.

———. *Who Speaks for the Negro?* New York: Random House, 1965.

———. "Why Do We Read Fiction?" *New and Selected Essays*. New York: Random House, 1989. 55–66.

———. *Wilderness: A Tale of the Civil War*. New York: Random House, 1961.

Secondary Sources

Abrams, M. H. *The Mirror and the Lamp: Romantic Theory and the Critical Tradition*. New York: W. W. Norton and Company, 1953.

Arac, Jonathan. "Repetition and Exclusion: Coleridge and New Criticism Reconsidered." *Boundary 2*, vol. 8, no. 1 (Fall 1979): 261–73.

Balla, Philip. "'A Dance on the High Wire over an Abyss." Rev. of *Rumor Verified: Poems 1979–1980* by Robert Penn Warren and *Chief Joseph of the Nez Perce* by Robert Penn Warren. *Parnassus: Poetry in Review*, vol. 12, no. 1 (Fall/Winter 1984). 267–80.

Barthes, Roland. *S/Z*. Trans. Richard Miller. New York: Hill and Wang, 1974.

Beck, Charlotte. "The Postmodernism of Robert Penn Warren." *To Love So Well the World: A Festschrift in Honor of Robert Penn Warren*. Ed. Dennis L. Weeks. New York: Peter Lang, 1992. 211–21.

———. *Robert Penn Warren: Critic*. Knoxville: U of Tennessee P, 2006.

Bedient, Calvin. *In the Heart's Last Kingdom: Robert Penn Warren's Major Poetry.* Cambridge: Harvard UP, 1984.

Berman, Art. *From the New Criticism to Deconstruction: The Reception of Structuralism and Post-Structuralism.* Urbana: U of Illinois P, 1988.

Bixler, Frances. "Robert Penn Warren's Varied Voices: An Approach to the Late Poems." *"To Love So Well the World": A Festschrift in Honor of Robert Penn Warren.* Ed. Dennis L. Weeks. New York: Peter Lang, 1992. 85–99.

Blanchot, Maurice. "Our Clandestine Companion." *Face to Face with Levinas.* Ed. Richard A. Cohen. SUNY Series in Philosophy. Ed. Robert C. Neville. Albany: State University of New York Press, 1986. 41–50.

Bloom, Harold. Foreword. *The Collected Poems of Robert Penn Warren.* Ed. John Burt. Baton Rouge: Louisiana State UP, 1998. xxiii–xxvi.

———. "Sunset Hawk: Warren's Poetry and Tradition." *A Southern Renascence Man: Views of Robert Penn Warren.* Ed. Walter B. Edgar. Baton Rouge: Louisiana State UP, 1984. 59–79.

Bloom, Harold, Paul De Man, Jacques Derrida, Geoffrey Hartman, and J. Hillis Miller. *Deconstruction and Criticism.* New York: The Seabury Press, 1979.

Blotner, Joseph. *Robert Penn Warren: A Biography.* New York: Random House, 1997.

Bowie, Andrew. *German Philosophy: A Very Short Introduction.* Oxford: Oxford UP, 2010.

Brooks, Cleanth. *The Well Wrought Urn: Studies in the Structure of Poetry.* 1947. New York: Harcourt, Brace and World, 1975.

Brooks, Linda Marie. "Sublimity and Theatricality: Romantic 'Pre-Postmodernism' in Schiller and Coleridge." *Modern Language Notes* vol. 105 (1990). 939–64.

Brown, Homer Obed. "The Art of Theology and the Theology of Art: Robert Penn Warren's Reading of Coleridge's *The Rime of the Ancient Mariner.*" *Boundary 2,* vol. 8, no. 1 (Fall 1979): 237–60.

Brown, Nahum, and J. Aaron Simmons, eds. *Contemporary Debates in Negative Theology and Philosophy.* Palgrave Frontiers in Philosophy of Religion. Ed. Yujin Nasagawa and Erik J. Wielenberg. Cham: Palgrave Macmillan, 2017.

Bruns, Gerald L. *Modern Poetry and the Idea of Language: A Critical and Historical Study.* New Haven: Yale UP, 1974.

Buber, Martin. *Ecstatic Confessions.* Ed. Paul Mendes-Flohr. Trans. Esther Cameron. San Francisco: Harper & Row, 1985.

Budick, Sanford, and Wolfgang Iser, eds. *Languages of the Unsayable: The Play of Negativity in Literature and Literary Theory.* Irvine Studies in the Humanities. Ed. Robert Folkenflik. New York: Columbia UP, 1989.

Burt, John. *Robert Penn Warren and American Idealism.* New Haven: Yale UP, 1988.

Butterworth, Keen. "Projections and Reflections in *Audubon: A Vision.*" *Southern Literary Journal,* vol. 36, no. 1 (Fall 2003). 90–103.

Callander, Marilyn Berg. "Robert Penn Warren's *Chief Joseph of the Nez Perce*: A Story of Deep Delight." *Southern Literary Journal*, vol. XV, no. 3 (Fall 1983). 24–33.

Cavell, Stanley. "In Quest of the Ordinary: Texts of Recovery." *Romanticism and Contemporary Criticism*. Ed. Morris Eaves and Michael Fischer. Ithaca: Cornell UP, 1986. 183–213.

Christensen, Richard P. "Annie Leibovitz: Utahns Get a Chance to See Photographer's Innovative Portraits of Celebrities." *Deseret News*. 20 June 1993. www.deseret.com/ 1993/6/20/19053219/annie-leibovitz-utahns-get-a-chance-to -see-photographer-s- innovative-portraits-of-celebrities#. Accessed 3 January 2020.

Cluck, Nancy. "Audubon: Images of the Artist in Eudora Welty and Robert Penn Warren." *The Southern Literary Journal*, vol. 17, no. 2 (1985): 41–53.

Coleridge, Samuel Taylor. *Aids to Reflection*. The Collected Works of Samuel Taylor Coleridge 9. Ed. John Beer. Princeton: Princeton UP, 1993.

———. *Anima Poetae*. London: William Henderson, 1895.

———. *Biographia Literaria, or Biographical Sketches of My Literary Life and Opinions*. The Collected Works of Samuel Taylor Coleridge 7. Ed. James Engell and W. Jackson Bate. Princeton: Princeton UP 1983.

———. *Collected Letters of Samuel Taylor Coleridge*. 6 vols. Ed. Earl Leslie Griggs. Oxford: Clarendon Press, 1958–1971.

———. *Confessions of an Inquiring Spirit*. Ed. H. StJ. Hart. London: Adam and Charles Black, 1956.

———. "Dejection: An Ode." *English Romantic Writers*. Ed. David Perkins. New York: Harcourt Brace Jovanovich, 1967. 432–34.

———. "A Lay Sermon Addressed to the Higher and Middle Classes on the Existing Distresses and Discontents." *Lay Sermons*. The Collected Works of Samuel Taylor Coleridge 6. Ed. R. J. White. Princeton: Princeton UP, 1972. 117–230.

———. "Lecture on the Slave Trade." *Lectures 1795 On Politics and Religion*. The Collected Works of Samuel Taylor Coleridge 1. Ed. Lewis Patton and Peter Mann. Princeton: Princeton UP, 1971. 231–52.

———. *Lectures 1795: On Politics and Religion*. The Collected Works of Samuel Taylor Coleridge 1. Ed. Lewis Patton and Peter Mann. Princeton: Princeton UP, 1971.

———. *Lectures 1808–1819: On Literature*. The Collected Works of Samuel Taylor Coleridge 5. Ed. R. A. Foakes. Princeton: Princeton UP, 1987.

———. *Marginalia*. The Collected Works of Samuel Taylor Coleridge 12. Ed. George Whalley. Princeton: Princeton UP, 1987.

———. *The Notebooks of Samuel Taylor Coleridge*. 5 vols. Ed. Kathleen Coburn. Bollingen Series L. London: Routledge and Kegan Paul, 1957–2002.

———. *The Rime of the Ancient Mariner. With an Essay by Robert Penn Warren*. New York: Reynal & Hitchcock, 1946.

———. *Shakespearean Criticism*. 2 vols. Ed. Thomas Middleton Raysor. Everyman's Library 183. New York: Dutton, 1960.

———. *The Statesman's Manual. Lay Sermons.* The Collected Works of Samuel Taylor Coleridge 6. Ed. R. J. White. Princeton: Princeton UP, 1972. 3–114.

———. *Table Talk and Omniana*. Ed. T. Ashe. London: George Bell and Sons, 1888.

Corrigan, Lesa Carnes. *Poems of Pure Imagination: Robert Penn Warren and the Romantic Tradition*. Baton Rouge: Louisiana State UP, 1999.

———. "Snapshots of Audubon: Photographic Perspectives from Eudora Welty and Robert Penn Warren." *Mississippi Quarterly*, vol. XLVIII, no. 1 (Winter 1994–1995): 83–91.

Cronin, Gloria L., and Ben Seigel, eds. *Conversations with Robert Penn Warren*. Jackson: UP of Mississippi, 2005.

Culler, Jonathan. *Structuralist Poetics*. Ithaca: Cornell UP, 1975.

Davis, Charles. "Our Modern Identity: The Formation of the Self." *Modern Theology*, vol. 6, no.2 (January 1990): 159–71.

Derrida, Jacques. "Différance." *The Continental Philosophy Reader*. Ed. Richard Kearney and Mara Rainwater. London: Routledge, 1996. 441–64.

———. "Edward Jabès and the Question of the Book." *Writing and Difference*. Trans. Alan Bass. Chicago: U of Chicago P, 1978. 64–78.

———. *Of Grammatology*. Trans. Gayatri Chakravorty Spivak. Baltimore: The Johns Hopkins UP, 1976.

———. "Plato's Pharmacy." *Dissemination*. Trans. Barbara Johnson. Chicago: U of Chicago P, 1981. 61–171.

———. "Structure, Sign and Play in the Discourse of the Human Sciences." *Writing and Difference*. Trans. Alan Bass. Chicago: U of Chicago P, 1978. 278–93.

Duane, Daniel. "Of Herons, Hags, and History: Rethinking Robert Penn Warren's *Audubon: A Vision*." *The Southern Literary Journal*, vol. 27, no. 1 (Fall 1994): 23–35.

Ealy, Steven D. "On the Creation of the Self in the Thought of Robert Penn Warren." *Modern Age*, vol. 43, no. 3 (Summer 2001). 202–10.

Empson, William. "*The Ancient Mariner*: An Answer to Warren." Ed. John Haffenden. *Kenyon Review*, vol. 15, no. 1 (1993): 155–77.

Felton, David. "A Conversation with Annie Leibovitz." *Photographs*. By Annie Leibovitz. New York: Pantheon/Rolling Stone Press, 1983. n.pag.

Franke, William. "Apophasis and the Turn of Philosophy to Religion: From Neoplatonic Negative Theology to Postmodern Negation of Theology." *International Journal of the Philosophy of Religion* vol. 60 (2006): 61–76.

———. "Franz Rosenzweig and the Emergence of a Postsecular Philosophy of the Unsayable." *International Journal for the Philosophy of Religion*, vol. 53, no. 3 (December 2005): 161–80.

———. *A Philosophy of the Unsayable*. Notre Dame: U of Notre Dame P, 2014.

———. "Varieties and Valences of Unsayability." *Philosophy and Literature*, vol. 29, no. 2 (October 2005): 489–97.

Fulford, Tim. "Coleridge, Bohme, and the Language of Nature." *Modern Language Quarterly, vol.* 52, no. 1 (1991): 37–52.

Gardner, W. H., and N. H. McKenzie, eds. *The Poems of Gerard Manley Hopkins.* 4th ed. Oxford: Oxford UP, 1970.

Goodson, A. C. "Coleridge on Language: A Poetic Paradigm." *Philological Quarterly*, vol. 62, no. 1 (1983): 45–68.

Graziano, Frank. "The Matter Itself: Warren's *Audubon: A Vision.*" *Homage to Robert Penn Warren: A Collection of Critical Essays.* Ed. Frank Graziano. Durango: Logbridge-Rhodes, 1981. 17–32.

Griggs, Earl Leslie, ed. *The Best of Coleridge.* New York: The Ronald Press Company, 1934.

Grimshaw, James A., Jr. "Introduction." *Robert Penn Warren's* Brother to Dragons: *A Discussion.* Ed. James A. Grimshaw, Jr. Baton Rouge: Louisiana State UP, 1983. 1–10.

———, ed. *Robert Penn Warren: A Documentary Volume.* Dictionary of Literary Biography, vol. 320. A Bruccoli Clark Layman Book. Farmington Hills, MI: Thomson Gale, 2006.

———. "Robert Penn Warren as Moral Philosopher: A Study in Hope, Love, and Endurance." *The Legacy of Robert Penn Warren.* Ed. David Madden. Baton Rouge: Louisiana State UP, 2000. 97–110.

Hagberg, G. L. *Art as Language: Wittgenstein, Meaning, and Aesthetic Theory.* Ithaca: Cornell UP, 1995.

Hall, Donald. *Poetry: The Unsayable Said.* Port Townsend: Copper Canyon Press, 1993.

Hawkes, Terence. *Structuralism and Semiotics.* London: Routledge 1992.

Heidegger, Martin. *Being and Time.* Trans. John Macquarrie and Edward Robinson. London: SCM Press, 1962.

———. "A Dialogue on Language." *On the Way to Language.* Trans. Peter D. Hertz. New York: Harper and Row, 1971. 1–54.

———. *The Essence of Truth: On Plato's Cave Allegory and THEAETETUS.* Trans. Ted Sadler. New York: Continuum, 2002.

———. "Language." *Poetry, Language, Thought.* Trans. Albert Hofstadter. New York: Harper and Row, 1971. 187–210.

———. "The Nature of Language." *On the Way to Language.* Trans. Peter D. Hertz. New York: Harper and Row, 1971. 57–108.

———. "On the Origin of the Work of Art." *Poetry, Language, Thought.* Trans. Albert Hofstadter. New York: Harper and Row, 1971. 15–88.

———. "Overcoming Metaphysics." *The End of Philosophy.* Trans. Joan Stambaugh. London: Souvenir Press, 1975. 84–110.

Hoy, David Couzens. "The Owl and the Poet: Heidegger's Critique of Hegel." *Martin Heidegger and the Question of Literature: Toward a Postmodern Literary Hermeneutics*. Ed. William V. Spanos. Studies in Phenomenology and Existential Philosophy. Bloomington: Indiana UP, 1976. 53–70.

Hummer, T. R. "Robert Penn Warren: Audubon and the Moral Center." *Southern Review*, vol. 16 (1980): 799–815.

Ivarsson, Soren, and Lotte Isager, eds. *Saying the Unsayable: Monarchy and Democracy in Thailand*. NIAS Studies in Asian Topics 47. Copenhagen: NIAS Press, 2010.

Jackson, Richard. "On the Horizon of Time." *Acts of Mind*. Tuscaloosa, AL: The University of Alabama Press, 1983. 53–60

———. "The Deconstructed Moment in Modern Poetry." *Contemporary Literature*, vol. XXIII, no. 3 (1982). 306–322.

———. "The Generous Time: Robert Penn Warren and the Phenomenology of the Moment." *Boundary 2*, vol. 9, no. 2 (Winter 1981): 1–30.

Jameson, Frederic. Foreword. *The Postmodern Condition: A Report on Knowledge*. By Jean-François Lyotard. Trans. Geoff Bennington and Brian Massumi. Theory and History of Literature 10. Manchester: Manchester UP, 1984. vii–xxi.

Jarrell, Randall. "The End of the Line." *Kipling, Auden Co.: Essays and Reviews 1935–1964*. New York: Farrar, Straus and Giroux, 1980. 76–83.

Jasper, David. "From modernism to postmodernism." *Major World Religions: From their origins to the present*. Ed. Lloyd Ridgeon. London: RoutledgeCurzon, 2003. 289–323.

———. "The Two Worlds of Coleridge's 'The Rime of the Ancient Mariner.'" *An Infinite Complexity: Essays in Romanticism*. Ed. J. R. Watson. The University of Durham 150th Anniversary Series. Edinburgh: Edinburgh UP, 1983. 125–44.

Jencks, Charles. *What is Postmodernism?* 3rd ed. New York: St. Martin's Press, 1989.

Justus, James H. *The Achievement of Robert Penn Warren*. Baton Rouge: Louisiana State UP, 1981.

Kearney, Richard. *Dialogues with Contemporary Continental Thinkers*. Manchester: Manchester UP, 1984.

Koppelman, Robert S. *Robert Penn Warren's Modernist Spirituality*. Columbia: U of Missouri P, 1995.

Langer, Suzanne. *Feeling and Form: A Theory of Art*. New York. Charles Scribner's Sons, 1953.

———. *Philosophy in a New Key: A Study in the Symbolism of Reason, Rite, and Art*. London: Oxford University Press, 1951.

Lentricchia, Frank. "Coleridge and Emerson: Prophets of Silence, Prophets of Language." *Journal of Aesthetics and Art Criticism* 32 (1973): 37–46.

Locke, John. *An Essay Concerning Human Understanding*. 2 vols. New York: Dover, 1959.

Longenbach, James. *Modern Poetry after Modernism*. New York: Oxford UP, 1997.

Lowes, John Livingston. *The Road to Xanadu: A Study in the Ways of the Imagination*. Boston and New York: Houghton Mifflin Company, 1927.

Lyotard, Jean-François. *The Postmodern Condition: A Report on Knowledge*. Trans. Geoff Bennington and Brian Massumi. Theory and History of Literature 10. Manchester: Manchester UP, 1984.

Marks, Emerson R. *Coleridge on the Language of Verse*. Princeton Essays in Literature. Princeton: Princeton UP, 1981.

McClatchy, J. D. *White Paper: On Contemporary American Poetry*. New York: Columbia UP, 1989.

McKusick, James C. *Coleridge's Philosophy of Language*. Yale Studies in English 195. New Haven: Yale UP, 1986.

———. "Symbol." *The Cambridge Companion to Coleridge*. Ed. Lucy Newlyn. Cambridge: Cambridge University Press, 2002. 217–30.

McNiece, Gerald. *The Knowledge that Endures: Coleridge, German Philosophy and the Logic of Romantic Thought*. London: MacMillan, 1992.

Miller, J. Hillis. *Illustration*. Cambridge: Harvard UP, 1992.

Miller, Mark D. "Knowledge and the Image of 'Billie Potts': A Reading Via a Reading of Strandberg's Reading." *To Love So Well the World: A Festschrift in Honor of Robert Penn Warren*. Ed. Dennis L. Weeks. New York: Peter Lang, 1992. 123–48.

Norris, Christopher. *Derrida*. Fontana Modern Masters. Ed. Frank Kermode. London: Fontana Press, 1987.

Olson, Elder. "A Symbolic Reading of the Ancient Mariner." *Critics and Criticism: Ancient and Modern*. Ed. R. S. Crane. Chicago: U of Chicago P, 1952. 138–44.

Palmer, Richard E. *Hermeneutics: Interpretation Theory in Schleiermacher, Dilthey, Heidegger, and Gadamer*. Northwestern University Studies in Phenomenology and Existential Philosophy. Ed. John Wild. Evanston: Northwestern UP, 1969.

———. "The Postmodernity of Heidegger." *Martin Heidegger and the Question of Literature: Toward a Postmodern Literary Hermeneutics*. Ed. William V. Spanos. Studies in Phenomenology and Existential Philosophy. Bloomington: Indiana UP, 1976. 71–92.

Parini, Jay. "The Lessons of Theory." *Philosophy and Literature*, vol. 21, no. 1 (April 1997). 91–101.

Perkins, David. "The 'Ancient Mariner' and Its Interpreters: Some Versions of Coleridge." *Modern Language Quarterly*, vol. 57, no. 3 (September 1996): 425–48.

Perkins, Mary Anne. *Coleridge's Philosophy: The Logos as Unifying Principle*. Oxford: Oxford UP, 1994.

Plato. "Phaedrus." *Plato: Euthyphro, Apology, Crito, Phaedo, Phaedrus*. Trans. Harold North Fowler. Loeb Classical Library. Cambridge: Harvard UP, 1914. 405–579.

Preston, John. "Introduction: Thought as Language." *Thought and Language*.

Ed. John Preston. Royal Institute of Philosophy Supplement 42. Cambridge: Cambridge University Press, 1997. 1–14.

Prickett, Stephen. *Romanticism and Religion: The Tradition of Coleridge and Wordsworth in the Victorian Church*. Cambridge: Cambridge UP, 1976.

Riefe, Jordan. "Annie Leibovitz on the Shots That Made Her." *The Guardian*. 31 March 2019. www.theguardian.com/artanddesign/2019/mar/31/tricky-dicky -arnies-abs-annie-leibovitz-rolling-stone?CMP=share_btn_link. Accessed 3 January 2020.

Rogers, Annie G. *The Unsayable: The Hidden Language of Trauma*. New York: Random House, 2006.

Runyon, Randolph Paul. *The Braided Dream: Robert Penn Warren's Late Poetry*. Lexington: U of Kentucky P, 1990.

———. *Ghostly Parallels: Robert Penn Warren and the Lyric Poetic Sequence*. Knoxville: U of Tennessee P, 2006.

Sanoff, Alvin P. "Pretty, Hell! Poetry Is Life." *U.S. News and World Report* 100 (June 23, 1986). 73.

Sarnowski, Joe E. *The Literary Achievement of the American Poet Robert Penn Warren: His Lifelong Struggles with Morality, Myth, and Modernity*. Lewiston: Edward Mellen Press, 2009.

Schulz, Max F. "Samuel Taylor Coleridge." *The English Romantic Poets: A Review of Research and Criticism*. Fourth Edition. Ed. Frank Jordan. New York: The Modern Language Association of America, 1985. 341–463.

Shepherd, Allen. "Chief Joseph, General Howard, Colonel Miles: The Context of Characterization in Warren's *Chief Joseph of the Nez Perce*." *Mississippi Quarterly*, vol. 39, no. 1 (Winter 1985–1986): 21–29.

Spanos, William V. "Heidegger, Kierkegaard, and the Hermeneutic Circle: Towards a Postmodern Theory of Interpretation as Dis-closure." *Martin Heidegger and the Question of Literature: Toward a Postmodern Literary Hermeneutics*. Ed. William V. Spanos. Studies in Phenomenology and Existential Philosophy. Bloomington: Indiana UP, 1976. 115–48.

———. "Martin Heidegger and the Question of Literature: A Preface." *Martin Heidegger and the Question of Literature: Toward a Postmodern Literary Herme-neutics*. Ed. William V. Spanos. Studies in Phenomenology and Existential Philos-ophy. Bloomington: Indiana UP, 1976. Ix–xix.

Steiner, George. *Heidegger*. 2nd ed. Fontana Modern Master. London: Fontana Press, 1992.

Strandberg, Victor. *A Colder Fire: The Poetry of Robert Penn Warren*. Lexington: U of Kentucky P, 1965.

———. *The Poetic Vision of Robert Penn Warren*. Lexington: U of Kentucky P, 1977.

———. "R.P.W. and T.S.E.: In the Steps of the (Post) Modern Master." *To Love So*

Well the World: A Festschrift in Honor of Robert Penn Warren. Ed. Dennis L. Weeks. New York: Peter Lang, 1992.

Szczesiul, Anthony. "'Language Barrier': Warren at the 'Inevitable Frontier' of Post-modernism." *Robert Penn Warren Studies* vol. 1 (2001): 1–23.

———. *Racial Politics and Robert Penn Warren's Poetry*. Gainesville: UP of Florida, 2002.

———. "Robert Penn Warren's *Audubon*: Vision and Revision." *Mississippi Quarterly*, vol. 47, no.1 (1994): 3–14.

Thiemann, Fred Russell. *Original Sin and Redemption: Philosophy of Language in Robert Penn Warren's Poetry*. Diss. Auburn U, 1995.

Van Dyke, John C. "A Critical Sense Worthy of Respect: John Marston and the Early Poetics of Robert Penn Warren." *Style*, vol. 36, no. 2 (Summer 2002): 203–21.

———. "Language at the End of Modernism: Robert Penn Warren's *A Plea in Mitigation*." *Mississippi Quarterly*, vol. LII, no. 2 (Spring 2000): 237–50.

Vanhoozer, Kevin. "A Lamp in the Labyrinth: The Hermeneutics of 'Aesthetic' Theology." *Trinity Journal*, vol. 8, no. 1 (Spring 1987): 25–56.

Walker, Marshall. *Robert Penn Warren: A Vision Earned*. Edinburgh: Paul Harris Publishing, 1979.

Watkins, Floyd C., and John T. Hiers, eds. *Robert Penn Warren Talking: Interviews 1950–1978*. New York: Random House, 1980.

Watkins, Floyd C., John T. Hiers, and Mary Louise Weaks, eds. *Talking with Robert Penn Warren*. Athens: U of Georgia P, 1990.

Wente, Margaret. "Angela Merkel says the unsayable on 'multikulti.'" *The Globe and Mail*. 19 October 2010. Web. 12 March 2011.

Westendorp, Tj. A. *Robert Penn Warren and the Modernist Temper: A Study of His Social and Literary Criticism in Relation to His Fiction*. Delft: Eburon, 1987.

Winchell, Mark Royden, ed. *Robert Penn Warren: Genius Loves Company*. Clemson: Clemson U Digital P, 2007.

Wolfson, Elliot R. "Heidegger's Apophaticism: Unsaying the Said and the Silence of the Last God." *Contemporary Debates in Negative Theology and Philosophy*. Ed. Nahum Brown and J. Aaron Simmons. Palgrave Frontiers in Philosophy of Religion. Ed. Yujin Nasagawa and Erik J. Wielenberg. Cham: Palgrave Macmillan, 2017. 185–216.

———. *Language, Eros, Being: Kabbalistic Hermeneutics and Poetic Imagination*. New York: Fordham University Press, 2005.

Wood, Edwin Thomas. "On Native Soil: A Talk with Robert Penn Warren." *Mississippi Quarterly*, vol. 37, no. 2 (1984): 179–86.

INDEX

GENERAL